TRAVAIL SO GLADLY SPENT

TRAVAIL SO GLADLY SPENT

Tom Price

To Frank Burns
Best Wishes

Tom Price

 THE ERNEST PRESS

Published by The Ernest Press 2000
© Tom Price 2000
Reprinted 2002
All illustrations in the text and on the cover
are by the author

For my Grandchildren

Paperback edition ISBN 0 948153 67 9
A CIP record for this book is available from The British Library

Typeset by Stanningley Serif
Printed by Colorcraft

CONTENTS

1. On Getting Out 7
2. Short of the Folding Stuff 8
3. On Failing 18
4. Long Walks 25
5. Mt. Blanc. The Tourist Route 29
6. Motorbike 32
7. Batura Mustagh 40
8. André Roch 47
9. Bird How 55
10. On Climbing Huts 59
11. A Grand Steyan 65
12. On Doing As You're Told 77
13. Almost Eliminated 80
14. Way Out West 83
15. In Scotland 90
16. The Skye Ridge 95
17. Reflections On My Slides 99
18. Louder And Funnier 102
19. Youth At The Door 105
20. Going Walkabout In The Alps 109
21. More Rainy Days in 1954 118
22. Training For The Haute Route 130
23. And Southward Aye We Fled 135
24. Bill Peascod 149
25. The Eskdale Mountain
    Rescue Team 154
26. On Outward Bound 178
27. The Stranglements 186
28. Look! No Boots 190

29. Bridging The Gap 194

30. Adventure By Numbers 198

31. Bingley College 205

32. And Some Have Greatness
    Thrust Upon Them 209

33. The Road To Mokhotlong 219

34. Ha Charlie 225

35. Of Horses And Hills 230

36. Idyllic Hills 238

37. A Northern River 242

38. East Buttress 252

39. Climbing Gossip, Climbing
    Friends 255

40. Old Soldiers 273

41. Fain Would I Climb;
    Yet Fear I To Fall 276

    Acknowledgements 280

ON GETTING OUT

'Stone walls do not a prison make, nor iron bars a cage.' What does, however, is the clang of the door closing, leaving no escape.

Looking back on my long and generally law-abiding life it is odd that I have the impression of having spent most of it on the run, like some miscreant of the Wild West trying to keep ahead of the posse.

A real life, as distinct from a life in fiction, is a jumble of random happenings and concerns, yet I suppose there is usually, if one can find it, some underlying unity or coherence arising from the values and disposition of the individual.

I have always been an associate rather than a full member of society, ready to cooperate, but not to belong. My school, for instance, was never my alma mater; it was a jail in which I was a compliant prisoner, counting the days to my release. Every time I have taken a new job it has been to escape from the old one. And not because I disliked the work – I have been fortunate in having one or two interesting jobs – but because I feared doors were closing and I might be trapped. I see myself as resembling some solitary grazing animal, placid and undemanding, yet always alert for flight.

In other words I have valued freedom, or at least the feeling of freedom, more than advancement or wealth, and consequently have spent a lifetime keeping an eye open for avenues of escape. When I was ten my family moved from a rural environment near Wharncliffe Crags in South Yorkshire, to a sprawling suburb of Liverpool. A door clanged shut on me then, and my eventual escape, when I was old enough, was into the hills or to wherever there was open space.

This book is in a way a collection of escape stories, escape for the most part into the open air, in pursuit of life's simple satisfactions and the succour that is to be found in the wilderness and the mountains.

SHORT OF THE FOLDING STUFF

I am not much given to looking back. My photographs, curled at the edges, and my diaries scribbled in pencil in weather-stained notebooks, are stowed away in shoe-boxes under beds and in attics. They come to light only when we move house. But when this summer I toiled up to a col in the Pyrenees, and scanned the new panorama, and saw the Pic du Midi d'Ossau standing there, dominating the skyline, it set up a train of reminiscence which on and off I have been reflecting upon ever since. It is strange how a mountain, once you have been up it and, so to speak, spent yourself upon it, becomes easily recognizable even when viewed from new angles. It is almost 40 years since I was last anywhere near the Pic du Midi d'Ossau yet it seemed almost uncannily familiar.

Not an enormously high mountain, the Pic du Midi. But there are more ways than one of calculating the height and remoteness of a summit. People now get to the Himalaya with less expenditure of time and effort than we put into that approach to the Pyrenees. It was not only that there were no motorways and fewer planes. It was a matter of money.

There is curiously little mention of money in mountain literature. Perhaps it is because the climber leaves the mundane world of work, money and home behind for loftier realms, which have their own realities and harsh imperatives but of a different order. And the early mountaineers seem to have been so well off that money was not a consideration. The question on arrival at a Swiss hotel was not whether there was anywhere cheaper to be had, but whether the entertainment was likely to be adequate to a gentleman's needs. Transport, guides and porters were all hired with an Olympian disregard for cost. Even Robert Louis Stevenson, a mere writer after all, scratching a living by the pen, when he spent a night sleeping out in the Cevennes, found nature's 'green caravanserai' so satisfactory that he left money on the turf, enough for his night's lodging. That has always seemed to me, anxiously meting out my cash to stay as long as possible in the hills, as something akin to blasphemy. Mountaineers when they have climbed a mountain by the easiest route seek further challenges by imposing various handicaps upon themselves. They choose harder routes, or winter ascents, or solo ascents, or ascents without oxygen, or ascents, if one is to believe McHaffie of Borrowdale, in boxing gloves and roller-skates. Presumably these carry a richer reward in terms of achievement and personal fulfilment.

The same can be said, in a way, for penniless ascents.

Just after the war the most you could take out of the country was £30. To us, however, that was so generous a ceiling as to be beyond our reach. We took £20 each, and subsisted for five weeks in the Pyrenees upon it. This penury led us into some memorable experiences. We never once slept in hired accommodation and so we were not just in the mountains for so many hours a day; we were there day and night, like the other animals. There is nothing like living out in the hills for bringing one into an intimacy with them. Coming down to a hut or hotel is like going home early from a good party: restful, perhaps, and prudent, but not so much fun. The fact that much of one's time and energy is expended on merely keeping alive and consequently less is available for getting up the peaks is not so great a disadvantage as all that. I think it was Sir Martin Conway who observed that climbers were on the whole too much interested in summits to the neglect of the rest of the mountains. Making brief sorties from under a roof and returning daily to the world of chairs and tables is being in the mountains, but not of them.

Not that living out is one long delight. On the contrary one often plumbs the depths. But after all, the same can be said of mountaineering generally; for all its moments of splendour, it is largely a catalogue of discomforts, dangers, tribulations and minor ill-health. But living out, one explores new levels of tolerance to the vagaries of the weather and the inconsiderateness of the natural environment. The great outdoors is a draughty place and full of insects, but there is something about it that soothes the savage breast.

On setting out for the Pyrenees, as my diary reminds me, though I had forgotten, I was visited by the usual misgivings about venturing forth from the security of home. My two companions had already left the day before, to hitch-hike to the Channel. I was to go by train since as the son of a railwayman I could travel for a quarter of the normal fare. So I had a day of fretful waiting before I began my journey. On a clear evening, under a green and blue sky which remained bright long after the twilight had invaded the Liverpool townscape, I lifted my rucksack on my back and set off, wishing I was bound only for Ogwen, or could just go to bed at home. It was my first holiday abroad, and late evening is a sad time for departure. With no jacket, and my warm clothing stowed away in my rucksack, I felt lightly equipped for a long journey, but on the train I was put in the shade by a fellow passenger clad only in shirt, pants and shoes. 'Are you a DBS?' he asks me. 'Not yet', I reply. He is, and drunk. En route from Curaçao to Montreal his only luggage is money and cigarettes. The latter he hands round and spills on the floor with great generosity. Always keen on travelling light I saw in him a new standard to aim for.

With half of one side of the compartment at my disposal I could lie down in the foetal position and so passed a tolerable night. Time was on my side. I drifted across central London and continued quietly, sleepily and sunnily to Newhaven. It was a beautiful fresh breezy summer's day, and before long my two companions appeared. They had been there since the night before and had slept on a hill overlooking the town. On the voyage across the Channel we had lunch in the saloon and made quite an occasion of it, as it was to be our only restaurant meal for weeks.

The long trail south continued, spells of boredom punctuated by bursts of activity. Taking our places in a train was no easy task as the corridors were barely as wide as our loads. Edging along crab-wise it was hard on the spur of the moment to think of the French for 'Kindly retreat, madam, into the compartment as I cannot squeeze myself past you.' We humped our loads across Paris to the Gare d'Austerlitz and boarded the night train for Pau. We sat up all night on the hard green seats, heads toppling forwards whenever we lapsed into sleep. While the train was hurtling and lurching across France, emitting that occasional demented long-drawn-out scream-ing sound that used to be such a feature of the SNCF *rapides*, one could drift into a state of complaisant torpor and pleasant waking dreams, soothed by a feeling of progress; but the stops were an agony of impatience and discomfort..

The night passed and at eight in the morning we alighted at Pau. Pau has a fine esplanade rather like a seaside promenade, but instead of the sea it looks out over a broad landscape backed by the Pyrenees. Prominent on the skyline we saw a splendid jagged peak, the Pic du Midi d'Ossau. It was the first we had heard of it. Our background reading for this trip had been an atlas and Hilaire Belloc's poem about the fleas that tease in the High Pyrenees and the wine that tasted of the tar. But we now recognized it as what we had come all this way for. In the town we found a mountain equip-ment shop and there bought a Guide Ledormeur to the Pyrenees. Its maps were sketch-maps without contours, ridges and spurs being indicated by thick black lines. We had no map and this book became our sole source of topographical information. We had been led to believe that food rationing was in force in France, though what we did not know was that no-one took any notice of it. We went to great lengths to find the appropriate office for obtaining ration cards. The man immediately in front of us at the *guichet* was having a passionate row with the woman behind the counter. She flew into a violent temper, and when the interview came to an end and he went out giving the door a slam that brought bits of plaster down off the ceiling, she thumped the counter and hurled abuse after him. She would have scant patience with us, we thought, with our halting French. Yet she turned to us with the utmost charm and urbanity, pulse normal, blood pressure a placid 120/80. I made up my mind that I would learn how to do that.

On the way back to the station we bought several feet of French bread, two bottles of red wine and a bag of peaches so ripe that they soaked through the paper and stuck our fingers together. By the time we boarded the local train with wooden seats we were getting very tired, and hungry, and hot, but spirits revived when we tucked into the bread and peaches, and passed round one of the bottles; and they soared when the other bottle, falling over on the luggage rack, exploded like a bomb and sent down a purple rain over Ken's head and shoulders.

At Laruns the noonday sun smote us like a hammer. From the dusty station an avenue led up a hill for half a kilometre to the village square. There was a fountain in the middle of it and by the time we reached it we were ready to drink it dry. The village lay stunned and torpid in the heat but life stirred faintly behind the bar of the Hotel des Touristes, and we laid out some precious francs for a pot of tea.

The weight of our packs was now a matter of immediate and pressing concern in that, when it came to the crunch, we could not carry them any distance. It was not that they were full of climbing equipment, most of which had not yet been invented, nor were they full of camping gear, for our tent was from a cheap offer in a newspaper, suitable for a child in a back garden, and we had brought it not to sleep in but to house our belongings while we were up in the mountains. What they were full of was food, and particularly coffee beans. We had believed postwar France to be seriously short of coffee, having naively accepted what was said in the newspapers, and in the hope of making a killing we had gone to Cooper's, an upmarket grocer in Liverpool, and bought a huge quantity of the cheapest coffee beans available. So our rucksacks bulged with ex-army biscuits, dried bananas, compressed dates, oatmeal, sugar and the like, but above all, coffee beans. Many of these beans had burst their paper bags and were running loose throughout our equipment.

The faint suspicion with which we were at first received in the bar of the Hotel des Touristes turned gradually to a fascinated interest as we unloaded our rucksacks on the floor and tried to gather up our stock of coffee beans. The patron kindly provided new paper bags. By some sort of telepathic communication the entrepreneurs of the village homed in on us. There was a good deal of amiable discussion but the consensus was that roasted beans were what everyone wanted. Green beans got the thumbs down. The auction, consequently, was a social success rather than a financial one, but we came away with fifteen hundred francs profit and a tumbler or two of the patron's red wine. There is nothing like trade between the great nations of the world for promoting international understanding and cooperation. Not only had we lightened our loads but had also been promised a lift up the valley in a lorry at some unspecified time in the late afternoon, from a nearby road junction. Waiting for that lorry I count as one of the most delightful experiences of my mountaineering life. It was a pleasant crossroads, with deep grass full of wild flowers and humming with insects of the more benign sort, under a generous, baking sun. We had our doubts about whether the lorry would indeed arrive, but we did not greatly care. Two girls came by and lingered with us, as though they too had all the time in the world. We had no past and no future, and the present was limitless.

When the lorry did come it was all the more pleasant a surprise for we had given it up. It was loaded with roof-tiles packed in straw, and on top of the load sat three picturesque characters whom we took to be drunken brigands but who were in fact drunken Portuguese workmen returning from a day off and singing, not altogether tunelessly. The afternoon was turning into a golden evening. The road climbed through a narrow defile, crossing from side to side of the torrent, tunnelling through crags and traversing tree-clad precipices. We passed through Eaux Chaudes, a village crammed in the narrows, and finally came out into a strath from which we caught occasional glimpses of our mountain, a formidable volcanic plug with almost vertical sides, the sort of mountain a child might draw from imagination.

Our lift brought us to Gabas. We walked straight through the village and made camp on the first bit of level ground we could find. This was at the bottom of a very steep field, hemmed in by trees and crags, and poised about 10m above a riverbed accessible only by a difficult rock climb. Everywhere there was the sound of cowbells. It was getting dark. We made a good fire, and after a frugal meal of biscuits, dried bananas and tea, we crawled thankfully into our sleeping bags close to the blaze.

'Night is a dead, monotonous period under a roof, but in the open world it passes lightly, with its stars and dews and perfumes.' So said old Stevenson, and there is some truth in it. Certainly it was an improvement on the last two nights which I had spent in railway carriages. Dreams and reality mingled together. At first it was too hot to sleep, later too cold. My weary mind was visited by romantic Stevensonian impressions of firelight, a large moon, bright stars. Later there was mist swirling among the trees and I groaned and buried my head in my bag.

In the morning Norman made a foray into the village and returned with a green bottle full of milk. He was proving very useful on the public relations front, what with his uninhibited French and his capacity for getting a favourable response, from girls particularly, to openings which if I had made them, would have earned me a thick ear. Ken and I, if pressed, would have had to say that Norman did not have the same commitment to climbing as we had. He was known to have expressed the view, for example, that a holiday should include a certain amount of enjoyment and indulgence. Over the porridge he argued strongly for a visit to the village inn, for diplomatic reasons as well as to further his acquaintance with the landlord's daughter. A glass of wine he said was not much to pay in exchange for all kinds of local information and goodwill. At the inn the patron talked readily about the Pic du Midi. We made a casual mention of a good route on the North Face. 'La Face Nord' he exclaimed sonorously, and held us with a glittering eye. "Sit down, monsieur," says Norman, and we make room for him on the new red leather settee.

"It was on October the 12th, 1923," he says, "a young Englishman, a fine strong type, an experienced alpinist, you understand, who called himself Monsieur Pop..." and he tells a graphic tale of a confident solo climber attempting the North Face and failing to reappear; of the efforts to find him; of the arrival of his family from England; of the summoning of first class guides from Switzerland; and of what they found of him ... "A small piece, you understand, messieurs, as big as that," says the innkeeper, picking up a glass. No, we shall surely kill ourselves if we go on the North Face sans guide. It was only years later that I realised that Monsieur Pop was in fact that distinguished young climber and Alpine Club member Hugh Rose Pope. Young climbers are not disposed to learn from the misfortunes of other people, and still less inclined to heed the advice of non-climbers, but one thing the innkeeper said stuck in our minds. There were some soldiers camping at Bious Artigues, and they knew the mountain well. We should go and talk to them.

After lunch – last of the army biscuits – we left our gear at the camp and walked up a steep side-valley through woods. Breasting a final slope we came out quite suddenly upon a broad high pasture ringed by wooded summits and dominated by the high rock towers of the Pic du Midi d'Ossau. Slightly right of centre of this delectable meadow stood three small marquees, with the Tricolour waving above them. It was a splendid and unforgettable sight, and it will never be seen again as the whole place now lies at the bottom of the artificial Lac de Bious Artigues.

The camp belonged to a small detachment of Chasseurs Alpins, most of whom were away on a parachuting exercise. We chatted about climbing to two slim bronzed youths stripped to the waist, and made mention of the North Face. They took us to a practice rock in the woods nearby and we did various boulder problems and hand traverses. The corporal, Jean, said he knew the North Face climb and would go with us if the lieutenant agreed. This excursion to the boulders had been to give us the once-over. On getting back to the tents we found the lieutenant had returned, a handsome and voluble Basque who received us formally but with great warmth and charm. We reclined in the sun on a large sheet of canvas, and smoked and talked. We seemed to have found our way into a delightful upland world where friendliness and liberality held sway. It was hardly with surprise that we heard the officer suggest that we go down to Gabas, return immediately with a few necessaries, spend the night in the camp, and climb the peak the next morning. "Do not bring any blankets," he says with a courteous sweep of the hand. "We have enough. You are welcome to our simple soldier's fare of soup and potatoes. But bring utensils." So we run downhill again in a state of great excitement, cram food and clothing for three into one rucksack, leave the other two at the inn, and hasten back to Bious Artigues .

It is Saturday and some weekend climbers have in the meantime joined the soldiers; two hard men, clanking with ironmongery, a middle-aged extrovert held in much respect by the others – "très fort, très très fort" we are assured in earnest asides by the soldiers – and a lively blonde in blue pants and scarlet anorak. We shake hands. The conversation flashes about our heads like a volleyball which we manage only occasionally to intercept. It is now quite late and the summer evenings are shorter in these latitudes than at home. The lieutenant explains that he has a mess table in the tent but thinks it more agreeable to have dinner round the camp fire. The fire, which has been smouldering all day, is now built up into a splendid blaze and blankets spread all round it. On these we take our places with some decorum, though the party very soon becomes informal and voluble. Darkness falls as the meal progresses, and the later courses are mysterious and delicious, particularly a rich, creamy, ambrosial substance piled high on slices of iron-hard rye bread which we later learn is made from cheese 'au petit lait' mixed with a tin of Lyle's Golden Syrup which we have contributed. The whole is enriched by copious draughts of 'le bon pinard', army issue, from a huge aluminium flask; the absence of the main body of the troops has created a surplus. It is a meal fit for the gods, and the good company, the great fire, and the magnificent towering face of the Pic du Midi, lit by a moon which has not yet itself come into \view, and Venus shining brightly to the right, make this an evening never to be forgotten.

Norman is in great form, and the climbers and soldiers all appear to be wags. There is an abundance of conversation on several planes, climbing talk, comparisons of prices, views on religion and politics, leg-pulling and vulgarity. We have seen today for the first time a new kind of climbing boot with a rubber sole called Vibram. The Frenchmen laugh at our nails and say that they are only for old men with long grey beards. The evening goes on and on, and none of us would miss it for the world, but I do mention to the lieutenant our projected early start next day. "Ah," he says, "but it is very 'sympathique' by the fire," and he is perfectly right. We finally turn in well after midnight, in a tent whose middle is a big shallow trough full of straw. The very strong mountaineer, M. Arruyeux, who has already climbed the Pic du Midi 41 times, is not ready for bed even now, and provides a largely unintelligible cabaret show with candles for footlights and a hand-generated torch for spotlight. Impossible to believe he intends to climb anything next day. Finally we quieten down, or rather move into the snoring mode, and I spend a very short night with long dreams. In the middle of it one of the hard men asks me the time, and he and his friend move stealthily about in the clammy comfortless dark. Someone drops what sounds like a hundredweight of old iron and the blonde wakes up and says something with a tolerant laugh. At daylight we drink a little cold earthy coffee, eat some bread and cheese, and set off with the corporal, our soldier guide, through steep dense woods. As the sun gets up the going becomes extremely hard. We arrive at the foot of the rocks at about 9am, "a little late," says the corporal. Anyone who feels he cannot do the climb, he adds, should say so now, for he is not prepared to descend from half way up. We all feel unfit but hold our peace.

We rope up on a short, stout Army rope. It is more an assertion of the principle 'One for all and all for one', than a protection, for it is much too short for proper rope technique. The climbing is continuous and open and a bit like climbing on Lliwedd. As last man I spend every moment when not actually climbing looking anxiously for something to belay on. It seems logical, and to some degree takes my mind off the stones that keep spinning down from above. After a few hundred metres we reach an airy ledge at the top of our buttress, and eat some dried bananas and sugar, then make an upward traverse right, over beautiful slabs giving very enjoyable climbing, into an amphitheatre. We stop at a snow patch and suck some of it avidly. The corporal wraps a big lump in a cloth for use later on. Ken and I take turns with the rucksack and find it makes us breathless.

Easy rocks lead to a gap between a pinnacle and the main face, which beetles above us alarmingly. From here we descend into an astonishing rock cwm whose back-wall is a huge vertical cliff of yellowed rock, and over whose lip is another precipice. Opposite, a great stone shoot, very deep and narrow, leads up to another gap. From the depths we suddenly hear the strains of 'Hi yi yippie yippie yi' and make out the two hard men of the night before, dwarfed to leprechaun size by their immense surroundings. 'She'll be coming round the mountain' was the song they liked best in our repertoire at the camp fire. Our route still trends rightwards and eventually an easy but tremendously exposed edge is crossed with a great vertical drop on the right and we attain the Fourche, the gap between the Grand Pic and the Petit Pic. It is time for more sugar, helped down by the corporal's snow. There is still a long way to go, but apart from a rather confusing section where a large rock-fall has occurred it is easy climbing. Moving all together makes for greater breathlessness, and the rocks, now in full sun, radiate a noonday heat. We reach the summit at three. We bask for an hour among the sardine tins, rich men, our minds still trying to encompass the splendours of the North Face, our bodies screaming quietly for water. There is a tin full of scraps of paper bearing the names of climbers. We add ours, giving the corporal his full title, Jean Miaille, Caporal I classe, and about ten letters denoting his army status. It is his sixth ascent. On descending the *voie normale* we are received with applause by the other climbers who are sitting by a spring. The water brings about a miraculous improvement to our health, the equivalent, say, of a good night's sleep, and we continue in company with the others through a long green valley, about an hour's walk, and back to the soldiers' camp. No sooner do we get into camp than the lieutenant orders Jean to put on a beret and assist with the simple ceremony of hauling down the colours. We stand to attention, feeling like ambassadors.

We wash and drink. The climbers depart. We have a frugal Army meal off a table of branches and pine-fronds. "Perhaps you would like to sleep" suggests the lieutenant, " shall we sit a little at the fire?" But we are still on a high and sleep is far from our thoughts. We liven up the fire, and all hands join in the French custom of jumping through it. Straw is fetched and a high sheet of flame produced and we leap through that too. The fire attracts some other campers and they join us sitting on the circle of blankets, a woman with two daughters and two or three lads. We sing songs, have French ones sung back to us, 'le bon pinard' circulates in the bottomless gourd, the girls tear our heartstrings with their harmonising of 'Au clair de la lune', and one wonders if the dark one, dimly seen through the blaze, can really be as pretty as she looks. The corporal's only English is 'OK boy', and the lieutenant's is confined to the phrase 'the food of a mighty race' taken from the carton of Scott's Porage Oats, but conversation flourishes nonetheless. Finally, after the company has dispersed with farewells and handshakes, I am left by the dying fire with the lieutenant, hopelessly waiting for tea-water to boil, and replying in worse and worse French to his political and religious views. I turn in very weary.

So that was the beginning of our vagabondage in the Pyrenees with many a night *à la belle étoile* and several undignified flights for cover in thunderstorms. We were to subsist largely on vegetable stews enriched by a substance from the butcher's called *matière grasse*, and as we grew more expert our cooking fires were to become smaller and smaller. We were to climb the Mur de la Cascade at Gavarnie, and the Mont Perdu, and seek shelter in the wretched hovel of the Refuge de Tuqueroye. We were to have the meal of a lifetime at Pierrefitte Nestalas, its sauce the accumulated hunger of a month out of doors. Norman was to end up between the starched linen sheets of a hospital bed, minus his appendix, tended by nurses much intrigued by his surname, Wildblood, while Ken and I slept under bridges, and on a heap of sand in a builder's yard, and the verandah of a little estaminet in a wood, waiting for visiting time. Our life had its squalid moments, but for the most part we were lifted above it by the beauty and sublimity of the mountains. The stony uplands were washed and sunbleached to an austere cleanliness. The alpine glades and meadows were full of purple irises, harebells, gentians, speedwell, vetches, cornflowers, clovers and orchids. We found bilberries and raspberries, and liquorice roots to chew. I suppose we saw comparatively few summit cairns bur we had a thorough acquaintance with lizards, flies, beetles, moths, ants, grasshoppers, butterflies and dragonflies. And clear running water was our constant delight.

Some day I think I must make a trip to the Lac de Bious Artigues, and try and recall once again the drowned meadow with the tents and the Tricolour waving over them, and Lieutenant Jauretche, dreamer and thinker cast in the role of man of action; and Jean Miaille, corporal first class, neat, compact, tough, efficient; and Blanc, the cook, friendly and 'sympathique' without ever smiling; and Perasseux, rough and wild with a bucolic wit; and of course the admiral's daughters who sang so well in harmony.

How many such delectable places have been drowned by reservoirs, I wonder. Perhaps, after all, it would be a better idea not to go back.

ON FAILING

'If a thing's worth doing it's worth doing badly.'
G.K.Chesterton.

MOEL SIABOD

About the first mountain I failed to get up was Moel Siabod in North Wales. I was a schoolboy, walking around with the aid of the One Inch Ordnance map, and thought to climb it on my way from Beddgelert to the Lledr Valley.

I had been out several days in variable weather and one more or less constantly wet boot had somehow pressed on my right Achilles' tendon until it became intolerably painful. Faced with the choice of curtailing the trip or sacrificing one of my boots I chose the latter. I made a vertical cut down the back of my right boot so that the tendon received no pressure from it, and I was thus able to continue in comfort

Moel Siabod was almost totally in cloud but I thought that if I kept going uphill I could not help but get to the top. It was not so easy as that, however. I found myself wandering through and around all kinds of hollows, and every time the ground fell away in front of me instead of leading upwards I feared I might be dropping down towards Capel Curig instead of into the Lledr, where I was hoping to stay at a youth hostel. It was all very wet and dreary, the more so as I came across numerous dead sheep. In the end, after what seemed hours in the mist, which always distorts time and distance, all I wanted to do was to get out of it. I came down on to the Capel Curig road, and, in the village, settled for a bed-and-breakfast at two shillings and sixpence.

The people were kind and hospitable but I was put to share a bed with the son of the house, a young man of eighteen who worked at the quarries in Llanberis. We talked pleasantly until he was ready to go to sleep, and I concentrated all night on keeping to the extreme edge of my side of the bed.

I found it easy to be philosophical about this failure. I had a lifetime before me, and innumerable hills yet to climb.

18

THE CUILLIN

It was almost the end of my second year at the university, and as soon as lectures finished in the summer term of 1939 I went to Skye with a fellow-student called Callaghan. We got there by persuading his brother to take us in his brand new car, on the grounds that a long journey would 'run it in'. He brought us therefore to Kyle of Lochalsh, and there turned for home. He was not pleased that our route had lain through Glen Moriston, which at that time had a single-track road with a high grass ridge in the middle. He claimed he had scraped the underside of his car once or twice.

Callaghan had an Itisa tent with flysheet, made by Camtors. He was very proud of it. We did not make it to Glen Brittle that night, so we camped on the saddle above the valley. The Black Cuillin lay before us, seven miles of jagged gabbro peaks. They were soon obscured, however, by bad weather, and we endured a night of storm and tempest. It became evident that we could not keep the flysheet on without risking its being torn to shreds, so we took it off. The rain was then driven so fiercely against the single fabric of the tent that a fine spray began to wet us. As we could not afford to get our sleeping bags soaked, we rolled them up, stowed them in our ruck-sacks, put on all our clothes and waterproofs, and spent the night support-ing the single tent pole, which was bending like a bow.

On nights like this one longs for the dawn. One cannot help thinking that daylight will bring an end to the nightmare and that the weather will change.

But the weather did not change, except perhaps to get worse. We began to feel that the storm had it in for us personally. In the late afternoon we packed up, dropped the tent, put stones on it and, fighting a ferocious wind with every step, made our way down into Glen Brittle. I knew Mrs. McDonald kept a bunkhouse there. We knocked on her door, which looked as if it was closed for the winter. After much drawing of bolts and moving of draft excluders it opened, revealing a very old woman.

We stood there, soaked, with the rain bouncing off us.

"Could we stay in your bunkhouse?" we said.

All she did was laugh. For some time she was helpless with mirth. "Just look at ye!" she said. "Just look at ye." And eventually, "Ye'd better come in by."

We got dry and warm and comfortable. She had a kitchen drawer full of cold cooked porridge, and she carved out a chunk of it and heated it up in a saucepan. "Parritch," she called it, and to her the word was in the plural.

"Are they all right?" she asked.

"Who?" we asked.

"The parritch," she said.

"Great," we said. "Delicious."

And they were.

The cost, modest though it was, of staying in the bunkhouse, cleaned us out and we had to leave after a brief foray into the Cuillin to the Window Buttress. When I got home there were two letters waiting for me. One was from Mr. Bonner, my Latin tutor, requesting an urgent meeting before the end of the term to discuss my failure in the Latin paper. The other, dated a week or two later, was from the Director of Education of the city of Liverpool. My scholarship, he regretted to inform me, was withdrawn owing to an unsatisfactory report from the University on my year's work.

It was hard at this time to take one's future too seriously. I had already had to register under the Militia Bill, and though my military service was deferred for the time being I knew that when war broke out I would be among the first to be conscripted.

MT ETNA

About half way through the six years of the War I was in Sicily for a time. The sight of Mt. Etna, eleven thousand feet, capped with snow, made me long to try and climb it. A fellow officer in our flotilla had somehow acquired an abandoned German motorcycle. I borrowed it, found a willing colleague who could ride it, and we set off one morning before dawn with a full tank and high hopes. We wore very warm clothing to cope with the altitude. Etna is a conical mountain, but of enormous breadth. We understood we could ride to within four thousand vertical feet of the summit. There were two things, however, that we did not reckon with. One was that most of the bridges on the mountain roads had been destroyed, and the other was that on the steep hills the clutch of the motorcycle began to slip. We had to manhandle the machine across the streams the bridges had spanned, an exhausting business for two overdressed climbers. On account of the clutch we had to go down the gears and eventually ran out of petrol. By the time this happened we had reached about five thousand feet and the day was well advanced. We accepted failure.

At this point, while our thoughts were turning to the problem of getting back home, we were invited into the house of an elderly man of gracious manners and aristocratic bearing. He gave us wine and fruit and cakes, which did wonders for our flagging spirits. At length we said our goodbyes, mounted the motorbike and began free-wheeling down towards the coast. It was evening and falling dusk. It was the time in the villages when people strolled along the main street, taking the air after the heat of the day. The silent ghostly passage of a phantom motorcycle with two muffled strangers on it caused several people to leap for cover and others to make jeering comments. Apart from crossing the stream beds where the bridges had been, it was almost all downhill, and we made good progress. But the time came when we reached the main coast road from Catania to Messina and free-wheeling was no longer possible. We had some thirty miles to go. Given petrol, we might on the flat have made it, even with a faulty clutch. But petrol was like gold and the chances of getting any were nil.

While we were sitting in the dark wondering what to do, a truck came along. We signalled and it stopped. To our delight it was full of sailors. We were saved.

Then we saw they were not British sailors, but Italian. We managed to explain that we were naval officers and needed to get to Messina. The officer in charge was polite and sympathetic, but well-adjusted enough to be able to bear with fortitude the misfortunes of others. He was willing to give us a lift, but as for the motorcycle it was clearly impossible. We knew that to leave the bike was to lose it forever. We took it to the back of the truck, made gestures and pleas to the sailors riding there, and in a moment had them jumping down to help us heave it up. Many hands made light of the job and soon we were safely on our way home.

Midnight found us pushing the dead bike through the streets of Messina to the harbour. It had been a long day.

I had not finished with Mt. Etna. My next ploy was to get the padre interested in laying on a truck and driver, ostensibly to take a group of ratings on an adventurous excursion, in the interests of morale. With about a dozen volunteers we set off again. There was a road, we were told, on which the bridges were not blown. If there was, we did not find it, but we got high up on the mountain and climbed on foot for two or three thousand feet. We had no map, but my theory was that if you kept going up a hill you were bound to reach the summit. We did in fact reach a summit, but it was not Etna. I later found that it was Monte Pomingiaro.

On the way down we had the pleasure of a long and most exhilarating scree run, bounding in enormous strides down a talus of soft volcanic ash. Another consolation on this abortive attempt was that we got among apple orchards. Apples strewed the roads like autumn leaves in Vallombroso, and our party filled their haversacks with them.

I never got back to Etna, and, now, I'm afraid, it is too late.

That was a long time ago, over fifty years in fact, but I remember it with affection and even a little pride. It was the only time in the six years of war that I set foot on a mountain, and it was an adventure quite different from, and in many ways superior to, the great communal adventure of warfare. Failing to reach a summit is not such an important thing after all. The journey is what matters, perhaps more even than the destination. Once a mountain top has been reached there is after all nowhere to go but down.

CLOUDY RIDGE

Cloudy Ridge is not a well-known mountain, and I imagine very few people trouble to climb it. The reason I chose it, and not one of its neighbours, such as Spread Eagle to its north or Dungarvon to its south was that it was the nearest summit to the ranch I was working on, which in fact bore the same name. This ranch ran right up against the Rockies and had one boundary in common with that of the Waterton Lakes National Park, (which in its turn was contiguous with the Glacier National Park in Montana). Some thirty miles to the south the border between Alberta and the U.S.A. was marked by Chief Mountain, a sharp peak held sacred by the Native Americans.

Cloudy Ridge Ranch was small by Alberta standards, about three thousand acres. I was no cowpuncher; I just looked after the goats and hens, and checked the fences, on foot. The mountain sent down a long ridge that extended across the ranch. The terrain was a mixture of open pastures, scrubby woodlands, swamps and beaver dams. It was divided into paddocks for managing the cattle, and the paddocks were separated by electric fences. Where these went through woodland, narrow breaks had been cleared through the trees. Wildlife in the area included moose and grizzly bears. When walking the fences I would carry, in addition to my voltmeter and tool kit, a pepper spray reputed to be effective against a grizzly bear at ten feet, provided the wind was in the right direction.

Cloudy Ridge Mountain reached a height of over eight thousand feet. The ranch house was at about three thousand. Forests of pine, spruce and aspen clothed the lower slopes, giving way higher up to juniper scrub and finally bare rock and scree, showing bands of horizontal strata

I set off one morning at about eight o'clock and at first was on familiar ground to the top of the ridge, a fine airy place commanding views up a wild river valley into the heart of the mountains. I then began to make my way along the ridge towards a dense belt of forest which I hoped to get through by sticking to the crest. This proved difficult going, however, with a steep vegetated slope to my left, and I was forced into the wood itself, which was dark and full of deadfalls, and, for all I knew, bears. I expended a great deal of time and energy getting through it, pepper spray at the ready, but at length emerged into a very attractive upland region of juniper and tussock grass providing new and inspiring views of mountains I knew well from down below.

Soon the ridge steepened and narrowed and became almost bare of vegetation. The rock was loose and friable, but I was helped here and there by patches of snow in which I could easily kick steps. On one of these snow patches, which lay in a long streak up a steep section of the ridge, I saw massive paw prints, heading upwards. It could only have been a bear, though what any bear would want on that empty and inhospitable slope I could not imagine.

I now had either to stay on the ridge itself, climbing questionable rock, or take to its right flank and go up scree-laden open slopes separated by horizontal bands of rock. These rock bands were easy enough to climb through, but each one added a little to the feeling of exposure as I got higher up this rather daunting slope. At the same time the wind began to increase and was soon blowing so strongly that I was glad to have rock to hold on to. I pressed on, and began to consider how much time I should safely allow myself before I turned round and headed for home, for the last thing I wanted was to find myself still out in the dark. I surmounted one more rock band and saw ahead of me a different and less trying terrain. I had reached a sort of *gendarme* near the top of the ridge; from here the angle lessened and I could see what was probably the summit. It was however still a considerable distance away and perhaps two hundred feet higher. By this time I was struggling against a strong and unfriendly wind.

I suddenly no longer cared very much about reaching the top. I was seventy-two years old and I was high up on a remote mountain in the Rockies. I was higher than the top of Chief Mountain and as high as Spread Eagle. I could see Montana off to my right, and before me Alberta stretching away to a far horizon as level as an ocean. I got out of the fierce wind behind a bit of rock and thought it wiser to spend time here in contemplation of the vast landscape below me than to fight on to the summit and once there turn hastily around again in an anxiety to get down in time. I thought if I allowed myself the same length of time on the descent as I'd taken on the way up I would get home well before dark. I wondered if the mountaineering bear had made it to the top.

I descended with care like the old man I was. As I got to the last bit of the steep part of the ridge I saw, twenty-five yards below me, a magnificent

Rocky Mountain ram with huge shoulders and great curling horns, making his way quietly across my ridge. When one travels alone it is a remarkably moving thing, like a boon or a privilege, to see a big wild animal sharing the same place.

I was not anxious however to meet other wild animals in the dense belt of forest that had given me such trouble on the way up, so I left the ridge and went down towards what looked like a series of open glades and grasslands leading in the general direction of the ranch. It turned out to be not nearly as easy a route as it looked. I had to circumvent swamps and beaver ponds, and since I was down in the lowest part of the country I could not see how the land lay. Plodding across glade after glade I began to fear I had already passed the ranch, but at last I came upon a place I recognised and soon after that I was home, with an hour of daylight still in hand. I had been out over ten hours.

A failure, one might call it. But it remains in my memory more like a success.

LONG WALKS

I once had the strange experience, in the dark at one in the morning, on the North York moors, of joining a long queue to get over a stile. Busloads of people from various parts of the north were doing the Lyke Wake Walk, the forty-mile trudge from Osmotherly to Ravenscar, which for many in the north of England has become a sort of rite of passage, a way of building up one's sense of identity. At the end of it you can get a little badge in the shape of a coffin to prove that you're still alive and walking.

The reason I was there – in addition to the compulsion touched on above, which I was not entirely immune to myself – was that the West Riding of Yorkshire was about to be carved up into twelve different authorities, and I thought my colleagues in the education department needed something to take their minds off the fear of redundancy. I had put out the suggestion of the Lyke Wake Walk as an office outing and been astonished at the response. It is a curious thing that people who are not fell walkers will decline an ordinary day's walk as too strenuous but eagerly volunteer for an outrageously long one. The party even included the County Solicitor, a man who would take a taxi to cross a street. He came to ask my advice about boots.

"Just whatever you find comfortable," I said.

"Well, that would be my old dancing shoes," he said. "I can dance all night in them."

"Wear them," I said, for I have always pioneered lightweight footgear. And he did. They served him very well except that at five in the morning he lost one in a bog, and we had the unusual spectacle of several people on their knees in the grey light of dawn probing the peat for the missing shoe.

The party got so exhausted on this walk that they pronounced it a tremendous success and asked me to arrange another one the following year.

So I laid on the Three Peaks Walk, Whernside, Ingleborough and Penyghent, twenty-one miles round trip. Two young members of the clerical staff were so pleased with their Lyke Wake performance that they declared they could do the Three Peaks in half a day, running. But they burned themselves out on the first hill and finished along with the rest of us, sustained by sandwiches begged from their friends.

There is something about the north of England – in the air perhaps – and particularly in Yorkshire and Lancashire, that encourages sports requiring the endurance of discomfort and even pain over long periods. Some clubs, and that august body the Yorkshire Ramblers is one, do prodigious walks of distances like a hundred miles over vast empty moors and often in terrain arduous to walk on such as the acreages of tussock known round Halifax and Huddersfield as bobbies' helmets. The Pennine Way, according to Tom Stephenson, was intended simply to make the grouse moors accessible to walkers and not as a long distance challenge, yet a survey in 1965, the year it was opened, found that almost a third of those walking on it were doing the whole length of some two hundred and fifty miles in one trip.

No one, not even a Yorkshireman, will court pain and discomfort purely for its own sake. There must be some other reward. Partly, no doubt, it is having one's strength and stamina measured and recognised, but mainly I think it is the feeling of invincibility that comes after the limbs have functioned for many hours like a well-oiled machine and seem all set to go on doing so indefinitely.

This feeling may give way suddenly to desperate fatigue, what people who do these things call The Knock or Hitting the Wall, but while it lasts it is like an assertion of immortality, a heroic dream of fluent, tireless movement over the landscapes of the gods. I have felt this occasionally myself, I must admit, but for the most part I have managed to resist the lure of the long walk. The longest I ever did in the Lake District was from Shap to Ravenglass, and what made me do it was this.

Diadem Press proposed a book entitled *The Big Walks*, a compilation. Richard Gilbert, the editor, approached various people to make suggestions and write descriptions. My friend Roger Putnam had offered to write up a walk that crossed the Lake District from Shap to Ravenglass, but finding himself too busy to meet the deadline, asked me if I would take it on. Since the only part of the walk I was not quite familiar with was the section from Dunmail Raise to High White Stones, that was the only bit I reconnoitred before writing the article. Anyone reading my account in The Big Walks will see that I nowhere state that I walked it all in one day, though I was happy enough to let it be assumed that I did.

In the years that followed the publication I got rather tired of being forced to admit, when cornered, that I had written the article without actually doing the walk, so I decided to have a crack at it, especially when a friend offered to help with the transport on the condition I took his fifteen-year-old son with me.

It was an ill-assorted party of four that eventually started out. There was myself, old and frail, my son, a climber and fell walker, the fifteen-year-old already mentioned and Etsu Peascod, lissom and delicate as a flower, the young Japanese wife of Bill Peascod. Two men of my acquaintance also expressed an interest but on hearing that we intended to do it in one day said they would rather take two days over it and stay Saturday night in Grasmere. More of them later.

We started in the dark at 3:30 in the morning. It was early May. We got lost almost immediately around Tailbert in the approach to Swindale and floundered into a bog which was a setback for me, for I was wearing what used to be called desert boots, lightweight suedes which did not take kindly to being wet. Going up Swindale we roused various dogs in farm houses and half expected some farmer to appear at a bedroom window with a shotgun, but soon we'd followed the old corpse road out of the valley and dropped over into Mardale where our support was waiting with early morning tea and biscuits.

We went up over High Street by way of Caspel Gate, and on the great open space of Racecourse Hill savoured that heady feeling of superiority that being up on the fells in the early morning brings, before going on down by Angle Tarn to Patterdale, where Mike Harvey, our support, again appeared and served us a full English breakfast, a memorable meal.

This was becoming a very enjoyable day. The weather was fine, the air crisp and clear, and there were still patches of old snow, but they did not wet the feet. We were about as lightly clad and lightly shod as fell runners, and I can tell you, and any plodding hiker with big boots, emergency food, first aid kit, giant plastic bivvy bag, waterproofs, whistle, map in large dangling map case, camera, sun screen, dark glasses, wallet, credit cards, Swiss army knife, mobile phone and kit for the treatment of anaphylactic shock, I can tell you there is nothing to beat being on the fells on a fine day with featherweight foot gear and the lightest of clothing, secure in the knowledge that wherever you cross a road there will be a car waiting with its tailgate open revealing an ample spread of food and drink.

We continued up Patterdale, past Grisedale Tarn and through a slot into the narrow valley leading to Dunmail Raise, where we had lunch – perhaps luncheon would be a better word – of beef stew and suet pudding, before tackling the steep flank of Steel Fell.

It was now quite a long way to the next road and further succour. We went across the top of Wythburn over High White Stones, and on to our second Angle Tarn of the day, in its dramatic rocky cirque. On the abrupt slope up to Ore Gap Etsu was inclined to grind to a halt – in fact so were we all – but she called upon her samurai ancestry and by repeatedly putting one foot doggedly in front of the other finally made it to the col.

In my article in *The Big Walks* I had referred at this point rather grandiloquently to stout Cortez on his first sighting of the Pacific, and to tell you the truth, we did in our modest way look at each other with a wild surmise, in the glad realisation that that faint streak of light at the horizon was the Irish Sea and from here to the coast it was all downhill. Much heartened, we plunged down into Green Hole, across the big boggy hollow, and down beside the waterfalls and potholes of Lingcove Beck, to the packhorse bridge at Throstlegarth. Another mile or two and we came out past Brotherilkeld to the road at the foot of Hardknott Pass, where we enjoyed a richly undeserved reception and premature congratulation from Bill Peascod and Brian Dodson, who were waiting there with a bottle of champagne.

We still had ten miles to go. The one thing no one can deny about champagne is that it goes straight to where it counts. We now took the path along the River Esk, than which I know no lovelier valley walk – and that is not the champagne talking – right through to Forge Bridge, and then the private lane beside Muncaster Fell to Muncaster Castle. We were flagging a little, I must admit, but only in the legs. We walked down the main street of Ravenglass, and though I was a bit sorry to get salt water on my suede boots, put our feet in the sea. It was nine o'clock. We had done forty-two miles and about nine thousand feet of climbing.

One of the most satisfactory things about this outing was that on Sunday morning we woke up to a day of pouring rain, and thought with a certain amount of unholy glee of the two who had decided to take an extra day over the walk.

Carpe diem is a good motto for mountaineers, and one I have often through indolence failed to live up to. For a long time I had another big walk in mind. I worked out its detail from the map but put it off for so long that I am now too old to attempt it. It starts on the top of Black Coombe and ends on the top of Skiddaw. Try it and the best of luck.

MT. BLANC: THE TOURIST ROUTE

To a climber heading for Chamonix those soaring rock peaks, the Aiguilles, are probably the main objectives, while Mt.Blanc itself is thought of as a mere snow plod. But when one actually stands beside the statue of de Saussure, gazing up at that airy and ethereal summit, it exerts a surprisingly powerful attraction and it is hard to resist the desire to go and stand upon it. It has a sublimity that seems to go beyond what a rock climb has to offer. On my early visits to the Alps we made two attempts on it. On the first we got as far as the Vallot Hut, that comfortless aluminium box you enter from below by a trap door. A strong and extremely cold wind had begun to blow, and the hut was full of unhappy climbers with blue lips and inadequate clothing, standing in a puddle of snow-melt on the bare floor, trying to decide whether to go any further. What lay ahead were the Bosses du Dromedaire, then the exposed final ridge to the summit. It was still early in the day and we thought we would have some food and drink and wait to see if the weather improved. We were now a party of three, having picked up a solitary young Frenchman who was not a mountaineer but had come to Chamonix and bought an ice axe and crampons for the express purpose of climbing Mt.Blanc.

Two hardy looking characters set off for the summit, but everyone else hung about in indecision. After half an hour these two came back and clearly had a story to tell. We caught the words "deux morts" and gradually pieced together the information that they had come across two dead alpinists sitting beside the track, partly buried in snow, and that this had changed their minds about continuing. It changed our minds too, and we were soon on our way down to the Grand Plateau and the head of the Bossons Glacier. A thousand feet or two of descent brought us into quite tolerable weather conditions and we took our time. Near the Mulets Hut we were overtaken by a couple of guides, descending very quickly and bringing with them what looked at first like two small toboggans but were in fact the bodies of the two climbers still rigidly frozen into a sitting position. They had climbed the Brenva Face the day before, it was assumed, and had been too exhausted to make it to the Vallot Hut. When we finally got off the glacier our young French friend declared that he would sell his axe and his crampons; he was finished with mountaineering forever.

I was in Chamonix again the following year, and the plan was to make another attempt towards the end of the holiday when we were well acclimatised. I was with S.B.Beck and F.J.Monkhouse, both Lake District rock-climbers, and this time we reached the summit without incident. In the crowded Aiguille de Goûter Hut we had noticed a French family party, husband, wife and two teenage children, with a guide. I had felt some admiration for them tackling a serious mountain climb *en famille*. From the summit we once more descended via the Bossons Glacier and on reaching the Grand Plateau at its head, became aware of a small group of people off to our left, who looked as though they might be in trouble. We went across. A guide, a small man with very black hair and a sunburnt red face, was peering down a hole in the snow. A rope led out of the hole and three or four other men were hauling on it. We recognised members of the family we had seen the night before. There was a lot of excited chatter and the guide kept shouting for silence while he tried to communicate with whoever was down the hole. At his request we joined the men on the rope and hauled away. Eventually the mother of the family group was brought to the surface, scratched and bleeding and with a broken arm. We learned that two of the party had fallen into the crevasse. The teenage boy had been the first to go through, pulling his mother after him, and the rope had broken between them and the rest. The boy had fallen through a narrow place further down but his mother had fortunately stuck there. The guide had climbed down to her with another rope but all attempts to haul them both right out failed. He had then gone down again, and the boy being now within reach, had secured him to a separate rope. We had arrived just in time to help haul the mother out. We now manned the boy's rope and heaved upon it while the guide knelt at the lip of the crevasse and peered into its depths. The more we pulled the more pitiful were the muffled screams of the boy – his name was Georges – down the crevasse. We pulled so hard I thought the rope might break. In a pause while the guide considered what to try next I went up to him, rehearsing my grammar school French. "Monsieur," I said, "Descenderai-je?" He looked at me. "Je suis foutu," he said. Taking this for assent, I uncoiled our rope, made sure it was held by my two companions and no one else and climbed down the crevasse. A foot or two below the surface it was all ice, sharp, spiky ice, melted and refrozen into a rigid honeycomb. I was in shirt sleeves for it was a hot day on the surface. As I was wearing crampons it was easy to climb down using back-and-foot technique. About forty feet down I came to Georges. At first I could do nothing as he seized my hands in his as though I was his sole lifeline. He was a drowning man grabbing his rescuer. His head and shoulders protruded through a narrow slot; the rest of his body and his legs were dangling in a dim, and as far as I could see, bottomless abyss. Every time they heaved on the rope he felt not only that he was being pulled in two but that the rope might slip or break and drop him into the awful depths. Looking up the ice chimney, which was lit by a blue and strangely beautiful light, I could see the red face and black hair of the guide outlined against the dark of the alpine sky.

It was the friction of Georges' body and clothing against the spiky ice that was making him immovable. I saw a way of overcoming it. I put my back on one wall of the crevasse, and my feet, wide apart, on the other, so that the boy's head was between my legs and I could grab his shoulders. I then rehearsed some more French. "Monsieur," I bellowed, (for the crevasse absorbed sound to a remarkable degree) "Ecoutez! Quand je dis 'Tirez,' tirez! Vous comprenez?"

"D'accord," he shouted.

I seized Georges by the shoulders and pulled him as hard as I could towards me and away from the ice that he was stuck on. "Tirez!" I yelled, and to my delight Georges shot up like a cork from a bottle. The guide now sprang into action.

"Tirez Georges!" I would hear him shout, and Georges would go flying up a few feet. Then, "Tirez l'Anglais!" and I would be hauled willy-nilly, blaspheming helplessly and getting quite scratched about the arms, when I could have climbed up carefully and without risk. In this way the two of us were hauled up like sacks of coal. In the end I stopped trying to remonstrate and just concentrated on fending myself off from the spiky walls of the crevasse.

Back on the surface I felt pretty pleased with myself. It was the first time I had ventured into the bowels of a glacier and I would not have missed it. Georges was none the worse and was received into the bosom of his family with much emotion. The guide was called Balmat, a name famous in the annals of Mt.Blanc. He carried the mother with the broken arm down piggyback, no mean feat. My friends and I followed slowly, savouring our day out in this splendid scenery. As we passed the Mulets Hut, Balmat came out, shook me by the hand and invited me for a drink. In deference to my friends, who were now wanting to get on, I thanked him but declined.

I have never ceased to regret that. He may well have taken my refusal as a slight and for my part I probably forfeited a brief interlude of friendship and bon accord.

MOTORBIKE

In my early days, when getting to the hills and crags was as big a challenge as climbing them, motorbikes were more commonly used by climbers. Nowadays almost everyone has a car. My friend and climbing partner Jack Carswell owned a Vincent Black Shadow, and no doubt put himself more at risk riding it than in his rock-climbing. To him it was much more than a mere means of getting about. On one occasion when he skidded on ice beside Bassenthwaite Lake and he, his bike and his wife went sliding separately along the slippery road, it was the Vincent he ran to first and not his wife. Or so she claimed. It seemed to me that about as many climbers were killed on motorcycles as on rock climbs. Helmets were not commonly worn, the preferred head gear being a cloth cap put on back to front. Hospitals often pointed out the alarming frequency of deaths and serious head injuries to young men on motorbikes. Nevertheless so much did I need to get to the hills that I bought a BSA B31, a 350cc single cylinder workhorse of a machine.

With me on the pillion, a friend rode it from the shop to the University quadrangle, where he gave me a twenty minute course in handling it. Like a pigeon I made two or three circuits of the quad before taking off for my destination four or five miles away through the traffic of Liverpool. I was determined not to be killed motorcycling. Getting killed climbing had a touch of distinction to it, but getting killed motorcycling was common.

I took my driving test in Workington and passed, which enabled me to take my bike to Eire during my Easter holidays. I rode south to Blarney and Cork, then over to Kerry, camping, or if the weather was bad, staying at youth hostels and hotels. My shining new motorcycle was much admired.

I had a notion to climb Carrantouill in the McGillicuddy's Reeks, 'the highest hill in all Ireland,' as people kept telling me. With my scarcely adequate road map I started towards it along country lanes. When I reached the end of all rideable tracks I called at an isolated croft. It was a two-roomed thatched cottage with a flagged floor, and occupied by an old woman and her niece. The niece, who looked between twenty-five and thirty, wore two or three men's jackets, each gone under the armpits, so that when she raised her arms you could see bare flesh. They were both the soul of courtesy and said yes, of course I could leave my bike there, and to be sure they could make me a supper. I set off up the hill.

The upper part of Carrantouill was still snow-covered, but I kicked steps up it without difficulty. By the time I got back to the croft my boots and socks were wet through. I took them off and put them near the fire. The old lady brought me the side of a cardboard carton to rest my bare feet on; it was the nearest she had to a hearth rug. The niece, I noticed, was now wearing a dress and looking quite attractive.

It was raining quietly, and getting dusk. I did not feel like putting my tent up and asked if I might sleep in the house. The old lady said yes, but was somewhat concerned about what she called the down-drop. It seemed that though their bedroom had a sound roof the living room thatch tended to drip and she feared that if I slept on the settle as I proposed I might get wet.

She kept referring to the meat that we were to have for supper. It turned out to be a hunk of bacon fat with skin on one side and a thin streak of salty meat on the other. But with boiled potatoes it tasted quite delicious. When she offered me tea, the blackest I have ever seen, she asked, "Do you take the colouring, Thomas?" The colouring was evaporated milk, which turned the tea from pitch black to rich mahogany. She was throughout both courteous and dignified, with not a hint of embarrassment about her poverty. She showed me a letter her mother had received from de Valera, the Prime Minister, on the occasion of her hundredth birthday – "and she'd never had the priest nor the doctor near the house," she declared. She herself was seventy-two.

The niece and I went out to scout for some firewood. She wore old wellingtons and a jacket, and picked up a saw as we left. She plunged downhill boldly and we went so far I began to think how laborious it would be getting back loaded with wood. We came to some trees and she felled quite a large one, sawing non-stop till it toppled. She put down the saw, came to me and smiled ....

We got the tree back up the hill. It was hard work and she had the heavy end. We shoved the end in through the door and sawed pieces off until we could get it all inside. The old lady showed a lot of skill in making it burn. "It's the vintillation, Thomas," she said, "the vintillation," as she raised the burning sticks.

Next morning when I left I offered money, rather hesitantly as nothing had been said. She took it graciously, like a queen accepting tribute.

Approaching Limerick I came off the bike on some loose gravel, tearing the shoulder of my cycling suit and bending the headlamp sideways. Though I pushed the lamp straight again the bike had lost its shop window perfection. For some reason I called in at the next police station to report the accident. The Garda was sympathetic and made me a cup of tea.

"Perhaps" he said, " you were getting just the least little bit too confident."

I cycled down the narrow winding coast road to Connemara marvelling at the tiny fields manured with seaweed and the low thatched cottages growing out of the rocks. I think it must all have gone now, or be turned into holiday homes, but then it was a real peasant community, with donkeys everywhere. I came to Clifden.

Heading east again, my time nearly up, I spotted a suitable field to camp in and called at a white-washed croft for permission. "And would you mind if I lifted a sod and made a little fire to cook my ham on," I asked. "I'll put it back and leave no mark."

"There's no need to make a fire," the crofter said. "We have a fire here. You're welcome to cook on that."

The little house was bare but spotlessly clean. A peat fire burned on a flat hearth. The back and sides of the chimney were whitewashed, except for the narrow streak of black that the smoke made. When I had cooked my slice of ham I found that a table had been laid with a blue-checked cloth, cutlery and crockery, slices of soda bread and butter and a pot of tea. We spent the evening chatting, their two children listening quietly.

In the morning I tried to give them something but they would not take it. "I've been kindly treated in England," said the crofter. "But there's one thing I'd like to ask you to do."

"What's that?" I asked.

"Just send us a postcard when you get back to say you've arrived safely."

During that summer I rode my motorbike to the Alps, with Keith Warburton on the pillion. Nylon climbing ropes had become available and studying the specifications quoted by British Ropes I came to the conclusion that the thinnest rope, with a breaking strength of a thousand pounds, would meet our needs, though it was no thicker than string. I bought a hundred and eighty feet, to use doubled as a climbing rope and to provide if necessary a ninety foot abseil. This, together with a couple of slings and karabiners, crampons and ice axes, comprised our whole climbing equipment. We carried sleeping bags but no tent.

It was raining as we arrived in Folkestone, and we slept that night – or more accurately spent that night – in an abandoned gun emplacement overlooking the town. As usual we were on a budget.

My memories of this trip are vivid but fragmentary and the spirit of the holiday is perhaps best represented by a few vignettes:

Though appreciative of the scenery, what we really have an eye out for throughout this trip is possible bivouac places. The countryside around Lille is very unpromising. For mile after mile ditches prevent us from leaving the road and getting into fields. Eventually, in the dark, we spread our sleeping bags on the grass verge. Every time a vehicle passes the ground shakes and we feel in danger of being run over. At one point a truck grinds to a halt and backs up. We feign sleep. The driver leans out of his cab. "Qu'est-ce que c'est?" he calls.

"Nous dormons," we reply.

"Merde!" he says. "J'ai cru que vous êtes en panne."

We find haystacks are good to sleep against in wet weather. On the lee side there is usually a scrap of dry ground.

In Zurich, the stress of trying to find the way causes me to forget to drive on the right, and I cross a river bridge on the wrong side of the road, to the accompaniment of an indignant fanfare of motor horns, and much shaking of fists.

Somewhere in Switzerland we get permission to sleep in a barn. We bed down on a big canvas sheet covering what we take to be hay. It is wonderfully soft. It turns out however to be silage, and during the night the weight of our bodies carries us down into its foetid depths. It becomes unbearably hot and we are convinced that internal combustion has already started, so we move out and find a little straw to lie on. Next morning a young girl comes out to us with a jug of milky coffee and an invitation to come in and have some breakfast.

We pass through Innsbruck and turn south into the Oetstal . It is raining again, but we press on to Vent. This little village is reached by a narrow cart track halfway up a precipitous mountain side, a mere ledge carved through the crags, with vertical drops on our left. We slither and slide on the wet surface. I am sustained by my happy ignorance of motorcycles and Keith, accepting his helplessness, hopes for the best. We arrive, put up at the little inn, leave the bike in a shed and take to the hills. We traverse the mountains moving from hut to hut, over the Wildspitz and others until we are driven down by a blizzard. Back in Vent after a week's absence, we learn that a bridge has been washed away. Though we can climb over the gap there is not the slightest chance of getting the bike across.

"When will the bridge be rebuilt?" we ask.

"Who knows," they say.

So we take off on foot for the Zillertal where, among other minor adventures, we have our first taste of alpine route-finding in thick weather.

Somewhere during this period, probably in the Oetstal mountains, we are having a rest day, sunning ourselves on the terrace of a hut overlooking a great flat glacier. We are alone in the place except for the hut guardian and a middle-aged woman with her eye glued to a telescope mounted on the terrace. Suddenly this lady becomes animated and urges us to look through the glass. Out on the plain of snow we see the figure of a man, straining back against the pull of a rope which disappears into the surface of the snow. He does not move.

We call the guardian and show him.

"Komm," he says.

We grab our ropes and ice axes, leap into our boots, and plod off as fast as we can across the soft midday snow.

We find a guide, holding a client. The client's head is only a couple of feet down below the glacier's surface, but his feet are kicking in space over a gulf of unknown depth. He is a big, stout German, and very upset. The rope has cut deep into the lip of the crevasse making it quite impossible to haul him out. We somehow pass a rope round him and attempt to pull him out from the other side but it does not work; the softness of the snow surface in which we are floundering makes rope engineering impractical, and the German has no strength or agility to assist. I go for a simple solution. "Cut a channel," I say, and we attack the lip of the crevasse where the rope has cut in, widening the groove until we've made a slipway up which to haul the unfortunate victim. The disadvantage of this system is that the snow we dig falls on to the poor fellow we're supposed to be helping; the advantage is that we do get him out. On the way back to the hut he is too busy composing himself to think of thanking us.

I have my own problems. I have rushed out to the rescue wearing shorts. I now tie handkerchiefs round my legs to protect them from the powerful high altitude sun.

We obtain a night's lodging in a house run by an old lady who speaks not a word of English and cannot understand our feeble attempts at German. We sleep under very short eiderdowns which, from the warmth of our bodies, inflate to a height of about two feet. It is like sleeping under hot balloons, with feet and shoulders out in the cold.

After ten days we walk back up to Vent and find a new wooden bridge in place, with a small Christmas tree tied to its rail. Our timing has been just right.

We cross the Brenner into Italy.

We spend a wretched, hot night, sweating in our sleeping bags on the side of Lake Como, with a cloud of mosquitoes whining to get in through the tiny breathing holes we have had to leave.

We go over the Grand St. Bernard and down to Martigny, then up over the Col de la Forclaz (the old road, the new one being not yet built). The bike overheats and takes two hours to cool down.

We climb the Aiguille d'Argentière. On the descent I slip on steep ice above a bergschrund. As I shoot down I think, in a detached sort of way, that I cannot help but pull Keith off too, and that we will both be swallowed by the schrund. But my nylon string is so elastic that he feels no sudden strain and stops me without difficulty, like a hooked fish.

Next we traverse the Grand Charmoz and the Grépon, two of the spectacular granite aiguilles that tower over Chamonix. Abseiling on our nylon string in this vertical landscape of soaring pinnacles and immense drops is a hair-raising experience. Our hands seem to have nothing to grip, and the thin cord stretches like elastic. Fortunately we are not aware how little friction against a rock it would take to abrade the rope to breaking point. Books on climbing technique have yet to be written.

One abseil I am unlikely ever to forget is the one off the Grand Gendarme on the Grépon. The flat granite top of this pinnacle has one large stone lying on it too heavy to move. It is the only thing to abseil from, and unfortunately it is not placed directly above the point one wants to descend to, an exiguous rock col with big drops on either side. The recommended procedure is to separate the two parts of the abseil rope and, taking one in each hand, back off down a steep rib grasping the rock between the knees, 'à cheval' as it says in the guidebook. (As I performed this manoeuvre once on a previous traverse of the Grépon, a French climber added the sardonic advice "Attention aux petits pois!") After descending a few feet, one's only handholds the two parts of the rope held one on each side of the rib, a small foothold is reached 'on the edge of all things,' and here one can marry the two parts of the abseil line, put them round a small knob of rock, and do a classic abseil straight down to the rock col.

With our rope, British Ropes No. 1 nylon, the thickness of baling twine, this method of descent feels extremely insecure. Keith goes first and is

soon down and perched on the rock col. I shuffle off backwards in my turn, breathing rather heavily, but when I get to the foothold, in bringing the two lines together I inadvertently let go of one of them and the wind blows it out of my reach. This leaves me standing with no handholds on a tiny ledge, with an unclimbable sweep of granite above me, and about a thousand feet of exposure below. I am very unhappy, but fortunately Keith down below still has hold of the end of the line, and by swinging it vigorously to and fro manages to bring it within my grasp.

Compared with this little incident such famous features of the traverse as the Mummery Crack, the Rateau de Chèvres, the Route aux Bicyclettes and the Venetz Crack seem almost second-rate.

Another place on this excursion where I become mildly terrorised is on the descent of the top of the Nantillons Glacier. We have left our crampons and one of our axes at the start of the rock climb, and consequently Keith goes first cutting steps and I follow, in vibrams, with no means of stopping a slip, not even a piton. I plead with Keith to cut bigger steps, and the delay this causes shreds my nerves even further, for I am feeling an urgent need to get down and away from all this steepness and verticality.

It is dusk by the time we get off the mountain. We continue down to Chamonix on a zig-zag path through the forest. It is easy to follow except where it comes out on to small areas of pasture from which the continuation is hard to spot in the dark. We are now very tired and thirsty, and the sole of one of Keith's boots has come adrift. He has to stop every so often to lash it on with a piece of string, and I use these pauses to fall asleep for a few minutes. In the end, in fact, we seem to be walking in our sleep, and when we reach Chamonix we spend a long time at a fountain, trying to drink it dry, before repairing to Snell's field to sleep.

We cross France again, at slow speeds, sleeping out every night. A motorcycle ridden slowly in summer weather is a most enjoyable means of travel. Each morning our sleeping bags are drenched with dew. We put them around our necks like scarves and dry them out as we ride. The roads are largely deserted; at one point we ride for miles abreast of a car, chatting with the occupants. And we sometimes sing as we go.

BATURA MUSTAGH

Looking through old papers and notebooks I have come across one bearing the words Batura Mustagh 1959 on its title page. All it contains is equipment lists, and a record of the firms, thirty-seven in all, to whom begging letters had been sent. The lists include climbing gear, tents, stoves and pressure cookers, clothing for expedition members and for porters, photographic materials, etc., all with prices. The prices, of course, seem very low by modern standards. The last entry is a simple summing up: -

Spent	£292 -12 -6
Committed	£403 - 0 - 0
To be bought	£ 78 - 0 - 0
	£773 -12- 6

Not that I need this discovery to remind me of the Batura Mustagh Expedition. It has always been with me, and will be, no doubt, to the end of my days. If I'd had the money and could have left my work, I would have gone with them. As it was I became the expedition's home agent.

We saw them off at Liverpool, for those were the days when people still went to foreign parts by ocean liner. The big ship towered like a cliff above the landing stage, its several decks lined with passengers, our six young mountaineers among them, waving and calling to friends and relatives ashore. When the lines were cast off and tugs nosed the huge vessel away from the dock so that water began to be seen between ship and shore, it was as always a rather moving moment, the gap widening between the travellers and their loved ones. In retrospect these farewells, cheerful and full of high hopes as they were, have a particular poignancy for we were never to see them again. Except for the one who was not going to climb.

The driving force behind the expedition was its youngest member, Harry Stephenson. I had introduced him to rock climbing some years before, when I took four senior boys from Workington Grammar School, all complete novices, to climb Scafell Pinnacle by Slingsby's Chimney. Having led the chimney I had to continue some distance further up to find a satisfactory belay, and this put me out of sight of the party. There was a long delay below, with a good deal of shouting, and a proposal, which filled me with misgiving, to change the order in which they were tied on. Eventually I was able to take in the rope, but the first thing to appear over the edge was a pair of boots attached to it by the laces. This was not a good idea, as the boots kept sticking in cracks. Next came Harry Stephenson, in his socks. With Stephenson belayed I was able to descend a little and help the rest of the party over the difficult bit. It all took much longer than I had expected and it was getting dark by the time we escaped from the crag. We were so late home that several parents had become alarmed and were baying at the heels of the headmaster.

Stephenson, apart from his miscalculation over the boots, proved a very cool and competent ally on this excursion and from that day on he was a climber. His father, sometime later when his son was at Nottingham University, expressed concern about this preoccupation, fearing it would interfere with his studies. "Bear in mind," I said, "that but for climbing he might not have made it to university at all. He worked hard for a university place because he knew the long vacations would give him plenty of opportunity for getting into the mountains."

Harry Stephenson was a quiet young man but he had big ideas. His first motorcycle was a big twin of enormous speed and acceleration. On his second trip to the Alps he climbed several impressive routes culminating in the Brenva Face of Mont Blanc. His companion on this occasion was the equally mild and self-effacing Richard Knight. Bad weather delayed them on the Brenva, and their food supplies exhausted, they were reduced to dining off Spangle Soup, Spangles being a popular boiled sweet of the period. It was during their incarceration in the tiny refuge that they met and made friends with two German climbers of considerable experience, Albert Hirschbichler and Martin Guennel. Hirschbichler had been the tenth man to climb the Eiger Nordwand. The party talked of their mountaineering aspirations and it was here, no doubt, that the idea of going to the Himalaya was mooted.

Harry now set about the task of researching the area, planning the expedition and finding a way through the political and legal obstacles that confront anyone trying to enter the realms of freedom and light that are the highest mountains of the world. Each member of the group was prepared to put in a substantial sum of money, but it was essential to secure the backing of the Royal Geographical Society and the Mount Everest Foundation. Consultation with Alfred Gregory and others had disclosed that the highest peak of the Batura massif in the north-west Karakoram was 25,540 feet and unclimbed. With this mountain the declared objective, an application was made to the Mount Everest Foundation, but it was at first rejected on the grounds that the party contained no doctor and no member with Himalayan experience.

When Stephenson told me of this setback I put him on to my old friend and climbing companion Keith Warburton, who happened to meet both criteria, though I doubted whether he would be interested, since he had just got married. Keith however found the opportunity too good to miss. He became the nominal leader of the expedition and the oldest, at thirty-one. The others were all in their twenties, ranging from Martin Guennel, twenty-eight, to Harry Stephenson, the prime mover of the whole enterprise, twenty-three. In addition to the two German climbers and the three English, John Edwards, twenty-six, was recruited as a glaciologist and surveyor. He did not intend to go further than the base camp. During the voyage out they made the acquaintance of Jamil Sherjan, an officer of the Parachute Regiment of the British army, the twenty-one year old son of a Pakistani general. He volunteered to join the party as assistant surveyor and glaciologist.

From Keith Warburton's letters I learned of the expedition's progress from Karachi by train to Rawalpindi, and by air to Gilgit. In Rawalpindi they were held up for seventeen days waiting for suitable weather for the flight in, but there was plenty to do repacking the baggage into sixty pound porter loads. They had the pleasure of staying with Colonel E.R. Goodwin, the retired Indian Army officer, whom Keith Warburton already knew and to whose kindness and hospitality many expeditions were indebted.

Keith's letters reflected the wonder and excitement of travelling in a foreign land and eager anticipation of what lay ahead, tinged, nevertheless, with anxiety at the seriousness of the undertaking. As they flew in the Dakota to Gilgit they saw for the first time such giants as Nanga Parbat, Haramosh and Rakaposhi standing above innumerable nameless peaks.

In Gilgit they stayed at the Mir of Hunza's guest house, delayed by a washout on the Baltit road, but the exotic charm of the place, with its bazaar full of traders from far and wide, and the invigorating air of the mountains, made the stay enjoyable. The road to Baltit is seven feet wide and clings to the precipitous side of the Hunza gorge, high above the tumbling brown waters of the river. Nine jeeps transported the expedition, with all their gear, in a five hour drive, no doubt full of interest. Safely arrived, they were welcomed by the Mir himself, ruler of Hunza, and generously entertained.

The next stage was to travel with a string of pack horses to the village of Pasu, which lies at the confluence of the Hunza river and the outflow from the vast Batura glacier. Here the baggage, totalling about three tons, was transferred from the horses to some forty yaks and the final stage of the approach began. Keith Warburton's next letter reflected anxiety and frustration at the recalcitrance of the porters. When I think back upon the quiet, stress-free nature of the times he and I had spent in the Scottish hills, and of his appreciation of the simple pleasures of camping and climbing, I wonder whether he regretted taking on the tribulations of such a serious mountaineering venture, and leaving his new wife at home. The journey from Pasu to their base camp took six days. Here, at 11,000 feet, at the foot of the prodigious ice fall, which seemed to be the most serious obstacle of the whole ascent, they were glad to pay off the local men, retaining only three high-altitude porters.

The ice-fall was about two miles wide, more than a mile high, and moving at about twelve feet a day, a monstrous creeping escalator of a glacier. Spending time on it was so hazardous that the party decided to be done with it in one big push, and establish an advanced base camp at the top, with twenty-eight days rations for the five climbers. This task was made more difficult by the behaviour of the three remaining porters who were making further demands for equipment and pay. After two temporary camps had been set up in the ice-fall at 13,000 and 16,000 feet, and before the serious ferrying of equipment began, the porters were all sacked, and the whole strenuous and dangerous business of establishing the advance base at 18,000 feet was done by the seven expedition members, Edwards and Sherjan having left their glaciological work in order to help.

This phase, from base camp to advanced base camp, took nineteen days, from 4 June to 23 June.

I still have Keith Warburton's last letter, dated 16 June, 1959. It is brief and factual, 'in a hurry to catch the dak wallah, or mail runner', and it is mainly a request for me to claim a rebate on the insurance taken out for the sacked porters. "Work on the mountain," he writes, "is going ahead. Albert and I have been right through the unpleasant and dangerous part of the climb, the ice-fall, to establish Camp III at about 18,000 feet, but without any HA porters there is a tremendous lot of hard work to put in. At present the weather is foul again with an awful lot of new snow." There follow one or two comments about communications with the Sunday Times. And he adds a postscript, "P.S. I wish you were here!!"

These words have a poignancy for me, not only because they are the last I ever heard from him, but because I read in them the loneliness of a worried leader. It is ironic that though this whole enterprise was not of his making, he now found himself saddled with its leadership. Though only a few years older than the rest of the party, I think he felt a certain difference in attitude. He belonged to an older school of thought, which regarded the preservation of life as an overriding factor in mountaineering ventures. He was a bold and sometimes an audacious climber, but prudence came high among his priorities. No mountain was worth dying for. His companions, his earlier letters had implied, seemed so hellbent on success that it worried him a little. Getting through the ice-fall would seem to him a sort of miraculous deliverance, and since there appeared to be no further obstacles ahead no doubt he was beginning to dare to hope.

There was now a whole month of silence and then a telegram from John Edwards saying that the party was overdue by several days. I passed this information on to the families of the climbers, with the comment that all kinds of unforseen circumstances occurred on expeditions and no news was probably good news. I had always dreaded hearing that someone had been killed, in crevasse or avalanche, but that a whole party should go missing seemed so extraordinary as to be unbelievable.

I meant this, and in the next few days the parents and dependents of the climbers were, I know, much more apprehensive than I. I confidently expected a happy ending. I was wrong.

The days dragged on. We heard that a severe spell of bad weather had struck the region from July 2-26. The German Karakoram Expedition had been routed and forced to retreat, as had the Swiss Distaghil Sar Expedition. Raymond Lambert sent up a high-altitude tent and other equipment and Edwards and Sherjan made a valiant but unsuccessful effort to climb the ice-fall. Three members of the German expedition also came to the rescue. They too were stopped by the ice fall, but they gained a point on its containing ridge from which they could see the site of Camp III. All that remained was an unbroken surface of snow. In the end we had to abandon all hope. It seemed likely that the whole party had been overwhelmed in a powder snow avalanche.

The only other clue to the climbers' activities was that on or around 28 June, a hunter had spotted through his binoculars two figures on a ridge some 1500 feet below the summit of Batura Mustagh. They were moving steadily upwards and he watched them, he claimed, for three hours. This raises the possibility that they succeeded in climbing their peak before disaster struck.

I had lost three good climbing friends, one of them my oldest and closest companion in the hills, another a youngster I had introduced to the sport and who had rapidly surpassed me in it. In addition I now had the sad duty of winding up the affairs of the expedition and trying to offer support and condolence to the families and friends of the missing men. There was some painful publicity of course. A journalist from Paris Match came over to see me, expecting to make the disaster the magazine's most sensational feature, but it was pushed from the front cover by some more newsworthy scandal.

In the high mountains and on the great rock faces the climber's life is urgent, vital, and supremely worth living, right up to the moment, I dare say, of the fatal fall or the oblivion of the avalanche; but at home it is a different story. The Batura misfortune made me shake my head sadly over the aspirations that drive mountaineers, and even now, nearly forty years later, I can only think what a waste it was.

I can seek some consolation in the words of Laurence Binyon:

They shall not grow old as we that are left grow old.
Age shall not weary them, nor the years condemn.

Once people are gone they need nothing; their troubles are all ended. It is those they leave behind that must be cared for.

It is strange how differently people cope with bereavement. Keith Warburton's wife, a hospital nurse, took the news of her husband's death gravely, privately, and with dignity. She needed to be left alone in her grief. Harry Stephenson's girlfriend, by contrast, was loud in her lamentations and clung passionately to her friends. It was his father I felt most sorry for; though he had another son, and a daughter, Harry, the youngest, was the apple of his eye, his joy and pride.

Mr. and Mrs. Knight lost their only child. They never told their grief, and when some time later my wife and I went to stay with them they never referred to him and there was not a photograph nor a memento of him to be seen in the house. They remained kind friends of ours until they died.

Martin Guennel too was an only child. His parents took refuge in a romantic and sentimental view of mountain tragedy, writing to us for many years until they too died, and always in terms of their son's 'glorious sacrifice' and the 'noble fate of those pursuing an ideal and a dream.'

Albert Hirschbichler left a wife and two children, a son and a daughter. He had been a customs man and his wife ran a small guest house. In winding up the expedition's affairs I found that the return fares of the climbers were refundable, and that there was in consequence a considerable sum to dispose of. Everyone agreed that this should go to Frau Hirschbichler. My wife kept up a correspondence with her throughout her life, and her daughter, a delightful and talented young woman, still keeps in touch.

Harry Stephenson's father collected all the information, photographs and slides he could, and gave lectures on the Batura Mustagh Expedition. He had a teak bench placed outside the climbing hut at Brackenclose in

Wasdale and he went to great lengths to get permission for a stone to be placed in the little churchyard in Wasdale Head. There, ringed by yew trees, in the heart of the Cumbrian fells, the names of the five mountaineers are commemorated, and words carved on a different grave at the opposite side of the graveyard could perhaps be taken as their epitaph too:

One moment stood they as the angels stand
High in the stainless immanence of air
The next they were not, to their gods
Translated unaware.

From such events one gains insights into one's own personality. From this and other bereavements and losses, I have found that the rituals of grief and the ceremonies of remembrance do not mean much to me. I am more pragmatic than I realized. But a small thing that still hurts me happened between me and Keith Warburton's family. On a visit to his home shortly after the disaster, his elder brother asked me if I would like to have his ice axe. I was touched. "Yes," I said, "I'd like that, and it would be very useful, as I often find myself going out with someone who hasn't got one." The brother left almost immediately. On a subsequent visit, though I was kindly enough received by the parents, this brother snubbed me quite pointedly. I realized too late that he thought I should keep the axe as a sacred relic. I felt guilty at my own insensitivity and at the same time wounded at his failure to appreciate the extent of my grief. I never saw him again, nor did I keep in touch with the family. I would not, like the Guennels, ennoble the Batura Mustagh disaster into a sort of high tragedy, though there was some tragic irony in it I suppose. I just saw it as a terrible misfortune, an accident that made no sense. 'As flies to wanton boys are we to the gods; they kill us for their sport.' My sorrow was a desolate kind of sorrow, and to unwittingly offend the brother of my best friend gave a bitter little twist to it.

ANDRE ROCH

'Everest is very easy to climb, only just a little too high.' A. Roch
Observer Sayings of the Week. 25 Jan. 1953

André Roch always claims that the day we first met I let him fall off Kern
Knotts Crack.

It was on the Sunday following the 1954 annual dinner of the Fell and
Rock Climbing Club of the English Lake District. Two years before, André
had been one of the Swiss mountaineers who reached the South Col on
Everest by the Geneva Spur, and he was now invited as principal guest to
the F & RCC Dinner in recognition of the expedition's achievements. That
was how I came to be climbing in such distinguished company.

It was a slightly drizzly November day and several Club members were
sitting among the rocks at the foot of Kern Knotts, watching with idle
curiosity as I negotiated the tricky bit of slab to the right of the Sentry Box.
My second, a very tall man called Bobby Files, was on sentry duty in the
Box and his head was about level with my feet.

I was climbing in nails.

My secret weapon for getting up this slab was to make a high step and
hook a No 6 tricouni over a tiny spike of rock on the edge of the Sentry
Box, then step powerfully up on it and reach the jugs above.

But this time it did not work. My foot shot off and I fell sideways.

I was suddenly in accident mode, reactions instinctive, everything in
slow motion. My left hand slapped against the far side of the Sentry Box
and I remained miraculously suspended, the nails of my right boot pressed
on a sloping apology for a hold on the slab, my only other point of contact
the flat of my hand against the edge of the Box. I was sure that if I so much
as batted an eyelid my foot would slip off the hold and I would plummet
onto the jagged rocks below before my second could arrest the fall.

Out of the corner of my eye I saw the balaclava helmet of my second.

"Bobby," I said in a slightly strangled voice. "Can you hold your head
still. I'm going to put my foot on it," and without delay I delicately ground
my tricounis into his scalp and reached up for the jugs in the crack above.

Along with the surge of intense relief I now experienced was a feeling
of embarrassment at having been seen in this predicament by the people
below, but the odd thing was that the whole riveting drama, which I was to
relive many times in years to come, had gone unnoticed by the spectators.

I belayed at the top of the Crack and Bobby followed. Third on the rope was André, and by this time the rock was a bit wetter. When he got to the slab his Vibrams failed to grip and he came off. He fell some two feet before I held him.

After we'd finished the climb he demanded to know why I had not given him a tight rope. I explained that being pulled upset a climber's delicate balance and spoiled the climbing, but he clearly thought it better mountaineering practice to give the second as much help from the rope as possible.

We went on to the Napes, and Bobby Files led the Needle, which he could do without much difficulty, since once on the mantelshelf he could reach the top. André followed smartly. When I reached the final slab as third man I saw that he was standing on the top block unbelayed, with the rope held simply in his two hands.

Now whenever I've climbed the Needle I've stood up on the top block with some temerity, and really only to show off, before thankfully sitting down again having lassoed the block by way of belay.

So I climbed the slab pretty gingerly, and when I was safely on top commented that he was not belayed.

"What do you mean?" he said.

"Rassurance," I ventured. "Pas de rassurance." He laughed and waved his arm through the empty air that surrounded us on all sides except for the exiguous point of rock on which we were perched.

"There is nothing to tie the rope to."

"Shouldn't you at least put the rope behind your body?"

He gave a Gallic shrug. "But then you might pull me off!"

"But like this I could pull you off."

"But no. If I cannot hold you, I let you go until I can." And he added, pointedly, "You see, if I keep the rope very tight, you cannot fall."

As for my near accident on Kern Knotts Crack, it was not until I got home and took my boots off that I discovered the cause. The No 6 tricouni in question was missing. When I had stepped up, my weight had torn it out, taking with it the chunk of leather it was attached to.

Over the years that followed a friendship developed based on a shared enthusiasm for the mountains. I felt great admiration for André's mountaineering achievements, which showed such a masterly blend of audacity and sound judgment, but what really distinguished him as far as I was concerned was his uncomplicated and generous spirit, his shrewd and lively humour, and his constant appreciation of how great it was to be alive, particularly in the mountains.

He was of course a lucky man. His father was an eminent surgeon in

Geneva, who introduced him to the mountains at an early age. He grew up fit and strong. In his youth he nagged his father for a swimming pool in the garden. To end the matter his father said, "All right. You dig the hole, and I'll provide the pool." To his surprise André laboured at it for a whole summer, and finished it. It was a course of training which no doubt stood him in good stead in the mountains.

He took a degree in engineering. He also became a Swiss guide, and applied for membership of the Alpine Club. The Alpine Club, believe it or not, turned him down on the ground that he was not an amateur. Most people, I imagine, would have sourly taken the view that if that was how the Alpine Club operated, one was better out of it, but André, with characteristic sweetness of temper, replied pointing out that he had become a guide in order to be able to afford to go climbing more often, and surely the Club was for people who climbed as much as they could. The Alpine Club had the good grace to reverse their decision.

André worked for most of his life at the Federal Institute for Avalanche Research on the Weissfluhjoch above Davos. In the winter he came home from work down whichever of several splendid ski runs he fancied, and I often accompanied him, thereby, I dare say, doubling or trebling the time it took him to arrive.

As an avalanche expert he was generous in sharing his knowledge with others, unlike some of his colleagues who jealously guarded their own expertise from foreigners and the uninitiated. After the terrible Yungay avalanche in South America, which buried many thousands of people, he invited the Peruvian glaciologist whose task it was to advise his government on avalanche control to stay with him in his home, and gave him every assistance. Another outsider he welcomed to the Institute was Colin Fraser, an expatriate Briton living in Trieste, the author of *The Avalanche Enigma*. He was the only foreigner to penetrate the Parsenndienst, the ski rescue organisation whose HQ adjoined the Institute. He wore the grey uniform and broad brimmed hat of the Dienst, was a formidable skier, and spoke German, French and Italian fluently. He and I happened to be guests of André Roch at the same time and I read Fraser's MS at the galley-proof stage, unable to put it down. It was full of strange and fascinating avalanche anecdotes, mostly supplied by André.

André had his own adventures with avalanches. One day, when he was skiing off piste with his son Jean-François above Davos, a small slab avalanche started and carried his son down over a cliff. This is how Jean-François described it to me in a letter (I retain his spelling and language):

I arrived in Davos in the morning from Zurich and went on the Meierhof with my dad in the afternoon ... As we arrived at the top of a very steep gully my dad tried to make an avalanche by traversing it but didn't succeed. I had a try and succeded but I went down with it. But firstly it didn't impress me although I was astonished about its speed. Then I cam to rocks and they helped me to a complete salto and when I was head up again and was instantly covered with snow. It was such a wet and heavy snow I couldn't move at all. I thought Don't get exited so you need less oxigene! and then I thought that it would last about an hour untill the first sondage would start and I didn't think I could hold out that long. Than I begann to feel the lack of oxigene and fainted. When I woke up I saw my dad before me breathing like a young horse who ran too much.

As he heard me shouting that I was sliding down he came back on his steps and went down as quickly as possible When he arrived to the rocky bit he took his skis of and half slided and half fell down on them. When he arrived at the bottom of the gully he saw one of my poles stiking out of the snow. He started to dig there to see if the hand was there too but he couldn't the snow with his hands, it was too packed, he had to use his ski to take the snow away. He heard me sounding like bubbling under the water and after ten or fifteen minutes he got my face out of snow and another three minutes and I woke up from my dreamland. 45 minutes to clear me completely. I had one ski and one pole broken and a foot got squashed by the boot and that hurted very much. I walked to the Wolfgang and the doctor said nothing broken and after three days I skied again.

André was more unlucky with his elder daughter. She was a keen rock-climber, and was leading a climb with a female friend, with André third on the rope, when she fell. They were not belayed and her friend was snatched from the rock. Whether André instinctively threw the rope over a rock, or whether it happened to snag in a crack I do not know, and never had the courage to ask, but it broke and he was left on the rock while his daughter and her friend fell to their deaths far below.

André climbed down the route, checked that the girls were dead, walked out, got help and returned to recover the bodies.

This terrible accident affected him for a long time and no doubt left a permanent scar. But he wrote to me perhaps a year afterwards and said that even in the face of this tragic event he could not renounce his love of the mountains.

At about the same time his wife confided in me: "You know, André is like a peasant. He accepts life and death, and doesn't question it." She spoke these words with a certain bitterness, but it was a bitterness that reflected her own pain, and was not a criticism.

She was right, and it was a profound comment on his nature. He was strong, sane, practical, down-to-earth; he saw things in simple terms. But more than that, he had something of the poet, artist and visionary about him. He was an adventurer. Mountains and mountaineering were his means of realising the splendour and beauty and privilege of being alive. He was a man who knew in his blood and his bones that great things are done when men and mountains meet.

On a Himalayan expedition, in retreat owing to accident and bad weather, he put his life at risk by staying in a high camp to look after an injured Sherpa. This later got into the news, and a clergyman wrote to the paper a letter of congratulation, commending this selfless act on the behalf of a native 'who was not even of our religion'. This, André told me, had turned him off religion for good.

He knew when to be bold and when to play safe. On a ski-trip once on the Haute Route we slogged our way up the Otemma Glacier in worsening weather, and, in the snowfall and poor visibility, could not see where to leave the glacier. Though we were only a mile from the Cabane des Vignettes, André would not leave the head of the glacier until the sky cleared. We waited. We built an igloo and sat in it for hours. When anyone commented on the tedium and discomfort of this long wait, André would come out with one of his favourite philosophical reflections: *La vie est dure, sans confiture*. In the end André said, "We have a choice. Either we stay here in the igloo for the night, or we go back to the Chanrion Hut." We of course decided to go back and it was a long and tiring plod, the slope too shallow for the skis to run in the deep new snow. Next day was fine and we retraced our steps reaching the Vignettes without difficulty. In the hut André spent a good deal of time telling people that the gardien ought to stick a pole in the snow at the point where you left the glacier. The gardien, meanwhile, was busy commenting that André Roch had written a book on the Haute Route, and had been unable to find the hut.

On the other hand when André was guiding a party of three, including a long-time climbing partner of mine, Jack Carswell, who was on his first-ever visit to the Alps, he took them up the famous Via della Pera, the Pear Buttress, a long and difficult rock-climb in the middle of the vast, precipitous

Brenva Face of Mt. Blanc, between beetling séracs and hanging glaciers. He saw that the conditions were right and seized his chance. What is more he chose Carswell as his second, in preference to the experienced alpinists Charles Tilley and Malcolm Milne. When questioned later about that, he said, "I saw he was a strong man."

He was no narrow Swiss nationalist. He was cosmopolitan in his attitudes and in his wide circle of friends. In America he advised on the layout of the ski-resorts at Aspen and Snowmass, Colorado. The main piste in Aspen is called the Roch Trail, though they somewhat spoil the effect by pronouncing Roch as Roach (instead of Rock). He found the Americans so open and friendly that on his retirement he considered going to live there, but his wife, who hailed from Tessin and was European to her roots, would not hear of it. They went back to Geneva to the family house overlooking the limestone cliffs of the Salève.

The companionship of mountaineers meant a great deal to André. He did not envy the triumphs of others but entered wholeheartedly in their praise. At the same time he was always delighted to have his own prowess recognised. He was a powerful skier and regularly came first in the veteran's class on the annual Parsenn Derby, from the top of the Weissfluh to Kublis, a distance of eight miles with a descent of over six thousand feet.

He loved sports and physical skills. He had a tightrope in his garden, was the first person I saw riding a skateboard and carved a large number of boomerangs. He built sail boats and sail boards.

When in 1954 he came as chief guest to our Dinner he was representing the Swiss mountaineers who had narrowly failed in 1952 to climb Everest. He spoke in English, warmly applauding the British success but was nevertheless eloquent in his insistence that mountaineering was not for the promotion of national pride, but for fun. 'Fun' was the word he used, but what he meant, I know, was that climbing was for personal enrichment, physical, aesthetic and spiritual. 'Joy' would have been a more accurate word, joie de vivre in its fullest sense.

It is ironic that after all his mountain adventures, such as the second ascent of the North Face of the Matterhorn, the first descent of the North Face of the Dru, his long fall down the North Face of the Droites, and all his Himalayan climbing, it was on a road that he came nearest to being killed. It was in a head-on collision with an army vehicle and it was only his physical fitness and strong constitution that enabled him to survive.

Military service is compulsory in Switzerland and André's took the form of giving mountain training to the troops. One of his most interesting exploits with the Swiss Army was to take a large detachment up the Bieshorn to spend a month in snow caves. They dug and constructed a whole HQ in the permanent snow and ice, with different messes, living quarters and offices, and even a chapel, which the Army chaplain consecrated. In the forties he introduced, and gained general acceptance of, a rope-coiling method particularly useful for long abseil ropes. This was a matter of doubling the rope, then, starting at the middle, laying it in long flakes over the palm of one hand, to produce a sort of hank which could be tied on one's back for carrying. He showed me this in the 50s and I adopted it but it did not gain acceptance in this country for years. Now, however, it is the normal practice.

Throughout his whole life André was concerned with snow and ice. He spent a considerable amount of time in Thule in Greenland as a consultant for the Americans, and became an internationally known expert in devising ways of controlling avalanches.

He was an expert photographer and on a Swiss Expedition to East Greenland, as on the Everest expedition, he was in charge of the film record, producing in 16 mm format a five-reel movie of the trip. Years later, knowing I was interested in canoeing, he gave me the twenty-minute reel that related to Eskimo village life and to hunting by kayak. It has captions in French and German. I still have it, and in case the film should become brittle with age I have had a video tape made from it. The quality of the filming is very good, though André modestly disclaimed credit for it by commenting that this was the village where a year or so before, they had filmed 'Nanook of the North' and the local Eskimos – or East Greenlanders as they preferred to be called – were well versed in demonstrating their skills in front of the camera. Besides some charming scenes of village life and seal-hunting by kayak among the ice-floes, the film shows an Eskimo wriggling double-jointedly into a kayak hardly wider than his hips, and securing his sealskin anorak firmly round the rim of the cockpit. He then rolls the canoe in various ways, culminating in a hand-roll. His anorak fits so well at the wrists and the hood that hardly a drop of water gets in during these manoeuvres. One of the Swiss climbers then has a try, but fails and has to be given the 'Eskimo rescue', that is the bow of another kayak to lever himself up on.

André told me that he was sixty before he could detect any significant diminution in his strength as a mountaineer. At the age of ninety-one, recognising that he was near the end of his life, he wrote a letter to his many friends all over the world, saying that before he left this planet he wished to put on record his appreciation of all the kindnesses he had received. He described how he fell in the bathroom, and, unable to get to the phone, made a forced bivouac on the cold tiles, 'as though he was on a mountain', and got to sleep only when the radiator came on in the morning. He was then found by his son.

In response to this letter I went to see him. He still had the same warm smile. Surrounded by his paintings of the Alps and Himalayas, equipped with a wrist alarm in case he needed help, and looked after now by Maria, a young and good-looking Brazilian, and his son who lives next door, he reads a little, watches sport on T.V. a good deal, and sleeps a lot.

He is a man I have been very proud to know.

BIRD HOW

As you go up Eskdale the last farms you pass before getting into the wilder upper reaches of the valley are Brotherilkeld on the right and Taw House on the left.

In the thirties Taw House was a youth hostel as well as a sheep farm, and the first time I ever went there it was as a schoolboy and a hosteller, walking from Black Sail Hut via Wasdale and Burnmoor. At the end of the day as I left the road and started on the cart track that led to the farm I felt dead tired and resigned myself grimly to plodding that final mile.

I was heartened after a few minutes to see ahead a chimney and a roof. The end, I thought, was in sight. But it was not the farm I saw; it was a tiny cottage. Taw House was half a mile further and I still remember the struggle I had making it. In youth one gets quickly exhausted. Fortunately one recovers just as fast.

The cottage was Bird How. Two rooms over a stable or cow-byre. It belonged to Mrs. Symonds, the wife of H.H. Symonds, who wrote *Walking in the Lake District*, the first of what was to become an avalanche of such books.

Bird How had escaped renovation. It remained a humble farm-labourer's cottage. Water was taken from a nearby beck. There was one fireplace. Oil-lamps provided light.

Some ten years later, just after the war, we of the L.U.M.C. were discussing the Christmas Vacation and where to go. We wanted somewhere different, quiet and above all cheap. I suggested Bird How. It was a long shot. Mrs Symonds would probably be none too keen to let it to a bunch of students but I found her number in the phone book, and asked her, diffidently, if she would hire her cottage for one week to our very respectable climbing club, whose president was none other than George Graham Macphee.

Without hesitation she said yes.

"How much would you charge?"

"Well, let's say ten shillings for the week, plus your estimate of how much coal you use. There's coal in the byre."

Since we were a group of twelve, that worked out at just over one shilling each the week. There were four beds, all with iron bedsteads, so there was a choice of places to sleep: either on a mattress, on the bare bedsprings, or on the floor.

The party reached Bird How by various means. There were one or two cars and motorcycles. Some of us hitch-hiked. Some walked over the passes from Ambleside.

Bird How was built on the side of a rocky mound and was what is now called a split-level building. The lower floor was the cow-byre, the upper floor the living space. There was no way of getting from the byre to the rest of the house except round the outside. You came out of the byre, turned right and followed the house wall in an upward spiral until you reached the front door. If you carried on past it your progress was halted by a dry-stone wall, which enclosed a tiny space on this side of the house, and formed a little yard in front of the door. From this yard you looked down into a field which fell away below to the River Esk. If from the byre door you turned left to go round the house, you got into a downward spiral and finished up in the field below. Before I knew any of this I went out for a bucket of coal in the black dark of our first night and tried to return the other way, groping along the wall. I finished up totally bewildered, half way along the wall of the field. A very late arrrival made a similar mistake. His plaintive voice came to us through the rain, and when we opened the door and shone a torch down over the wall he cried, "I could see a light in the window but I couldn't find any way up."

It rained the whole week. January rain, as cold as snow, only wetter. Heavy rain clouds made the short days even shorter; in fact twilight seemed to last all day long. But youth and good company – mixed company at that – made it a happy time. Every day we went out and sloshed about the fells, and every night we came back and hung our wet clothing on makeshift clothes-lines all around the house, which soon resembled Fagin's den in *Oliver Twist.* The coal fire, enthusiastically stoked, produced the humid warmth of a tropical rain forest, the clothes on the lines assuming a uniform dampness.

On our last day the weather looked as though it might relent, and for the first time we left Bird How in dry though cloudy conditions. Now was our chance to make the Eskdale Horseshoe, over Crinkle Crags, Bowfell, Esk Pike, Scafell Pike and Scafell. But by the time we got to Bowfell the rain was with us again, and we continued in worsening weather over Esk Pike, across Esk Hause, and eventually on to the top of Scafell Pike. It was already getting dark, and the prospect of getting the whole party up Broad Stand on to Scafell was so unattractive that we were forced into the application of a bit of common sense. We abandoned the Horseshoe objective and picked our way down through the rain and darkness into Upper Eskdale. We descended the rocks that flanked Cam Spout, the dashing water resounding in our ears, though only faintly discernible to our eyes, 'pouring a constant bulk uncertain where'. When we reached the sheep-fold at Sampson's Stones we paused in its shelter and reviewed our position. We were all becoming tired and cold. We knelt in a tight circle on the sodden turf and placed everything we had left to eat on the ground between us. By the light of a fading torch that one unusually provident member had brought we divided the food up and devoured it. It included, as I recall, a large slab of butter, which we cut into chunks and ate like chocolate. All is grist that goes to the mill.

The River Esk beyond this point drops into a gorge through numerous waterfalls and deep pools. An alternative route down the valley is via Silvery Bield, through two or three boggy hollows, to rejoin the Esk at Cowcove Beck. Following the river one could hardly get lost, but there was a danger of falling into the gorge, whereas the only real hazard on the Silvery Bield route was losing the way.

We chose Silvery Bield.

I knew there was a path that skirted the boggy hollows, but I recommended heading straight across them. It was one of the darkest nights I can remember. The sky, with its great weeping rain cloud, was as dark as the land, and all we could see, apart from an occasional gleam of water under our feet, was a faint band of lesser darkness between the rain cloud and the horizon. This enabled us to pick out a slight dip towards which to aim.

As we splashed across the springy bogs I had in mind that through most boggy hollows there meandered a stream of some depth, and after a while a faint gleam indicated we'd found it. It was too dark to see how wide it was but we launched ourselves into the void hoping to fall forwards rather than backwards.

Most of us were across when we heard a startled yelp.

"Help!"

"Where are you?"

"I'm down here."

We felt about and grasped the hands of one Peggy Sloan, medical student, who was up to her chest in water, laughing. We hauled her out.

"You should try it," she said. "I was getting really cold before and that warmed me up no end."

Fortunately we were not far from home now. When at length we sloshed through Taw House farmyard, the barking of their dogs was music to our ears, for it told us that Bird How was close at hand.

We stoked up the fire, brewed endless hot drinks, devoured a meal of huge calorific value and enjoyed a long last evening of warmth and well being.

Bird How is still there, property now of the National Trust. It is let to National Trust holidaymakers for sums very different from what we paid. But now of course it has the amenities of civilisation, which we were very happy to do without.

ON CLIMBING CLUB HUTS

Nowadays in what I suppose is my old age, though it does not feel like it, I prefer a tent to a climbing hut. It is more private, closer to nature, and has the inestimable benefit of the Thermarest, compared with which sliced bread pales into insignificance.

In the past, however, climbing huts – some of them at least – had for me a glamour of their own, what with their stone floors and thick walls, their old climbing books and dog-eared magazines, and open fires. And there was the pleasure of finding out from the hut logbook what pundits of the sport had graced the place with their presence.

At that time, gaining access to a network of climbing club huts was something we saw not only as a great convenience, but also as an indication that we had arrived as mountaineers, and were accepted in the climbing world. We sought therefore, a group of us in the L.U.M.C., to get into the Fell and Rock Climbing Club.

First of all we had to get a member to invite us to a club meet. After that we had to find a proposer and seconder. We had already been up enough fells and done enough rock-climbing to qualify.

There was a weekend meet in December, we learned, at the Haweswater Hotel. Expensive though it was to stay there, we did not baulk at it; it was, after all, worth casting a little of our bread upon the waters. We planned to walk over from Garnet Bridge on the Friday, climbing en route on Buckbarrow Crag in Longsleddale. We planned with the optimism of youth, and we were disappointed. It rained steadily all day and there was not the slightest chance of climbing. We slogged doggedly over Gatesgarth Pass, turned up bedraggled at the hotel, and made ourselves known to the leader of the meet.

We were not the only aspirants to membership; there were several, but most of them were rather coy about it and disinclined to discuss the matter. The exception was a cheerful small man called Jack Tucker, who let everyone know that joining the club was the sole reason he had come on the meet, and he was anxious to know what his chances were.

It rained the entire weekend and it was the spectacular kind of rain that causes even keen walkers to stare glumly out of windows waiting to see if it is going to moderate a little. It kept on relentlessly, however, falling like stair rods and bouncing off the ground. The hotel was a dull place to be holed up in, having none of the atmosphere that we knew climbing huts to have, and we were forced to make do with each other's company for the whole of Saturday. On the Sunday too we stared at the rain for most of the day, until at about two o'clock we came to the view that though getting soaking wet was a bore, it was less boring than staying another minute in the Haweswater Hotel. We would walk round the lake and then go home.

It is surprising how many weekends stay wet until Sunday afternoon, and then fair up just at the point when people have to depart, and it happened on this occasion. As we were leaving the road at the end of the lake we began to sense a faint amelioration, and on the strength of it struck up across a waterlogged moorland, Brampton Common, toward the ridge of High Street. The ceiling of cloud opened and a bit of blue sky appeared. The clouds were turning pink, for the day was at an end and the long December twilight had begun. By the time we reached the ridge to the north of Wether Hill, it was quite dark, but the dispersing clouds made available some of the light from the western sky, and we could just about see where we were putting our feet. This was the darkest part of our walk, as it turned out, for soon the clouds broke up to reveal a full moon. The transformation was remarkable, especially to people who had spent two days in the grey gloom of a wet weekend. All the fells and ridges of the Lake District stood out clearly before us and the whole scene was dappled, piebald rather, with great cloud shadows. And here we were, up on this fine high ridge, the world at our feet, and striding along with the joyous arrogance of youth, as though we owned the place. As, in a way, we did.

We walked exulting over Red Crag, High Raise, the Straits of Riggindale to Racecourse Hill and the High Street cairn, then down over Froswick and Ill Bell to Garburn Pass, to Troutbeck and Troutbeck Bridge. We felt as though we had been out all night but it was in fact only nine o'clock. We now had to address the problem of getting home to Liverpool. Fortunately one of our number had a mother who was Medical Officer of Health for Westmorland and lived near Kendal. She was prepared to come out and fetch us and after an interval she did so. We spent the night in various holes and corners of her spacious house before making our way by one means or another to Liverpool. Missing a lecture or two was a small price to pay for that moonlight walk.

I did not get into the F&R.C.C. until years later. Instead I joined the Wayfarers' Club. But it was a good try, and since clubs owning huts had reciprocal arrangements with each other, I soon had access to climbing huts up and down the country.

Huts were meeting places, where one could enjoy congenial company among like-minded people, for climbers are generally more sociable than they claim. In huts one could escape the tyrannies of home life and leave behind the indignities of having to work for a living. For a few days, life could become a matter of mountain air, good company and deeds of valour on the crags. It was like being transported into the fictional world of the cowboy film, with its simplistic values and unspoken codes.

Helyg, the Climbers' Club hut in the Ogwen valley, had plenty of atmosphere. In fact, detractors at one time used to claim you could smell it down wind for miles. It was simple and had all the advantages of a bothy, without the drawbacks. It was frequented by men who preferred climbing to housekeeping.

I was once staying there and had just drifted off to sleep at about eleven at night, when I was roused by the opening of a door. Someone spoke in a clear, confident voice.

"I say, old man. Could you give me a hand? I've put my car in a ditch."

The speaker was at the far end of the room, no doubt shaking one of his pals. Nothing to do with me. I pulled my sleeping bag round my ears and settled down to sleep.

"I say, old man. Could you give me a hand? I've put my car in a ditch."

There was another groan and a mumbled assent.

"I say, old man. Could you give me a hand? I've put my car in a ditch."

The fellow was moving systematically round the dormitory shaking each sleeper in turn, whether he knew them or not!

I cowered in my bag and flattened my slender body in the vain hope that I might go unnoticed but the voice got nearer and nearer repeating exactly the same words. It was a voice clearly accustomed to command.

A hand shook my shoulder. I've always hated being actually shaken from sleep. A quiet word is enough.

"I say, old man. Could you give me a hand? I've put my car in a ditch."

I feigned the stupor of sleep, made some vague, slurred remark, but I nevertheless climbed out of my bunk and joined the roomful of grumpy men getting dressed. There were at least six of us and he conscripted us all.

We expected to go out onto the A5 road outside the hut and push the car out of its ditch, or at least make it safe, but it now transpired that the car was actually back at the other side of Capel Curig, some five miles away. A friend had driven him to the hut. Someone volunteered another car and we drove to the scene. To our further chagrin, we found his car was not on the main road, a hazard to traffic or in danger of being vandalised, but on his friend's private driveway with one wheel in a drain. We lifted and pushed, the car came quite easily out of the ditch and we all went home to bed.

This man's name was Gilbert Peaker and I make no apology for revealing it. He was not unknown in climbing circles.

I had occasion to come across him again at Helyg. He had two guests at the hut, and it became evident that they were being initiated into the mysteries of climbing. Peaker, sitting with them at the fireside, was at his most expansive, holding forth in his confident, patrician voice, on the subject of ropes and footgear. Opposite him, staring gloomily into the fire, sat the legendary J.M. Edwards.

Peaker sought to draw him into the conversation.

"Which do you favour, Menlove?" he asked, "clinkers or tricounis?"

Edwards looked up, sadly. "I don't have either," he said. "These days I'm just using these old gardening boots."

"But if the rocks are wet? Greasy?"

"I try not to go out in the wet," said Menlove, and even Peaker fell silent for a while.

We shared the hut with Menlove Edwards for several days. He hovered quietly in the background, saying not a word, but somehow emitting a faint sense of unease. We were a party of four or five, and we all ate together from a communal stash of food. Halfway through a cheerful and garrulous meal we heard, subliminally, Edwards asking another occupant of the hut if he had seen anything of a large tin of pilchards.

He seemed quite concerned about them and an awkward silence fell upon our table as it gradually dawned on us that we had had pilchards for our first course. As we'd each contributed various items to the commissariat it took us a minute or two of murmured discussion to establish that we had indeed taken his. There followed a brief debate about who was to go and tell him and I, as the oldest, was voted the most suitable. So I went, bearing a large tin of bully beef by way of compensation.

He took the tin of beef but he was not to be consoled. He seemed more downcast than angry.

Of course at that time we had no idea of the troubles that beset him. All we knew was that he was a brilliant climber. One entry we noted in the Helyg logbook recorded a day's solo climbing. If we had accomplished in a whole week what he had done in that day, we would have gone home well pleased with ourselves.

There was another hut in the Ogwen valley that we frequented in the late forties. It was called Glandena and belonged to the Midland Association of Mountaineers, a club brave enough to let a university climbing club make occasional use of it.

In those days, Glandena was a conspicuous and unattractive feature of the landscape between Tryfan and the Glyders on the one hand and the

Carnedds on the other. It stood in the middle of a broad moorland, a large modern wooden bungalow with a suburban look about it, like its name. Today it lies hidden in a clump of conifers, I'm glad to say.

We would go there sometimes for the weekend, from Liverpool, catching a bus on Friday evening from Leece Street at the side of Lime Street Station and I would sit, with a bit of luck, with one of the female members of our party for the two and a half hour journey to the hills. We would tumble out from the drowsy warmth of the bus into the chill and maybe rainy dark, shoulder our rucksacks and feel our way down the rough track to Glandena. The first task was to turn on the water. This was done at a point half a mile or more away, beyond Tal y llyn Ogwen farm and uphill into the beginning of the Carnedds where by torchlight we would find the holding tank in a streambed, and a tap. But the hut had electricity, and coal for a fire, and we would soon turn the dark and cheerless building into a place of warmth, good food and good company.

We would then climb all day Saturday and Sunday on the old classics that are now insignificant at the bottom of the long lists of routes in the modern guide books, the Gashed Crags, the Belle Vue Bastions, the Monolith Cracks, the Gargoyle Traverses, the Grooved Arêtes, and as darkness fell on Sunday evening we would stop the Liverpool bus at the Glandena road end, and drowse away the miles home, cocooned in the warm dark fug of the bus, gratified – speaking for myself – by the proximity of the young women with whom we had shared the weekend's adventures.

A little later, when I was a member of the Wayfarers' Club, I would sometimes go on my own to Glandena. I went there once just as a New Year's Meet was coming to an end. There had clearly been great carousing and feasting, and many members were glad to be able to leave the remains of their lavish provisions with me rather than take them home or otherwise dispose of them. I lived in considerable style for some days.

On another occasion I was imprisoned there by foul weather, until I had built up such a head of steam that I had to go out in spite of the wet, to expend it somehow. I went up over the Glyders, following no path most of the way, and came down on a compass course to Pen y Gwryd. By this time my boots were squelching so uncomfortably full of water that I lay on my back on a rock with my legs in the air in an attempt to drain some of it out. It did not work, and I had to take my boots off and wring my socks out, before making the short ascent to the Gorfwysfa Hotel at Pen y Pas. I continued up Crib Goch, still in heavy rain, and made my way along the long sharp ridge, feeling quite lonely in this hostile, wet, precipitous world where the spiky ridge seemed to go on forever. At length, way ahead in the dense cloud, I began to hear the purposeful panting of some strange Welsh monster and sure enough it eventually it loomed into view, breathing fire and smoke. It was the Snowdon railway engine and I was glad to see it.

On the summit I made a brief stop among the disconsolate passengers crowding into the shelter of the cafe, anxious not to stop long enough to start feeling cold, then went out again into the harsh world of rain, mist and slippery wet rocks, and made very sure with the aid of the compass that I was on the path to Lliwedd. Even in those days I knew that whereas to find a summit there is only really one way to go, and that is up, when it comes to leaving it there are three hundred and sixty possible directions to go in. I slithered down a steep and rocky slope and began to wonder whether I'd gone wrong, but eventually the ground levelled out and I was soon on the Lliwedd ridge with glimpses on my left of the plunging faces of the great crag, the scene of the earliest exploits of British rock climbing. By the time I reached the road and the Pen y Pas hotel I was too wet to do more than get a quick cup of tea before tackling the Glyders once again. Only by taking exercise could I keep reasonably warm. I climbed straight up behind the hotel, passed the llyn, and took a slanting course uphill until I came across the old miner's track. I followed it over the height of land into the head of Cwm Tryfan, and then headed straight down the cwm to the A5 and Glandena.

It never stopped raining. I had seen nothing much except wet rocks, bogs, heather, running water and sheep. The splendid views from the Glyders and from Snowdon summit were denied me. The leather of my boots was as soft and pliable as wet felt. My feet were white and wrinkly. My clothes, with the water they contained, must have weighed ten pounds. But as for me, I felt assuaged and powerful. My mind was comfortable in my body. The hut seemed the height of luxury and the fire I lit a boon and a blessing. I felt like a gentleman of earlier times, taking his ease at his inn.

A GRAND STEYAN

Since I lived fairly close to it for some years, Pillar Rock has been for me the scene of a good deal of drama. More comedy than tragedy on the whole, I am glad to say.

On my very first visit to it I was repulsed by being hit in the eye by a falling stone. Someone above shouted a warning, and naturally I looked up. I saw a flat, spinning stone about three inches in diameter, so close to my right eye I hadn't even time to blink. It got me on the eyeball and bounced on down the crag.

It was acutely painful. When the first shock of the blow subsided I took my hand from my eye to check out the damage and, to my horror, saw blackness. Thinking I might faint I bent over to put my head down. This brought a cry of alarm from my companions, but falling was the least of my worries. I had lost an eye.

Somewhere further up the rope – we often climbed with several people roped together in those days – was our president, Dr. Graham Macphee. He came down and tied a handkerchief over my eye, and we climbed back down to the foot of the Rock.

I was filled not so much with self-pity as with self-blame. No one had forced me to go climbing. I had done it against advice and against the express wishes of my mother, wantonly, in a spirit of stupid bravado, and now I was going to pay the price. I was going to go through life with one eye. While the others ate their sandwiches I brooded along these lines.

Before we set off back to Wasdale, Dr. Macphee had another look at my eye. To my surprise I could now see some light. No shapes of any kind, just fog. This was so much less awful than blackness that I began to take heart.

That evening Macphee took me in his car down to Gosforth, and from the post office telephoned a colleague of his at the Liverpool Eye Hospital. I sat glumly in the car. He came out two or three times to look at my eye, and each time went back to the phone to report his observations. Following this remote control consultation with a specialist, he found a chemist and obtained some castor oil and cocaine drops, put one or two in my eye, and said there was no point in tearing off to Liverpool until next day.

At the eye hospital my injury was described as a corneal abrasion and I had to wear an eye patch for six weeks. No permanent disability ensued.

That was early in 1939, and it was not until after the War that I returned to Pillar Rock.

It is now high summer, 1946. We are staying midweek at Brackenclose, the F. & R.C.C. hut in Wasdale Head and have the place to ourselves. The trouble with L.U.M.C. meets is that since students are of course a largely nocturnal sub-species, we enjoy sitting round the fire in a climbing club hut so much that we never get to bed until the small hours of the morning. We have not yet been to the Alps, and consequently lack that haunted awareness of the passage of time that alpine climbers develop. We take our time getting up. We take our time over breakfast, and even on the fells we are not inclined to fill the unforgiving minute with sixty seconds worth of distance run. It is all too enjoyable.

So by the time we reach the foot of Pillar Rock it is well past midday. I am the only person in the party who has been here before, but we have the guidebook and take the view, born of inexperience, that we can get up anything less than a Severe. We disperse to different parts of the crag and since the day is well advanced we agree to do our climbs and return to the hut independently.

I am with June and Jean, medical students. June has done a climb or two before. Jean is a complete beginner.

June feels it is about time she led something. We pick the North Climb, and she sets off. After two or three pitches she encounters a difficulty, and spends a long time trying to overcome it, while Jean and I sit chatting and relaxed on a comfortable stance. Eventually June comes back down.

"I can't do it," she says. "My arms are tired. I think you should lead."

So we switch places on the rope. It all takes time.

So does the Stomach Traverse, which is the next notable feature of the route. I squirm up it easily enough, but my companions, both a good deal heavier than I, and a different shape, find it strenuous. The next little pitch, the cave pitch with a capstone, shows how seriously tired in the arms June has become. I have to arrange a rope stirrup for her at one point.

So far, the climb, though it has had its little problems, has not been intimidating or very exposed, but it now assumes a more serious character. We climb the Split Blocks, then traverse left by way of the Strid, to a corner from which there seems no escape. To our right is a vertical wall. On our left a precipice. Ahead, the Nose.

There is no satisfactory belay on our ledge, and we have our rope and nothing else, no slings, nuts or karabiners. The rope is L.U.M.C. property, manila, dating from before the war. Fortunately for our peace of mind we have not been subjected to disquieting information about the ageing of ropes or their breaking strains. To us a rope is a rope, our justification, our talisman, our safety.

What we are not short of is guidebook information. Almost two pages in the F. & R.C.C. guide are devoted to the problem of surmounting the Nose. "From the corner," it says, "work out on the projecting flake until standing on its tip. By feeling round the Nose with the left hand, a good side handhold can be secured. A man of moderate height can reach a good flat hold for the right hand overhead. By pulling on these and throwing the left knee round to a good but concealed hold, the Nose can be surmounted without further difficulty.

"The second man can safeguard the leader whilst he is climbing the pitch by jamming himself in the corner with his foot against the flake, and belaying himself to the rock by wedging the rope in the crack overhead."

It is all very steep and exposed. With my nose on the wall in front of me, my hands spread and palpating the rock for comforting rugosities, I gingerly move out along the flake until I am standing on its tip. I am pretty unhappy. We have no belay to speak of and my companions are inexperienced. My left hand feels a side hold but how anyone could describe it as good beats me. My right hand, groping above my head, can reach nothing deserving a moment's consideration.

"Can't find anything."

"Perhaps you're a man of less than moderate height," says Jean, maybe to ease the tension. If so, it fails, being too near the truth. I am inclined to be enamoured of this Jean, and though I have other things to worry about at the moment, the remark rankles.

I shuffle back to the ledge. The second option, says the guidebook, is the Hand Traverse. I go to the other end of our ledge, climb with difficulty a steep ten-foot wall, and get my hands on the perfect holds of the hand traverse. But at this point I wonder what is going to happen when I get to the other end. One thing my cautious approach to climbing has taught me is not to get into a place from which I cannot retreat. There flashes on my inward eye the following scenario: I cannot get off the end of the hand traverse, I reverse it using up my remaining finger strength, fail to make it down the wall, plummet into space with a last despairing cry ...

Thinking these craven thoughts I descend the difficult wall, little realising that in fact it is a good deal harder than the traverse itself.

Back to the guidebook. "Descent into Savage Gully," it says. Almost a whole page is devoted to this manoeuvre. The leader is lowered by his companions some forty feet down a wall into the Gully. I am a veteran of the War and my companions are only recently out of school. Medical students though they are, I would not trust them to take my appendix out. I suppose I am less worried at the prospect of their lowering me into Savage Gully, but not much. It has to be done, however. I check my bowline and soon I am dangling rather ridiculously in space, to touch down after a while in the unfriendly bed of the gully. I now instruct them to untie from the rope and drop it down to me, which they do with about as much misgiving as I have shown over being lowered. I coil it up, put it over my shoulder and disappear from their view round the corner, leaving them sitting cragfast on their ledge without a rope and without a leader. After scrambling about for quite a long time wondering whether I am going the right way, I reappear suddenly, within ten feet of them, on top of the Nose.

"What kept you?" they want to know, but I sense they are glad to see me.

The reunion over, we set about the next task which is to get them over the Nose. June ties on to the rope again, and I sit like an eagle on its eyrie, right on top of the Nose, with a waist level belay round a rock immediately behind me. It is not a good belay but I have too little rope to go back for a better.

She edges out onto the flake, and explores the rock for handholds. Though she makes several attempts to haul herself over the Nose she cannot do it.

"I have no strength left in my arms," she says, and goes back to the ledge.

I arrange a bight of rope for her to use as a handhold. She tries again. No use.

I take up the bight of rope and make overhand knots in it at intervals of one foot, then secure it like a rope ladder from my waist belay. It all takes time.

"Forget the proper holds, " I say. "Hold the rope. Lean out as on an abseil, and walk up round the corner."

She has courage all right. She grabs the knotted rope, leans out over space, plants her feet on the rock and struggles upwards, her eyes bulging with effort. The strain on my waist and my belay is intense. As she gets higher, and we are staring into each other's eyes only a couple of feet apart, I feel my backside being lifted off its ledge. The pull is no longer downwards, but outwards, and in another moment it is going to be upwards, and that might well result in my belay being lifted off.

Time seems to stand still. Goya could paint a good picture of this scene. I am a fatal accident about to happen.

"Oh," groans June. "I can't do any more," and subsides back onto the Flake. I breathe again.

All this time Jean has been sitting quietly in the corner looking a bit woebegone.

"What about letting Jean have a go, " I suggest, though without much conviction. But I am underestimating the strength of her desire to escape out of that corner and off that ledge. She attacks the Nose furiously and shoots up like a cork out of a bottle. We are jubilant. I get her tied on to a good belay some yards back, taking in the rope, then stand on top of the Nose and haul June up by main force.

We are out, and although the girls prefer to remain roped for the descent of the Old West, we have no further problem. It must be getting late, we think, but we might as well stick to our original plan of going back to Wasdale via Wind Gap, so we go up over the summit of Pillar and down that way. It is still quite light up on the hilltop but as soon as we begin to descend we realise that in the valleys it is already getting dark. We are glad to get to the easier ground in the floor of Mosedale, and though tired we feel enchanted by the balmy summer night and quietly exhilarated by our adventure on the rock. As we approach Brackenclose we see lights. We are glad they have not yet gone to bed, as we have quite a bit of eating and drinking to do and would not wish to disturb them.

To our surprise they are getting ready to come out and look for us. "Were you getting worried?" we ask.

"Well, it is one o'clock," they say.

There is something fine and remote about Pillar Rock, and the fact that you have to climb off it as well as up it adds to its seriousness. I once went there with a party of LUMC members who were staying at Buttermere. This was in the 1950s and I was still in touch with the club through my friendship with its longtime president, Graham Macphee. I joined them one morning in Buttermere with the idea of going out with them for a climb.

They were going to climb on Pillar, they said. This was a bit more than I bargained for. As it was winter and the morning was already far advanced, I assumed that these youngsters must be super fit and I wondered if I would be able to keep up with them on the walk over. I nevertheless went along.

Within an hour or so it became obvious that they had underestimated the walk to the crag. They were surprisingly slow, a motley bunch, and all strangers to me. It was going to be afternoon before we reached the Rock. I asked them what climbs they had in mind and they mentioned the North Climb and the New West.

By the time we got there we had only a couple of hours of daylight left. I put it to them that the only feasible thing to do was to go up the Old West, and down the Slab and Notch, routes most climbers would do unroped. It now appeared, however, that the majority had never been climbing before, and that out of the eight in the party, only two were prepared to lead. They were also seriously short of rope.

We made three ropes of three, and set off up the Old West. It was an unwise move; we should have turned round and gone home. They were disastrously slow, and there were hold-ups in the most straightforward passages. At one point I considered retreating, but thought that might take even longer than going on. It was dark by the time we all reached the summit.

We would abseil into Jordan Gap, I thought. But it now transpired that only one of the party knew how to abseil, and the prospect of teaching people how to do it in the dark was altogether too daunting. The Slab and Notch way off, though easy, would be hazardous for beginners in the dark. I decided to lower everybody off into Jordan Gap. I am by no means a dominant personality but I found that I was now in charge of the whole party.

These were the days before harnesses. A bowline or a figure-of-eight was all we could offer. I got myself seated and firmly belayed, then each of the party, one after the other, tied on to the rope and was lowered, from a shoulder belay, into the dark void.

"Don't try and climb down," I said. "There isn't time. Just let me lower you. And when you get to the bottom, untie, and stay there. Don't try and move off."

It took a long time. The girls were much better at it than the men, for they were more trusting. One of them, tied on and sitting with her feet over the brink, said, "And you mean I've just to go over this edge?"

"Yes," I said, and she shoved off like someone starting a parachute jump, putting a sudden ten-stone load on my shoulder.

Some of the men, by contrast, remained grasping the edge, unable to consign themselves to perdition by letting go. I was near enough to the brink to be able to kick their hands off with my heels, but managed to refrain from doing so. Of course they could not see what they were being lowered into, and who, I suppose they thought, was this stranger whom they were being compelled to trust. Eventually, however, they were all down.

Except me. I could of course feel my way down the Slab and Notch. I could climb down the East Jordan, as I'd often done before. But I was tired and fed up and wanted to get off the rock by the simplest means. So I abseiled down, and since I couldn't flick the rope off, abandoned it. It was an old L.U.M.C. rope, and probably past its sell by date.

We had now to scramble round the back of Pisgah, and down rock and scree to the foot of the New West. We then struck out across steep ground, well clear of the Rock, to avoid getting into the gully below the West Face

of Low Man. It was all very tiring and tedious as we had to be bent double
to see where we were going. No one had a torch.

It seemed endless creeping down towards the forest.

"When are we going to get to the trees?" someone asked. As it happened I had just noticed a solitary holly bush we had passed on the way up.
Except for that I would have had no idea.

"In under five minutes," I said confidently. The party was quite
impressed when, four minutes later, we came to the top edge of the planta-
tion.

"How did you know?" someone said.

"Local knowledge" I said nonchalantly.

We still had a long way to go, but we made it in the end. I said goodbye
and went off home, glad to escape.

Macphee joined the meet the next day. He was pretty scathing about the
abandoned rope, and went and fetched it. He was like that. A stickler.

Then there was the time I offered to introduce my headmaster's seventeen-year-old son, Robin, to rock climbing. We would go and camp in the
Doup, and have two days on Pillar Rock. It was a visit neither of us is likely
to forget.

On the first day we do the North Climb and one or two shorter routes,
and the boy does well. The weather is good, the rocks dry.

Next day I think we might try something a bit harder, and we go to the
West Face of Low Man and start on the Ledge and Groove route. Robin is
for some reason performing less well today. Perhaps he has slept badly on
the hard ground. Perhaps yesterday's exercise has left him a bit stiff, less
supple. And, one must admit, the West Face of Low Man has a rather
intimidating look about it, rising, concave and beetling, out of a rocky gully.
The stances are narrow compared with those on the north and east sides,
and it is unnerving to a beginner to be left on them while the leader is
messing about above. We climb several pitches – short ones by today's
standards – and the higher up the face we get the more I gather, from
telepathic messages along the rope, that Robin is not enjoying himself much.
A little of his unease spills over to me.

We reach a point from which it is necessary to make a slightly downward traverse, then get round a corner to the next belay. I am faced with a
dilemma. If I go first round the corner I leave my inexperienced second
above me on the crag, poorly protected. If he goes first I have to rely on his
making a satisfactory belay out of my sight.

I decide on the latter course.

"Just go down this traverse, and round the corner," I say. "You'll find a good belay."

He goes. At the corner he hesitates. He tries something, comes back. "Can't see how to do this," he says.

"Work it out," I say. "It's not hard. Feel round the corner for a good handhold."

He tries again. He is now spread eagled, one foot round the corner, one on the end of the traverse. His hands are similarly spread. His nose is against the rock.

"I can't move," he says.

He remains motionless for some time, clinging on, rigid with alarm.

"Okay," I say after a bit. "Come back and I'll do it."

He moves now, but he moves like a door swinging open, his left hand and left foot the two hinges. He faces the void and with a blood-curdling cry plunges into space like a skydiver and disappears from sight.

I have not been altogether happy about my belay. It is round a good rock but a bit too low down, with only a couple of inches of rock above the rope. I am now wrenched violently away from it, and in the slow motion that takes over in these situations, take a detached interest in whether it is going to hold or not. It does, and I come to rest with Robin's dead weight straining round my middle.

I cannot move, and I cannot see anything except the taut rope leading over the edge. There flashes through my mind the thought 'What if he's unconscious?'

"Robin," I shout, and feel a tremendous relief when he answers.

He is panic-stricken and incoherent, crying like a child.

"Shut up," I bawl. "Listen! Are you listening?"

"Yes," he calls.

"What is just below you?" I am desperate to lower him on to something, to get the weight off his waist. Hanging from a bowline round the waist he could asphyxiate.

"Nothing," he wails. "There's nothing."

"There's got to be," I yell. "Look. I'm going to lower you. Slowly, until you get somewhere."

I do so. When he fell I did not let the rope slip so my bare hands are not burnt. In a few feet the weight eases.

"Now," I shout, "We rest a bit. Just calm down. We've plenty of time."

We are alone on the Rock. It is midweek and we have seen no one.

He quietens down. I ask him what the damage is. His elbow is stiff and swollen, that arm useless. Otherwise nothing much. I get him to describe where he is, and tell him he must get to some place where he is unsupported by the rope. At first he says there is no such place, and we have a lengthy argument about it, but eventually I get him to admit there is a crack and some sort of ledge nearby. He is able to shuffle on to it and tie a bight of his rope round a chockstone in a crack. I get him to describe it all in detail, and when I am satisfied that he is secure I take off my belay and at last move down to where I can see him. I am keyed up myself, and feel cornered on this hostile rockface, but full of fight. I move round the corner that he fell off – it is exposed but not very difficult – and reach a good belay more or less above him. I now have to decide whether to go down four pitches, or up two. The route we have come up is a twisting one, with another traverse. It would be awkward for a one-armed man. We would no doubt be a long time getting down, and Robin is still on the verge of panic. Above us there are two pitches, one of them the crux of the climb, but they are straightforward. I decide that if I can get him up to my present belay, I will continue up the crag and finish out.

We do it. After his initial terror and demoralisation, he comes round very well, and realises that we have a fight on our hands to get off the crag. His elbow is hugely swollen, but the swelling has immobilised the joint and it is not very painful. Wherever he can he uses footholds and does what he can with his right hand. But for the most part I haul him up by main force, putting the rope over my shoulder, bending forward, then straightening my back. I bring to my own climbing such determination, born of fear and adrenalin, that I find it quite easy.

Once we are up, on Low Man, we feel we have won, and take a long rest. Getting down the Old West is slow. I take belays the whole way, but at length we are clear of the Rock and make our way back to our camp for a good meal.

From being petrified with alarm, and still anxious while ever we were on the rock, I now seem to have the strength of ten. I pack up the tent, load the two rucksacks and everything else on my back and we set off down into Ennerdale.

On the drive out to the hospital I reflect that the sooner I tell his father about the accident the better. I also think it will be more reassuring if Robin speaks to him himself. It will show him immediately that he is not unconscious or dead.

If my first mistake of the day has been sending Robin first round that corner the second is suggesting that he is first to tell his father. It goes something like this:

"Hello, Dad. Is that you, Dad?"

"Yes."

"It's Robin."

Squawking sounds from the phone.

"Well, Dad. I've got some bad news."

Louder squawks.

"Well, perhaps you'd better sit down, Dad."

It now sounds as if an excited group of Japanese is on the line.

"I fell off Pillar Rock! Yes. I'm on my way to hospital ... "

And so on. After a while I take the phone from him and give my headmaster the simple facts of the case.

I did not get sacked. Robin spent six weeks in hospital, for the elbow is a difficult joint to mend. He later became an outdoor pursuits instructor, but he specialised in sailing.

Pillar Rock was a splendid place to be in winter conditions, when it was like a bit of the Alps transported to Cumbria. The whole mountainside, and the area around the Shamrock, gave plenty of interesting snow-climbing. Once, shortly after I was married, keen to introduce my wife to the delights of the winter fells, I proposed a trip up the Old West. We went up Ennerdale on my motorcycle, crossed the River Liza, mostly frozen over, without getting our feet wet, and went up through the forest into the Great Doup. The Rock itself was so plastered with snow and ice that I fought shy of tackling it with a complete beginner and settled for an ascent of the fellside to the summit of Pillar Fell. The slope became steeper as we got into the broken ground to the right of the Rock. I began to think we ought to rope up, especially as my wife was getting nervous.

It was at this point that she began sliding downhill. "Use your axe," I shouted. She plunged the pick into the snow and the axe was immediately wrenched out of her hand. She continued sliding and built up speed. It was a perfectly safe run-out and after a hundred feet or so she came to rest, with me only a second or two behind her in a standing glissade, but having no means of assessing the danger she was convinced her end had come.

We found an easier line to the felltop where the winter sunshine did something to mollify her.

On the way home on the motorbike my wet gloves froze round the handlebars, and this journey was undoubtedly the most hazardous part of our day out, though not in the opinion of my wife.

When I was at the Outward Bound Mountain School at Eskdale, we would have regular rock-climbing sessions for the students. In summer we would set up climbing camps near suitable crags, and in winter occupy various climbing huts. Langdale, Borrowdale, Dunnerdale were the usual venues, and sometimes when the weather looked promising we would camp at places like Sty Head Tarn for Gable, Hollow Stones for Scafell, and the Great Doup for Pillar. It was always our ambition to climb multi-pitch routes with the students, though all too often we had to content ourselves, owing to poor weather, with single pitch climbs on valley crags like Shepherd's in Borrowdale.

On one occasion when we were camped in the Great Doup below Pillar Rock, the weather turned extremely stormy, and we had to bowse down the tents with climbing ropes to prevent them from blowing away. It was not good either for the ropes or the tents, because of the friction and abrasion. Climbing too was limited to the easiest routes on the crag.

We were experimenting at that time with a design of waterproof anorak which we hoped would cause less condensation. These garments were bright yellow and made very roomy so that air could circulate underneath them.

While taking a group of students up to the summit of Pillar from Jordan Gap, we found the anoraks a hindrance in the high wind, and since it was not now raining we stopped to take them off. One boy let go of his, the wind filled it and it took off into the air like a hang glider gone mad. It rose rapidly for a couple of hundred feet, looking quite grotesque with its arms and its hood stuck out, like a legless human figure that had suddenly discovered the secret of flight. It performed remarkable aerobatics over the Rock, diving headlong down the New West, swerving just before it hit the ground, to come soaring up the South West and do cartwheels above the summit of the Rock, before swooping off to have a look at Walker's Gully. We watched these manoeuvres for almost half an hour with awe and admiration, and not without a slight thrill of horror at the resemblance to a truncated human being. At last it touched down in the combe above Walker's and we were able to retrieve it.

One remembers vividly enough the climbs and excursions that went wrong, but the successful days tend to merge into each other to form a composite memory of golden summer days or winter rigours. A climb on Pillar that was one of my favourites was a combination of the New West and the Rib and Slab, avoiding the most difficult bits of each while retaining the most open and delightful sections. Walker's Gully too made a wonderful expedition, the escape at the top over its capstone being for me, a short man, extremely difficult. On the approach from Ennerdale we saw the Rock at its most impressive, an enormous aiguille, with one of its finest routes, the North West, going straight up the middle. The North Climb has for me continued to be an attractive and quite serious route. Anxious to demonstrate that I was 'a man of moderate height' I soon learned how to surmount the Nose, though I found the Hand Traverse a good deal easier. An interesting discovery was how much easier it is to climb down the Nose than up it. We found, in fact, that the North Climb in its entirety made a very interesting way off the Rock. In the days when we aimed to climb down as many routes as we climbed up I remember a most satisfying day out when we climbed up the North West, down the West Wall, up the South West, and down the New West, some hundreds of feet of superlative rock.

They tell a story of a group of climbers extolling the virtues of Pillar Rock, when an old Ennerdale shepherd had the last word: "Aye," he said, "it's a grand steyan."

ON DOING AS YOU'RE TOLD

Picture the foyer of the Royal Oak Hotel in Keswick on a Sunday morning in November 1952. The hotel has since been split up and put to various uses, but at that time it dominated the centre of Keswick, and was every year the venue for the Annual Dinner of the Fell and Rock Climbing Club of the English Lake District.

Five or six men in outdoor clothing stand in a row opposite a larger group who sit on the arms of chairs or lean against walls and doorways. Between the two a small man with a bent nose and a fierce eye consults a sheet of paper and issues his instructions. It is the F. & R.C.C.'s custom to invite representatives of kindred clubs to the Dinner and also to arrange some rock climbing for them on the following day. A number of active club members now stand ready to be of service to this end, and the man organising it is A.B. Hargreaves.

Outside it is a grey day and rain is falling. Not heavily, but with a quiet persistence common to the Lake District.

We receive our orders. Two of us are despatched with our respective guests to Gillercombe Buttress, one of the fine old classic Severes of Borrowdale, five hundred feet of sound rock standing high up on the south-east flank of Grey Knotts. It is a climb I know quite well, and one I have sometimes done after work on a summer evening, driving out from Workington to the top of Honister Pass and then walking over the fell to its foot, to delight in its warm grey rock and its splendid position high above the combe, while the rest of the world was at supper in the valleys. It is not, in my view, a very suitable choice for a wet November day, but I hold my peace. A.B. Hargreaves is a man of great authority in the Club. His manner is brisk and peremptory. Small he may be, but he has the power of command of a gunner's mate from Whale Island, and I still, at this stage of my life, believe in the importance of important people. Mine is not to reason why, mine is but to take these two guests from kindred clubs up Gillercombe Buttress.

We go by car to Seathwaite, and take the steep path up the side of Sourmilk Ghyll, hoping the rain will ease off, but as we slosh over the combe above the waterfall it seems to be getting if anything more persistent. One of my new companions, evidently a man of abundant good sense, announces at this point that he prefers to go for a walk, and departs in the direction of Base Brown. We two who are left arrive at the crag to find the other party already at work. The leader has taken his boots off and is climbing in socks. When their third man has got clear I start on the first pitch. It has a difficult move out of a corner, from a ledge that leans uncomfortably outward. I surmount it and take heart, for I have always regarded this move as the crux. Further up I make a belay and pass the time of day with the party ahead. In this weather I am glad they are there, for it makes me feel less lonely and the climb more justifiable. My second spends a good deal of time in the awkward corner, and after a while, though I forbear to point out that my hands are getting cold through remaining motionless on the stance, I give the rope a little tug to suggest it is time he made a move, but his only response is to say he is very sorry, he wants to abandon the climb.

If he had said this before we had started I would have applauded the notion, but now the thing uppermost in my mind is a reluctance to go back down that difficult corner. I am equipped with two slings and two karabiners but to abseil off leaving one of them behind is a defeat I am loth to accept. Furthermore having managed to get up the first pitch I have got the bit between my teeth and cannot easily be reined in. I call to the people above, their third man being still only a few feet above me. Have rope, will climb is the burden of my remarks, and they kindly consent to my tying on at the rear of their *caravane*. The guest for whom I am responsible is now safely off the crag, and waving goodbye to him I turn to the undemanding task of following as last man.

Gillercombe Buttress is within a mile or two of Seathwaite, which is reputed to be the wettest place in England. What that means of course is that it is the wettest place to have a rain gauge, and there may be places a good deal wetter, such as Mickledore, or Lingmell Cove, where no records are kept. Nevertheless it is undoubtedly a rainy place, and we really have no reason to be surprised that now the rain has set in in a very purposeful fashion, and though not pelting has a searching and penetrating quality that suggests it is not so much falling as transforming the atmosphere to a liquid. The temperature is not particularly low for the time of year, but the chill factor is considerable and its onset insidious.

After the first couple of pitches the rocks of the Buttress are easier, but toward the top there is another crux. From a commodious ledge a steep ridge rises with narrow vertical grooves running up it. The leader finds it difficult. After a struggle he descends and blows on his fingers. Another has a go with no better result. They discuss it coolly, in measured tones, determined to see it as a small problem whose solution happens for the moment to elude them; nothing to get excited about. The rain meanwhile continues its inexorable penetration into the recesses of our clothing.

I feel I have no business as a mere interloper and hanger-on to express an opinion, but I see that switching the order in which people are tied on takes time so I say why not reverse the cordée and see if I, as last man, can get up the pitch in my nails. Nails, while not as comforting to climb in as vibrams, are less affected by wet and greasy rock. Climbing in nails on wet rock it is the hands, not the feet that seem in danger of slipping.

The suggestion is adopted. When one has been waiting and longing for action, driven by a desire to break out of the impasse, it is surprising what determination and even skill one can find. I get up the difficult bit 'like a rat up a downspout' as Bill Peascod would say, and climb on, well pleased with myself, only to be brought to a halt by an unforeseen shortage of acceptable holds at the top of the pitch, with a lengthy run-out below me and nothing to hang a sling on. I am faced with two possible ways upwards, both equally unattractive. This is the kind of choice, psychiatrists say, that drives people into severe depression. I spend some time in craven indecision, for I am not a gambling man, but I eventually take my heart in my mouth and make a dicey step upward on to what turns out, fortunately, to be a more friendly bit of rock. Well belayed, I bring the others up and they all stream past me so that the original order on the rope is restored. Third on the rope comes Jack Longland, of Everest 1933, no longer young but climbing with calm and fluid competence, intent on wasting no time. He is bareheaded, the rain running down his straggling hair and off the end of his nose and doubtless down his neck. I am amazed at his apparent indifference to it.

By the time we get to the top I am very tired as well as wet and cold (and I have not fully recovered even when we get to the evening socialising). But up on the hill, as we coil up the wet ropes with awkward fingers and make our slithering descent down the side of the crag, there is at the centre of my chill and ill-used frame a small source of warmth and satisfaction, an assertion of the joy of life and its inestimable value. The hard things I have been thinking about A.B. Hargreaves I can now laugh off. It has been a good day out.

ALMOST ELIMINATED

If you look across Goats Water and select the steepest and most challenging main line up Dow Crag, that line will be Eliminate A.

"It keeps going all the way really," said Len Muscroft when I consulted him, way back, about what was the hardest bit. "There's always something there – except maybe the Rochers Perchés bit – but it keeps going all the way." And he smiled his sardonic, kindly smile.

It is hard in these days when VS climbing is the norm to appreciate the aura that surrounded a climb like Eliminate A. Even now, over forty years later, I would have to wind myself up for it. In those days it was like trespassing on forbidden ground. But my companion that weekend was Frank Monkhouse, a sanguine spirit, and Friday's post had brought me a new hundred foot hawser-laid rope from British Ropes, my first in nylon.

On the Saturday we did Eliminate C, a delightful exhilarating climb, exposed, with small positive holds and a tricky bit on the second pitch. It was not a natural line like Eliminate A and wound about the buttress as though looking for difficulties, but it had a euphoric effect upon me, and since Frank was enthusiastic about it we came back next day to do Eliminate A.

It was a fine warm day in May like the one in 1923 when Herbert Spencer Gross and George Basterfield made the first ascent. I did up the laces good and tight on my basketball boots, tied the new rope round my waist with a bowline, put my two hemp slings over my shoulder, wiped my fingers on the seat of my pants and set off. First a steep open wall with no recesses to scuttle into. Holds to me were of two kinds, ones you could stay on and ones that were for transit only. I moved circumspectly from perch to perch. Some perches were so exiguous as to make it desirable to move on to the next, others comfortable enough to be rather hard to leave. But it was all steep and exposed and it looked steeper above. Always one quested hungrily for somewhere to hang a sling. It was as Len Muscroft had said, there was always something there but it kept going. As my exploring fingers palpated the rock tiny surges of elation, dismay, qualified approval, alarm or satisfaction passed through me, in response to the nature of the little holds encountered, but nothing seriously hindered my upward progress. On the second pitch an exposed and committing move to the right with a kind of mantelshelf worked out well, alarm giving way to exhilaration. I reached the Raven's Nest. "You're climbing well, looking safe", said Frank on arrival at the stance. I was glad to hear it.

We were approaching a big steepness, not to say overhang, which had to be circumvented to the left. In a corner hung some big blocks, stuck on by nature's araldite. The Rochers Perchés, and the crux moreover. We contrived a belay near enough to be reassuring (for in those days we were not aware of the especial dangers of falling after a short run-out) and I made the mental adjustment needed to treat the difficulty as a boulder problem. Winning across the Rochers Perchés was rewarded by gaining access to a magnificent easy ramp rising leftwards on huge jug handles.

We began to feel exultant having broken through that forbidding steepness on to the upper stretches of the buttress but halfway up the next pitch I made an unpremeditated divergence from the route. In other words I fell off.

Or 'came off' as the phrase then was, some euphemism being required, since falling by the leader was simply not done in the best climbing circles. Moving up on a small finger hold and a foot scrape I must have exerted a prising action, for a thin leaf of rock flaked off under my fingers, revealing a white patch.

The next two seconds were a long and interesting experience. At first I seemed to hover in midair. I went through the motions of discarding the leaf of rock and getting a fresh hold, but I was of course too late. There followed a brief period during which I seemed to be going down in a lift close to the surface of the rock. This phase gave way to one in which I lost all orientation and was conscious of only two things. One was a dazzlingly clear view of Goats Water and the other was a feeling of tremendous acceleration, as though fired out of a cannon. Though I had not the slightest awareness of it – until told later by Eric Arnison, who saw me fall and remembered having looked down on the red rubber soles of my basketball boots – I was performing a back somersault. This would explain the vision of Goats Water. There is only one word I can find to describe the end of the fall and that is kersplatt!

My only feeling throughout these events had been surprise. But now, spread like margarine over a bilberry ledge and emptied of every single drop of energy I possessed, I became terrified at the ugly consequences of my injuries and was convinced that if I moved my head my brains would spill out. I felt demolished, and responding to the anxious shouts from above was one of the most exhausting things I've ever done.

A climber from an adjacent climb traversed across to me and said, predictably, "It's okay, I am a doctor," to which I replied, unpredictably in the circumstances, "Then you must be Jim Joyce and I think we have a common acquaintance in Betty Monkhouse who told me you might be on the crag today." He laughed and started assessing my injuries. It was the realisation that I was alive and not permanently maimed that brought about a feeling of well-being and euphoria which lasted several days. For years, ever since I began climbing, the dread of a fall had been lurking unobtrusively about the back of my mind, and now I had done it and lived. In those days people did not fall very often and when they did they were likely to be killed. With a little help from my friends I crawled on my knees sideways across the buttress to easier ground and eventually off the crag. A bunk bed was borrowed from the tiny 'Barrow lads' hut and I was carried down to Coniston and then to Workington hospital, feeling extremely well. A friend rode my motorbike home.

I had lacerations to the scalp, fractures to ribs and one ankle, sprains to both. My new rope was ruined, its first twenty odd feet abraded to about two thirds of its thickness by scraping over the rock behind which Frank was belayed. I had fallen forty feet and since the rope saved me from falling another two hundred, I felt it had been money well spent.

Nowadays Eliminate A no longer stands near the top of the list in terms of difficulty, but in quality it is still one of the finest face climbs in the Lake District. The last two pitches are open walls and they sustain the uniformity of standard that is one of the main qualities of the climb. It was only many years later I went and finished the climb, and I was unable to identify the exact point at which I fell. I think I may have got slightly off route.

WAY OUT WEST

Though the Lake District has become an important part of the nation's heritage, the pride of the north of England and known throughout the civilised world, the industrial strip in the west – Coronation Street transplanted on to the Cumbrian coast – tends to be passed over and ignored like a poor relation. Traditionally as a community it looked west and north rather than east, but nevertheless it has always had its climbers and devotees of the hills. When I came to live there after the war, not many people had cars, and so the Sunday bus of the Workington Ramblers was a useful facility for climbers, and offered the added attraction of a rendezvous in the evening at some tea-room or pub, and congenial company on the way home. We used to think that the acquisition of a car would bring about an increase in climbing, but I doubt if it did. When travelling was difficult we were much more inclined to come out for both Saturday and Sunday and stay at a hut, and it was surprising how well one could manage on public transport. The railway line from Workington to Penrith was open at that time. You could on Saturday mornings buy a return ticket to Penrith or Foxfield for two shillings (i.e., ten pence). It was a workman's ticket valid only on the 0630 train but with no restriction on the return journey. For a further half-crown you could take a bicycle along. Using the ticket made a day out into quite an expedition, especially in winter. The stealthy departure from home, the gruff greeting at the station, the sleepy ride to Keswick, and then the eight miles of pedalling to Seathwaite, gave an importance to the occasion which was quite absent when, later, we did the same journey by car. Eight o'clock would generally see us at Edmonson's, where we would treat ourselves to a second breakfast of bacon and eggs before going on to the Napes, or Great End, or even Pikes Crag or Scafell. We generally headed for the higher crags in those days, though the routes we did might be modest enough. On the return journey, waiting for the train, or, worse, hurrying to try and catch it, could make a chilly or tiring end to a long day, but our reward was to return home to an evening of warmth and ease, drugged with fresh air, and the memory of rocks competently scaled.

Climbers in those days were I think less well accepted by the general public then they are now. There was an undercurrent of feeling abroad that the sport had something perverse about it, as though scornful of ordinary human concerns. This may in part explain the incident that took place one evening on Keswick Station. The train drew in and we stood by the guard's van waiting to put our bicycles on board. Two porters were hurling parcels out on to the platform. I was with Jack Carswell, and those who know him will not be surprised that he turned to me and in a flat voice made the remark "Handle with care". The porters gave not the slightest indication of having heard, except that one of them picked up a parcel, examined it elaborately, and said to his companion:

"Can't see owt that says 'Handle with care', can you?" "No" said his mate, "I can't".

They went on unloading and when they had finished we stepped forward to put in the bikes. The guard was already unfurling his green flag. But one of the porters barred the way. His face showed no expression and his voice was mild and impartial. "Can't put them on without a label" he said.

I was inclined to expostulate and eat the necessary humble pie, but Jack said "Hold my bike" and disappeared at a full run into the booking hall.

Within seconds he reappeared with two scraps of a discarded cigarette packet. "Pencil", he rapped. I hadn't one. Charging back into the booking hall he borrowed one from the clerk and scribbled Workington on the bits of paper. We stuck them on the saddles with spit and presented the bikes again. They were accepted and we caught the train. It was one of those fortunate outcomes where both parties feel they have won.

Occasionally we took the Foxfield option on our workmen's tickets. From Foxfield we would cycle up to Coniston, leave the bikes in the village and climb all day on Dow. This gave a long but inspiring day. On one such occasion, heading for the last train at the end of a summer's day on which we'd climbed several classic routes, Jack Carswell lost a pedal from his bicycle, and his only recourse was to keep on trying to kick the crank round until the other pedal came into position for downward pressure. His riding was erratic but we made progress. Unfortunately his corduroy plus-fours kept catching and tearing in the machinery and on arrival at the station looked more like a divided skirt. But we caught the last train.

One of our ways to climb on Gimmer was to go by bus to Borrowdale and walk over from Stonethwaite. Gimmer took on a new and more impressive appearance when one started climbing from the top. Setting off down A or B Route made an alarmingly abrupt transition from fell-walking to climbing. Buttermere and Ennerdale, however, were our nearest climbing areas, and attainable by bicycle. Following Bill Peascod's development of the climbing there, Buttermere was probably our most frequented valley. The roadside cottage at the foot of Fleetwith Pike was then occupied by Miss Nelson, who would serve teas with home-made scones. Her front room became the rendezvous for many a cheerful gathering of damp and pungent climbers, their patched knees stained with moss and their fingernails black with dirt and lichen. Miss Nelson spoke with a high-pitched fluting daleswoman's voice, and gave a warm welcome to climbers. She kept hens and her life was an endless battle of wits against the foxes, which, nevertheless, she was fond of. She reared several fox cubs at different times, and they were free to depart into the fells when they felt the call to do so. Her charges for tea and scones revealed a disdain of trade. Another meeting place was the Travellers' Rest Inn in Workington, where, on Tuesday evenings, we got into the habit of foregathering. On Monday we would still be licking our wounds or coping with the shock of returning to work, but Tuesday was the evening for reliving the exploits of the weekend and for planning the next. It was a pleasant and informal arrangement and could well have gone on for years.

But alas for mutability someone one evening made the remark:

"You know, we've become a sort of a club" and from that moment on the conversation moved away from climbing talk and centred tediously on the formation of a club. Though our climbing was modest enough we felt proud of our status as rock-climbers, and we envisaged a club wholly devoted to rock-climbing and not to be infiltrated by fell-walkers. We proposed a continuing membership qualification like that of the Groupe de Haute Montagne. Anyone failing to attain an annual quota of climbs – on a points system taking account of difficulty – automatically relinquished membership. We would call ourselves the West Cumberland Rock-climbing Club.

There was no debate as to who should be the first president. It was Bill Peascod. A treasurer was found without too much arm-twisting: George Rushworth. But the secretary, the man who was to do all the work, took several meetings to determine. A sustained effort to get S.B.Beck to do it failed in spite of a wealth of blandishment and flattery. In the end Ronnie Wilkinson, a reporter on the local paper, and a warm, companionable man who could recite the poem 'I have been faithful to thee, Cynara, in my fashion' in its entirety, allowed his good nature to get the better of him and consented to do it. The founder members paid a first subscription.

Headed writing paper was ordered. The club was set fair to make its contribution to climbing history, and it began with a grand inaugural dinner at the Fish in Buttermere, to which all the flower of Lakeland climbing was invited.

The dinner was an immense and unqualified success. The notion that social events go best late at night in the winter season is quite mistaken.

Conviviality smiled upon by a summer sun has a special warmth and luxury. It was a lovely June weekend and we stood in a long line outside the inn, glasses in hand, for a group photograph. Speeches were made after dinner forecasting a distinguished future for the club. The President, in his, kept finding his way round to the same lines time after time, repeating them word for word, but this spoiled no one's pleasure and he was warmly applauded. It was one of those occasions which show how gregarious a sport climbing is in spite of its claims to individualism. At the end we walked through the balmy and night-scented dark to Gatesgarth, where we slept in the barn.

The interesting thing is that that inaugural dinner proved to be the one and only function of the West Cumberland Rock-climbing Club. It was as though the dinner's great success consumed the club like a fire, blazing with such splendour as to leave nothing behind. Or almost nothing, for somewhere, I imagine, there may be a forgotten stack of headed writing paper, and in some bank or building society, perhaps, a small stagnant pool of club funds.

But of course climbing went on exactly as before, and though in quantity and severity it was of little account compared with what is done today, it filled our imagination just as much and called for the same concentration and commitment. On the day after the dinner, Bert Beck and I walked over to Pillar, climbing up the North West, down the West Wall, up the South West, and down the New West. Down-climbing was considerably in vogue among those of us who pursued the ideal of competent cragsmanship. At one stage we sought to climb down as many routes as we climbed up. In the days of comparatively little dependence on rope technique this led to a useful increase in mobility on the rocks and made retreat a more acceptable option. 'Going for it' was really against our climbing philosophy, and when as sometimes happened we took a chance and got away with it, I for one would be troubled in conscience by it and brood about it in the night with superstitious dread. I remember climbing one day on Pillar in bad weather. We were descending the west side of the Rock in the rain, and the West Face of Low Man, that unfriendly and slightly concave crag rising out of a steep gully, gleamed wetly through the murk, its top lost in mist. Strung out towards the top were five climbers, with Joe Williams from Whitehaven in the lead. They were on the West Wall Climb, which has a difficult exit on the last pitch. Joe, within a few feet of easy ground, decided to come down. His calm and methodical retreat, with such a large party, in ever worsening conditions, commanded our admiration, as did his decision not to 'go for it' on that last move.

Long ropes of climbers were more common in those days. It maximised the leader's contribution. Once I was at the end of such a *caravane* in an ascent of Stack Ghyll, and had time, while the leader was fighting it out ahead, to brew tea half way up, using water from the back of the Ghyll.

But most of my climbing was in a leading-through partnership with Jack Carswell, which lasted several years. We were so used to each other's climbing that we seldom needed to communicate by word of mouth and we were embarrassed by people who shouted to each other on crags.

We climbed quite often in bad weather and since the current wisdom was against impermeable fabrics for climbing we got wet. I remember one occasion when Bert Beck and I, at the end of a dry spell, were just approaching the top of C Gully on the Screes when the weather broke. We finished in pouring rain, and, already so wet it did not matter, drove up Wasdale in Bert's open tourer with the hood off, knowing that the comforts of Brackenclose were to hand. The rain settled in in earnest, and with the satisfaction of C Gully snatched in the nick of time we were quite resigned to the prospect of spending the rest of the weekend in the simple enjoyment of being under a sound roof with a good fire. But on Sunday morning the only other occupant of the hut asked us if we could recommend a suitable solo rock-climb for the day. Our advice was to read a climbing book in front of the fire, but in spite of the fierce spattering of rain on the windows he seemed determined to go out. Conscience smote us. After all he had come all the way from London for this weekend. We offered to go with him, chose Upper West Wall Climb on Scafell, and put on plenty of clothes. It was I believe the wettest climb I had ever done, and it was hard work dragging all that sodden clothing upwards. When we got to the top we just had enough left in us to be able to raise a grin and turn to our friend with the question: "What shall we do next, then?" But he had had enough too. When we stripped off our wet clothes in the hall at Brackenclose I found a small round spot, about the size of a ten pence piece, on the front of my innermost vest that was still dry. It made me very careful in the use of such terms as 'wet through' and 'saturated'.

Another West Cumbrian I climbed with was Frank Monkhouse.

Whereas Jack Carswell's approach to climbing was one of sober judgment, Frank went in more for audacity. One winter's day we went to Dow. The crag was well plastered with snow and ice but it was not freezing. We started up Woodhouse's Route on B Buttress. There was a slanting icy chimney up which I struggled to a bay. Frank followed. The next pitch, a crack in a corner, was deeply buried under a vast festoon of icicles, which hung down like a candelabrum: our way was barred. "What about this slab up here?" I asked. "That leads to Giant Grim on Eliminate B" said Frank.

"But", he added brightly, "there is Abraham's on B! The only difficulty is moving round that corner on to a roof. After that it's straightforward." A preliminary look at the hard move and I came back down and took off my boots. I returned to the corner, spent some time scratching the snow out of the holds, and swung up and round on to a new and inimical aspect of the crag. I was now on my own, out of sight of Frank, on the bottom edge of a steeply inclined roof that rose above me for thirty or forty feet. Round my waist, tied in a bowline, was my Kenyon three-quarter-weight manila line, not a rope one could put much faith in. Through the waist loop was stuck my long ice axe, ready to gore me in the event of a fall. I stood there in my socks, unable to believe my ill-fortune. My chief enemy became a creeping paralysis of the will. The line from Henry V: 'Would I were up to the neck in Thames, or anywhere but here' kept running through my head, hindering my efforts to face up to the task in hand. Meanwhile my toes and fingers were getting colder. I made one move by hooking the pick of my axe over a little hold. Gradually I goaded myself upward. Every new perch I reached, comfortless though it was, seemed preferable to moving on, so I fought inertia all the way. I was also wooed by spurious ways sideways off the slab. Every hold had to be cleared of snow, and I found nowhere to place a runner. My last move was a kind of mantelshelf.

Supported on the heel of one hand I groped above my head with the other, and found the jug handle that represented the end of the ordeal. I remained motionless for some time before I finally made use of it and hauled myself into safety. Frank came up Giant Grim using the rope, and helped me on with my boots.

Nylon ropes were available but hemp and manila were still much in use. Vibrams had not finally taken over from nails. As late as 1954 I climbed Kern Knotts Crack in tricounis. There was a shoemaker at Grange in Borrowdale who made me a pair of boots nailed with Ortler clinkers, and after that I switched wholly to vibrams. It was not easy to get stiff-soled boots and a Whitehaven climber, Frank Crosby, had a pair of clogs planed flat and fitted with Vibram soles. This gave a rigid sole plus a pointed toe and was a precursor of the modern rock-boot. Nails came into their own in winter climbing, crampons being unheard of except for the Alps. Long bouts of step-cutting could turn a simple gully into a worthy expedition. I remember one such ascent when except at the top there was nothing but water-ice in Central Gully, Great End and we had to cut steps all the way. On the main pitch a big ice-bulge produced an overhang. By standing on Jack Carswell's shoulder I was able to cut hand and foot holds and over-come the bulge. Ahead now lay a cataract of transparent ice, up which I kept cutting, desperate for a runner. I'd taken every inch of rope out by the time I reached a belay. For Jack there was no rope left for manoeuvre, and I wasn't for descending. Darkness was only an hour or so away. With the rope twanging taut between us we were at a stand-still. Providentially at this moment another party appeared from below. As they cast a jaundiced eye on the options Jack said, in a matter-of-fact way that precluded refusal: "Just stand here a second and give me a shoulder" and the next moment he was on his way, and we reached the top at dusk. We often wondered how the other two got on.

And so, weekend after weekend, we made our small pilgrimages out of the west, returning homeward again with the evening sun in our eyes. In this way the Lake District retained its magical quality, and our concept of the picturesque remained unimpaired by too much familiarity. We went home to the ordinary world which began at about Frizington or Cleator Moor or the top of Fangs Brow, and in parts so resembled L.S.Lowry's Salford that he occasionally painted there. Where we picked up this clear awareness of where the mundane ended and the picturesque began I cannot think, but it was in our consciousness like a fundamental truth. They were good days in West Cumberland. One remembers fondly many names like Jack Carswell, Bill Peascod, Bert Beck, Ronnie Wilkinson, Stan Dirkin, the brothers Banner-Mendus, Brian Blake, Austin Barton, George Rushworth, the Monkhouses, Jim Joyce, and young fellows like Don Greenop and Eric Ivison; and one forgets many more. One looks back and wonders what it was all for, all that passionate interest and energy, and where it sprang from. Just as one wonders why one still keeps responding to the siren song, even when one is old enough to know better. Perhaps it has something to do with that warm golden light that floods Scafell Crag on about one summer evening in a hundred.

IN SCOTLAND

Now that roads and the motorcar have caused Britain to shrink one can get to the north of Scotland in half a day, and so it is harder to feel the lure of those distant hills and the romance of the Highlands. It was different in the forties and fifties when a weekend in Scotland was a considerable expedition.

We would set off after work on the Friday and try and get as far north as we could before midnight. There were no motorways and hardly any double highways. Getting through Glasgow was never easy; nor was finding the Erskine Ferry. Once across the Clyde we would revive our flagging spirits with a late-night call at some fish and chip shop, and then, before the benefit of the meal had worn off, snatch a few hours' sleep in a roadside bivouac, before continuing to our chosen area. A typical bivouac place was near Crianlarich, and in wet weather there was a convenient road bridge there, under which one could sleep on the sand and gravel beside the river.

In this way we could get two full days on the hills before taking the long road home late on Sunday night. A good proportion of the working week that followed would be spent recovering.

Scottish weather of course is something that calls for optimism. These trips were not for the fainthearted. One had to travel hopefully and believe in the possibility of hitting upon the kind of halcyon days that made the north-west of Scotland so incomparably beautiful. Frequently we were disappointed, and there are few places more pervasively wet than Scottish hills in bad weather. To an English ear the Scots pronunciation of 'hill' sounds remarkably close to 'hell.'

Yet looking back on these raids across the Border that we used to make I cannot remember a single one that was not worth while. Every trip was an adventure of some sort, and had its reward, either in some heroic struggle against the elements, or some splendour of mountain scenery, or some unexpected meeting.

The trip that came nearest to being a failure – and, indeed, was a failure in that we cut it short, turned tail and ran for home – was not a weekend sortie but a longer visit. We intended to camp in Glencoe for a week and climb the hills in that area. It was just after Christmas.

Considering that in midwinter we could expect only eight hours of daylight or partial daylight out of twenty-four, it might be thought remarkable that two men in their right minds would consider such a holiday. But what in our view made the whole thing viable was the Bialaddin Pressure

Lantern, a device which, pumped up like a Primus, would provide us with a brilliant light and raise the temperature of the tent to that of a sauna. The long dark evenings could then be spent luxuriating in the warmth, reading books in comfort and generally taking our ease.

We had two tents, one rainproof but vulnerable to wind, the other a mountain tent past its best and known to leak. A sheltered site, not far from the car, was what we were after.

The weather was drear. As we drove up the side of Loch Lomond towards Crianlarich, we passed a solitary figure plodding northwards, a tramp. He wore a big heavy overcoat, carried a hessian sack on his back and had no hat. Thick tousled hair came down over his collar and no doubt stopped the rain from getting straight down his neck. Compared to him we were royally provided. The rain was cold; higher up it would be snow. The sight of him, alone in that bleak landscape, made an impression on me and in the days that followed I thought of him more than once.

We crossed Rannoch Moor, and, reluctant to go down into the deep trough of Glencoe, cast about for a campsite. Eventually we found a small roadside quarry in which to put the car, and, some distance up a nearby burn, a level bit of greensward close to the water, out of sight of the road and sheltered in the little valley through which the burn flowed. There we pitched our tent. And the Bialaddin lived up to its promise, banishing the darkness.

Next day it was still raining and the only way out of it, apart from remaining in the tent, was to get uphill into the snow, for we saw that two or three hundred feet up the side of Buachaille Etive Mor there was a snow line, showing where the snow turned to rain. We took the ordinary route up the mountain, and though we soon lost the path, we did find the snow less wetting than the rain, and kicked our way upwards until we reached the summit ridge and then the summit itself. We were in mist all the way of course and saw nothing, but that did not worry us much; we did not climb mountains just to see the view. On the way down we were at pains to make sure we stuck to the same route as on the way up.

The weather next day was much the same. We kept it under close observation for a while, but had to conclude that the faint lightening of the gloom was brought about only by the sun – up there somewhere – getting higher in the sky. In the end we packed sleeping bags and a little food and made for the Aonach Eagach Ridge. The plan was to find somewhere to bivouac in Glencoe village and return to the camp next day, by some interesting mountain route if the weather improved.

We set off across the sodden moor and by the time we got to where the rocks began my feet were so cold, wet and numb that I declared myself unwilling to start on a long ridge scramble. There was one thing I could try, I said, and if that did not work we would have to call it off. I sat down on a stone, took off my boots, and removed one of my two pairs of wringing wet socks. This did the trick. With only one pair of socks on, my feet soon warmed up, having more room in my boots, and I had no further trouble from them.

We had a rope and ice axes, no crampons, for in those days most people only used them in the Alps, and in any case here they would have balled up in the soft snow. It now snowed steadily, which we found preferable to rain, and we made our way quite happily along the ridge, clearing the snow off the rocks or kicking steps in it where it formed solid plaques. Daylight we knew was short but we could afford to be slow and careful until we got clear of the narrow crest of the ridge.

At one point we seemed to be going down rather too much, and what was more, the angle kept getting steeper. We were on a convex slope and at length came to the conclusion that this could not possibly be part of the long crest we knew Aonach Eagach to be. The fact was that we were heading straight down Am Bodach into the great trench of Glencoe, and, very likely, an early demise. So we turned round and kicked our way laboriously back on to the ridge proper, to continue the miles of scrambling and step kicking. We finally got off the crest and out of the mist. There was now only a drizzle of sleet and we went endlessly down and down through it until we reached the village. It had been a good day, testing us a bit, and we were pleased to have wrested something worth while from the dismal weather.

We toured the village looking for a barn. We asked at two places and were refused, but in the end we found a small house with a disused cow byre adjoining it. The byre was clean and dry and a kind old lady gave us permission to sleep in it. We had brought a primus stove and a pan, and a candle, and though we missed the Bialaddin we made ourselves tolerably comfortable with soup and hot drinks. In the prevailing wet-cold of the environment, to be in a dry sleeping bag was 'paradise enow'.

We had no stomach for anything next day except to walk back up the road to our camp. In those days SAD – seasonal affective disorder – had not been discovered, which is perhaps as well, for I'm sure we would have had it. And in the midday twilight of our walk up Glencoe, with the rain beating in our faces, who should we meet but the tramp we had passed near Crianlarich, wearing the same rain-sodden overcoat, his thick hair still hanging over the collar. He passed us by without a nod or a word. At least he had the wind behind him.

Back at the camp all seemed snug and dry, but when we got in the tent and our weight pressed down on the floor, we found that the greensward we were camped on was now nothing but a sponge full of water. I had a lilo airbed, which floated with an inch or two of freeboard, but my friend Keith had a kind of thin mattress that rapidly became sodden and was wetting his sleeping bag.

It was already dark, raining heavily and blowing, but we had to act. Pumping up the Bialaddin – once hot these lamps absolutely refused to be blown out – we took it to the car and there cleared the floor of the little quarry of stones and put up the mountain tent. We then transferred all our camping gear and settled in. We still had dry camp clothes and dry sleeping bags and while the Bialaddin was blasting away we were warm. But of course when we were ready to sleep we had to turn it off.

After a couple of hours we realised we were getting seriously wet from the fine spray that was penetrating the tent fabric. Keith said there was a tarpaulin car cover in the boot. We could put it over our sleeping bags. Determined not to get any more of my clothing wet I stripped naked and darted out into the icy rain. It seemed to take me a long time dancing up and down and trying to find the way to open the boot, but I suppose it was only seconds. I found the waterproof sheet, threw it into the tent and followed it, wiping myself off with a bandana.

Keith was a junior doctor working at the Liverpool Royal Infirmary. His car had stood for weeks in the parking lot there, covered by the waterproof sheet, which as a result was coated with the industrial grime of the city, and in the morning we found our hands, clothes and sleeping bags were filthy.

This was the last straw that broke the camel's back. The Scottish rain was cold but it was clean. The darkness was only the effect of the earth rolling around in its orbit, and we had no quarrel with that. But the grime of inner city Liverpool was not what we were here for. We turned for home.

We went back via Lochearnhead, in pelting rain. Keith had been working with Dr. Charles Evans, the mountaineer, who, on hearing he was going to Scotland, had told him he should try and call on an uncle of his, a retired university don, who lived alone in a wooden hut on the Braes of Balquhidder. We now thought we might look him up, if only to get out of the rain.

He took some finding, and it took a good deal of hammering on the door before we heard him removing all the barricades he'd erected against the wind and rain. We entered a wonderfully warm, wonderfully dry house lined with books.

Mr. Ker spent a good deal of his time sailing in the Mediterranean and every summer stayed for several days at the Col du Géant, walking up the glacier early in the morning and skiing back down as soon as the sun had softened the top inch of the snow. He said these ski runs worked out at five pounds a minute and were worth every penny. Since he never drank alone he was glad we'd called, and opened a bottle of Graves. He also invited us to sample a rich fruit cake he had made, and wrapped up a similar one for us to take back to Charles Evans for the Kangchenjunga expedition he was about to go on.

We stayed for the whole afternoon and it was a visit that brought us back into the civilised world.

But I have never quite forgotten that tramp we saw.

THE SKYE RIDGE

The Yorkshire Ramblers in the early 1950s had one or two very inter-esting Whitsuntide meets at Loch Coruisk on the Isle of Skye. The partici-pants met at Mallaig, to be taken by boat to Loch Scavaig, and fetched back a week later. I joined George Spenceley for two of these trips. Our ambition was to make the celebrated traverse of the Cuillin Ridge, and in the early part of the week we made our plans and deposited bottles of water at two places on the route in preparation for the big day. On the eve of our attempt we turned in early in my small army pup tent intending to set off at one in the morning. On such occasions I need no alarm clock; I keep waking up every half hour or so. When we looked out at one o'clock it was obvious the weather was changing. The wind was rising, the sky starless and overcast, and there was already a hint of rain in the air. We cancelled the trip, and when in the next hour our predictions were confirmed and the tent began to be shaken by wind and rain we sank deeper into our sleeping bags and were soon fast asleep. It was a rough night, and we were aware once or twice of movement about the camp, but we were snug enough and slept on.

We turned out next morning, however, to a rather hostile reception. Our companions, assuming we were battling it out on the hill, had conscien-tiously checked our tent during the night, replacing pegs where necessary, making sure it did not blow down.

We had better luck the following year, and once again the plan was to leave Coruisk at one in the morning. This time we were a party of three, as we had been joined by Crosby Fox, a sea captain by profession and a keen mountaineer.

Our first objective was the summit of Gars-bheinn, and we reached it at 3 a.m. after a scramble straight up its flank. In the dark on the way up something hissed loudly at us and we persuaded ourselves that it was a wild cat. By the time we got to the top, daylight had already arrived, and all around us, so it seemed, lay the sea, dotted with islands and headlands, an inspiring sight. There is nothing quite like being up on the mountain at the dawning of the day. One feels not only favoured but virtuous, as though the pleasure one experiences is deserved, and not simply a gift from heaven. We had some breakfast and moved on quietly enough, conserving our energy, for we had much to do. We had brought a rope and a sling or two and plenty of food and drink. I had even brought a sleeping bag, not against the possibility of bivouacking on the ridge, but in preparation for our night out at the end. We made good progress over Sgurr a'Choire Bhig, Sgurr nan Eag, Caisteal a'Gharbh-choire, Sgurr Dubh Beag and the Dubhs, to the Thearlaich-Dubh gap, where we met our first bit of difficult rock, and roped up for it. We were pleased, we were doing well, and we were soon on the summit of Sgurr Alasdair, the highest mountain in Skye. It lay off the main ridge but we were soon back from it and over Sgurr Mhic Choinnich and An Stac to our next obstacle, the Inaccessible Pinnacle, or In Pin as we always called it. The long exposed scramble along the top edge of this remarkable blade of rock brought us to an abrupt drop. A number of old furry slings marked the abseil point. Not one of them looked worth risking one's life on, but taken together they seemed reasonably safe. To avoid having to add to the collection, we arranged one of our own slings in such a way that when we passed the rope through them all, ours was too long to bear any weight, but was there ready in case the others gave way. The heavier members of our party then went down, and since the old slings bore their weight, I, the lightest, was able to take our own sling off and trust to the old ones.

To be out on this splendid ridge, the rockiest of any in Britain, was rewarding on several counts. The panorama was magnificent with great hills standing out of the sea and going on, range after range, it seemed, into the far distance. The rock, gabbro, was as rough as sandpaper so that we stuck to it easily, and so steep as to convince us that these were mountains, not hills. The day was hot and sunny; one might have been among the isles of Greece. It was good to be alive.

Our way now led over Sgurr Dearg and the various tops of Sgurr na Banachdich, the smallpox peak, to Sgurr Thormaid and Sgurr a'Ghreadaidh, the peak of the mighty winds. It was about midday now and we were still going well. George, a great believer in food as a means of combating fatigue, kept making sure we were well stoked up. One item of food we'd brought was eleven raw eggs beaten up with sugar and carried in a glass jar. When it came to the pinch neither of my companions could face this delicious concoction, so I had it all to myself and I must say it slipped down easily and proved a highly efficient fuel.

It was about this time that we began coming across men stationed here and there along the ridge, not appearing to be going anywhere. We passed the time of day and went on over Sgurr a' Mhadaidh. Somewhere along the ridge, perhaps in the bealach by Harta Corrie, we stopped to chat with two such loiterers, and found that they were members of the Alpine Club on a meet at Sligachan Hotel, and that in recognition of his conquest of Everest, they were giving John Hunt a celebratory treat by enabling him and his wife to do an unencumbered traverse of the Cuillin Ridge. The pair were wearing espadrilles, and carrying no ropes, food, drink or spare clothing, as these were to be provided en route.

This piece of gossip had an interesting effect upon our little group. By our steady and purposeful progress along the ridge we had made satisfactory time, had had no serious hold-ups, and were clearly going to make it to Sgurr nan Gillean quite comfortably. We could now afford to slow up a little, take some of the pressure off, take full note of the incomparable rock scenery. But Crosby Fox became obsessively anxious not to be overtaken by the Hunts, and the fact that occasionally they could be discerned in the distance behind us gave a particular urgency to his fears. We were urged to step up the pace, and when we got to the Basteir Tooth and roped up for the rather intimidating pitch up from the little col, the presence of another Alpine Club man waiting there with a rope at the ready was like a goad to drive us on. I for my part, notwithstanding the eleven eggs, was getting tired having been on the go since one o'clock in the morning, and I had little sympathy for the idea of this finishing spurt. But we made it and avoided the ignominy of being overtaken.

On the way down across the moor to Sligachan in the heat of the afternoon we stopped at an inviting-looking dub, stripped off and plunged into the peaty water.

We ordered dinner at the hotel. The idea was to sleep in the heather and set off at five in the morning so as to be up Glen Sligachan before the sun began to beat upon it, for the heat wave weather seemed certain to continue. My friends had been offered sleeping bags by two of the Alpine Club men we had spoken to on the ridge, and they thought it only civilised to take a shower before using them. For my part I went straight out into the heather, full of good food, got into my bag, and was blissfully asleep in minutes. George and Crosby fared less well. Livened up somewhat by the shower, they were pestered by midges and kept awake for hours. Consequently when I awoke at five, eager to get going, they were very difficult to rouse and very grumpy. It was for their own good, I pointed out, and in the end they had to admit it, for we got to Lochan Athain in the cool of the morning and were up on Clach Glas by the time the full heat of the day struck us.

We were all fairly drowsy on this walk, but the interest of the rock scrambling kept us from nodding off, and we still felt quite strong. As we went down the ridge of Blaven towards Camasunary an eagle lifted off a ledge just a few feet immediately below us, and sailed off leaving us in no doubt of its size and power. We continued on down, with the fine panorama of the sea before us and the jagged seven-mile ridge of the Cuillin to our right. We still had the walk round to Loch Scavaig to do, but the hard work was over, and we felt well pleased with our two days of mountain travel.

When, a day or two later, the boat came and took us all back to Mallaig, I walked down the quay to see if I could get a herring or two for our supper. Some fishermen were unloading their catch into barrels. They were quite willing to let me take a few but laughed when I tried to get hold of the slippery fish. "Put your hand like this," one of them said, holding his own hand, palm up, with the fingers spread out and bent up like claws. I did so and he hung a herring by its gills on each finger.

George and I, travelling in my open top Austin tourer, pulled off the road at the white sands of Morar, and in the golden afternoon sunshine we fried the herrings in butter over a driftwood fire, the air full of screaming gulls clamouring for the guts and leftovers. What I remember about that delicious meal is how rich I felt, and how favoured.

REFLECTIONS ON MY SLIDES

When I look back on my life and wonder what I have to show for having picked my way up so many crags and 'crooked the pregnant hinges of the knee' so many times on so many hills and mountains, all I can produce apart from a pile of dog-eared diaries, most of them incomplete, is an enormous jumbled mass of photographs and slides.

I am by no means alone in this. I know people whose photograph and slide collections far outdo mine. And I cannot think of any climber of my acquaintance who has none. The person who comes nearest to it is my friend Tony Bomford, a cartographer by profession, who used to say that he preferred binoculars to a camera; they made the present more enjoyable, your appreciation of the day out more intense, whereas with a camera you sacrificed present enjoyment for the sake of the future. Instead of soaking up the view and losing yourself in the sublimities of nature, you were fiddling with apertures, your mind on shutter speeds. So he argued. But even Bomford has not persisted in that view. He is now taking photographs like everyone else.

There is something about enjoyment, I suppose, that makes one want to immortalise it. On a wonderful day out on the hills you feel the experience is so valuable you cannot bear to let it disappear into the mists of time. Taking photographs is a kind of protest against the transience of human life and the fleeting nature of one's passions and enthusiasms.

And so what one is left with is this enormous heap of slides and photographs.

Every so often I think I might sort them out, but I never get very far with it. Not only is the task tedious, especially in the case of slides, which have to be individually held up to the light or placed in a viewer, but it also produces in me a vague sadness, as of dreams and hopes that somehow proved illusory. Another thing is that for every photograph or slide of a friend or friends, there are twenty or more that depict scenery and mountains. Yet it is the pictures of people that now seem most worth having. There is little need to take pictures of mountains. If you want to see them again all you have to do is go and look at them; they will still be there. But people change, and go away, and die.

I had a good friend, a Swiss guide, Louis Wuilloud, who on any excursion in the incomparable scenery of the Valais, would use his camera only once in the day, and that was to photograph the party standing in a row at the lunch stop. I used to think it a wasted opportunity, but now I think he was wise. He has gone, but he has left behind reminders of the friends he climbed with.

Photographs are of course more than records. They are works of art, pictures, whose colour rendering and composition can be admired. There must be in existence many thousands of picturesque mountain scenes, all with someone in a red anorak in the foreground or middle distance, standing not in the middle but to one side, and looking into the picture rather than out of it, in compliance with accepted standards of composition.

Slide viewing has become a sort of hallowed communal activity among people who go on the hills. I remember, in the early days of my enthusiasm for the mountains, we in the L.U.M.C. were always invited to the Wayfarers Club slide shows, and would go in the same spirit as I suppose people go to church, more as an act of devotion than for entertainment. The slides were black and white in those days, and they were all of alpine mountains we had never seen and could therefore not properly comprehend, but we admired them dutifully, and stuck it out even when the lecturer agreed at the end of his talk to run through the pictures once more.

Most slide shows, and especially private viewings offered by friends, are too long, and one of the great hazards of a climber's social life is the evening when several people bring their slides along, say a hundred each. I have known such events to go on until well after midnight. My friend Louis Baume once invited me and three or four others to such an evening, but he was wise enough to stipulate that we bring "up to ten slides each." It was a most enjoyable show, the feast of reason and the flow of soul, an excellent sufficiency.

It used to be often said that the camera never lies. This is far from the truth. I know the Lake District well, it is my home turf, but I am constantly finding myself unable to identify places from photographs. The hills come out either too flat or too steep, tricks of light obscure features plainly visible to the eye, contrasts of tone are disastrously exaggerated. The art of photography is to a large extent the art of falsification. A clever photographer can create beauty out of squalor, invent nocturnal scenes in broad daylight, make people long-legged or dwarflike at will. The Abraham brothers, great photographers though they were, were not above tilting the Needle to make it more picturesque, and the easy route up it more desperate.

In my brief involvement in cartography, my job was to assist the surveyors by taking panoramic photographs from mountaintop survey stations and also drawing each panorama in a notebook in four ninety degree sections. The photographs were of course more accurate than the drawings, but provided much less information, since without reference to the drawings you could not tell where ridges separated or intersected, or what the relative distances were between mountains. In short, we could have managed without the photographs but not without the drawings. This in spite of the fact that the photos were taken with a Leica, and the drawings done in cold and wind, the 'artist' wearing two or three pairs of gloves and trying not to let his nose drip on the paper.

Skiing photographs are particularly misleading. They make precipitous slopes look like level prairies and the awkward postures they freeze you in fail to capture the fluid grace of your actual – or imagined – performance. A basic falsity in photographs is that they make something static and motionless out of what is essentially a matter of movement.

In the same way, though to a lesser extent, rock-climbing shots are seriously uninformative. They not only give no indication of the size or shape of the holds, but they present fly-on-the-wall pictures that convey no clue to the climber's movement.

The time will come, perhaps, when everyone on the crags or ski slopes is carrying a camcorder. And that is one step nearer to the time when we accept 'virtual reality' as preferable to reality.

I am still no nearer to sorting out these slides.

LOUDER AND FUNNIER

As autumn begins to turn into winter, the climbing clubs arrange their annual dinners. It is part of the age-old march of the seasons, like the departure of the swallows and the preparations for Bonfire Night.

Early in the planning for these events comes the task of finding principal guests, whose distinguished presence will grace the top table, and who will make entertaining speeches. Such people are thin on the ground, and the more famous they are the less likely they will be to accept the invitation. Nor does prowess on the mountains and the crags guarantee excellence as an after-dinner speaker. The public-spirited club member who takes on the job of organising the dinner must agonise long and hard over this. Quite apart from the difficulty of making a choice, there's the fact that during November practically every hotel in Wales and the Lake District will have its Saturday nights booked for climbing club dinners, and all those dinners will require speakers. When one considers that there are three hundred or more clubs affiliated to the BMC one can see the size of the problem.

Many years ago I was approached by my friend George Spenceley and asked if I would speak as principal guest at the annual dinner of the Yorkshire Ramblers' Club. I was surprised. And flattered, for it did not immediately occur to me that probably they could find no one else and were scraping the barrel. Like many people who on the quiet have a fairly good opinion of themselves I was at that time painfully shy about speaking in public. It had been the biggest hurdle I had had to overcome to qualify as a naval officer. The thought of having to confront a sea of faces from the top table of a prestigious climbing club was frightening enough. This club's modest title did not reflect its seniority and importance. What is more, it was full of Yorkshiremen. And Yorkshiremen are not easily impressed.

Deep down in even the most unassuming personality, however, there lies concealed the wish to be applauded. Put on the spot, backed into a corner, I accepted the invitation and for the next three weeks passed my nights not so much in sleep as in trying to think of what on earth to say.

There are after dinner speakers who can stand up and speak straight off the cuff and strike the right note. There are those so practised in the art that they can trot out well tried anecdotes time and again with success assured. At the other end of the spectrum there are those who write out their entire speech, and if they are drunk enough, get the pages mixed up and flounder desperately. I was none of these. I worked assiduously on my speech, got it off more or less by heart, then wrote the opening words of each paragraph on a post card, which I placed in the pocket of my dinner jacket.

The dinner was in Harrogate. I spent the day with George Spenceley, feeling much the same as I would on the eve of a major surgical operation, or of a marriage I had grave misgivings about. The venue was one of the most imposing hotels I have ever ventured into. It was filled on this occasion with a throng of excited club members, all in evening dress, most of them with one hand holding a glass and the other either slapping someone on the back or wringing his hand with crippling force. It was as noisy as a youth club.

For my part I was preoccupied by the problem of how much to drink. I needed enough to stop my mouth from getting dry with apprehension, but not enough to make me incoherent or forgetful.

At length we all moved into a dining room of quite remarkable splendour. The candelabra alone filled me with awe, and except for the absence of women the glittering assembly put me in mind of Byron's description of the ball that preceded the battle of Waterloo.

The meal itself, one of the perquisites accorded to the speaker at a climbing dinner, was good but largely wasted on me. The roast turkey might have been cardboard. The wine was for me a form of medication to keep me capable of speech. A fortunate diversion at the top table was the last minute inclusion of Peter Boardman, just back from the summit of Everest, first Briton to get there. There was no question now as to who was the chief guest. The presence of this pleasant young man brought a welcome atmosphere of informality to the proceedings. The president invited him to say a few words, which he did, to great applause.

Then my turn came. I was introduced with the usual flattering inaccuracies about my past which I decided not to attempt to correct, and I stood up, post card in hand.

The president had done his stuff admirably. The audience were primed and ready to be amused. I cannot remember what I said but somehow I struck the right note and my speech was a success. Many people came up to me afterwards and said so. My cup was full. What I did not then realise was that a lively bush telegraph exists among the dinner secretaries of the various clubs, and if a speaker has been anything better than a disaster he is likely to be asked again. From climbing obscurity I found myself suddenly quite sought after for a few years, but I was never as successful again, and my poorest performance was at the Wayfarers' Club dinner in Langdale.

At that time I was living in Yorkshire and on that particular weekend I took with me to Langdale two female American students who were on an educational exchange visit. They booked in at a bed and breakfast while I went to the hotel and to the dinner, but I undertook to meet them next morning.

I badly misjudged the mood of the Wayfarers' dinner. Those were the days when the clubs were beginning to admit female members and there was much jocular speculation on the subject. The president gave a long speech full of lewd allusions to the possible results of becoming a mixed club. If they made the change, he said – and I quote this only to illustrate the tenor of his remarks – the entry qualification for new members would be a stiff one. He went on for some time in the same vein, to uproarious applause, transforming the atmosphere of the gathering into something more like a rugby club night out than a climbers' annual dinner. My own speech fell pretty flat and was listened to with tolerance rather than enjoyment. Nor was it helped by the fact that the hotel staff were by this time clearing up at the back of the dining hall with much clattering of dishes. I was reminded of an after dinner speech described by P.G. Wodehouse at which someone at the back shouted, "Louder, please," and someone else added, "And funnier."

Next morning my kind hosts were slightly put out when instead of joining them for a walk over the hill to Grasmere, I told them I had a date with two young women staying at Chapel Stile. I would follow, I said, and hope to meet the party later. In view of all the chauvinism and machismo of the night before I was a little shy of showing up with the two young Americans and I rather hoped I would fail to catch up with the group. I took these girls, who had never seen the Lake District before, over the hill, down into Grasmere, and into the Red Lion. To my embarrassment that is where the Wayfarers had foregathered. I thought they might give me a cool reception, but instead they fell upon the two girls with such an excess of courtly attention and gallantry that I half expected them to roll over on their backs on the floor of the bar like dogs and kick their legs in the air. They extended their stay in the pub, they bought the girls more drinks, they told climbing stories and claimed to know Salem, Massachusetts, where the girls had come from. Leaders in this, as in so much climbing, were A. B. Hargreaves and Ivan Waller, whom age had not wearied nor the years condemned. Ivan, in fact, accompanied us all the way back to Langdale, leading off up the hill at a cracking pace. At stiles he would hand the young ladies over with old world courtliness, then spring nimbly over himself. It was fascinating.

Driving home to Bingley that evening I grieved over my poor showing at the dinner, but took some consolation from the reflection that I'd at least livened the proceedings up a bit next day.

YOUTH AT THE DOOR

Whenever I go into Brackenclose in Wasdale and into the men's dormitory, my eye roves up to the top bunk in the far left-hand corner of the room, and to the rafters above it. I'll tell you why.

The time is long ago, and the place is Langdale on a fine December afternoon. The occasion is an unofficial meet of the L.U.M.C. As students, when we came to the mountains for a weekend, our behaviour was very similar to that of small children let out into the playground at playtime. We burst upon the scene with just the same mixture of elation and surplus undirected vigour. We also took enormous pleasure in each other's company and experienced all the cheerful solidarity of the gang.

This explains, though it will hardly excuse, the extraordinary decision we made to hike over Esk Hause and Windy Gap to Ennerdale in order to force an entry into Black Sail Hut which we knew to be closed. We somehow persuaded ourselves that we could enter the building without causing damage and naturally we would leave it in as good condition as we found it, if not better.

The idea came to us as we sat expansively over a farmhouse tea at the foot of The Band. It may well have originated from one member of our group who became a highly respected officer of the F&RCC but who at that time had a propensity for lighting the blue touch-paper.

The farmhouse tea, which we were having as a late lunch, was too enjoyable an occasion to hurry and when we rose from it it was nearly three o'clock. We were already in shadow but the sunlit bracken shone like copper on the slopes of Pike of Stickle and walking in darkness was part of the idea. We filed up the side of Mickleden and by the time we reached the foot of Rossett Ghyll darkness had advanced upon us, assisted by a huge black cloud which had been forming in the west. We climbed up the steep and rocky slope into an altogether different and forbidding region of gloom, darkness and incipient storm. What had started as a delightful lark was changing rapidly into a serious undertaking.

By the time we reached the top of Rossett Ghyll we were in a tempest. The rain came at us downwards, sideways and even upwards. The wind buffeted us in a brutish and unseemly manner. Angle Tarn was seen as a livid blur in the general blackness. Progress was slow. Our party was seven or eight strong. Or seven or eight weak, it would be truer to say, for keeping everybody together was not easy. We had regarded the path over Esk Hause as an unmistakable highway. In the roaring dark, however, and with patches of snow across it, it proved surprisingly easy to lose. We also lost the capacity to estimate time and our walking, and waiting, and struggling seemed interminable. To an observer we would have looked like a demented, squabbling rabble, but we were only trying to make ourselves heard, and keep our feet in the savage wind. We had frequent discussions about the route, yelling our opinions, staggering in the wind, occasionally clustering round a wet map by the light of a failing torch. Somewhere on the top of Esk Hause my balaclava flew off my head in a violent gust of wind and disappeared forever, leaving me with a strong feeling of outrage. I wrapped my scarf round my ears and we pushed on. A dangerous-looking void ahead turned out to be the nearby waters of Sprinkling Tarn. No doubt a ragged cheer went up from our wretched little band. All should now be plain sailing to Sty Head. But a curious thing about walking the hills at night is an unconscious reluctance to go downhill. Visibility on a very dark night is limited to little more than a yard. One can generally see or sense the ground at one's feet, but anything lower than that is indistinguishable. One's tendency then is to step where one can see something to step on and that is usually something slightly higher than foot level. In this way one unconsciously prefers going slightly uphill to going down.

We lost the path but the feeling of knowing where we were was strong after leaving Sprinkling Tarn, and we hoped to run across it again. We set a compass course. Some time later we came to a drop. Those in the rear cried 'Forward!' and those at the front cried 'Back!' Cautious probing suggested we were on the top of a cliff. Tossing a stone into the blackness confirmed it. We tried more to the left. More cliff. We tried to the right. Cliff again. Those in charge of the compass protested that we had now tried all reasonable directions and that it made no sense. These conjectures, of course, were made at the pitch of our voices on account of the storm. In the end we took the only course open to us, which, as the compass-men bitterly pointed out, was back the way we'd come. We scrambled and slithered downhill and eventually found the path. After that whenever we lost it we would send our scouts in various directions until we found it again. In this way we got down to Sty Head Tarn.

The plan of continuing up Aaron's Slack into Ennerdale was now unanimously rejected while a proposal to get the hell out of our present difficulties was carried unanimously. Finding the start to the path to Wasdale was not easy however. We came to the col where nowadays the mountain rescue box stands and here I expressed the view, at the pitch of my lungs, that we needed to go up a little to make sure of hitting the track. My friend Wildblood disagreed, on the ground that we would then be in danger of taking the

Gable Traverse path. We became surprisingly heated for two people on the brink of hypothermia. It was like a scene out of *King Lear*. I do not know how it ended but after we'd torn a passion to tatters for some time we did eventually find the way and went lurching down in the teeth of the storm until we reached at last the levels of Wasdale Head. Endless columns of rain still swept up the valley from the Irish Sea. We trudged on until we came to the lake. There was a light showing in Brackenclose. We looked at the time and found to our astonishment it was only nine o'clock. We thought it must be at least one in the morning.

We knew Brackenclose, having stayed there with our president G.Graham Macphee. We now stood at the door, a forlorn, hapless crew, wet through. We knocked. It opened, revealing a vision of dryness, warmth and light.

We explained that we were a university mountaineering club, that our President was a member of the Fell & Rock and though he was not at present with us would no doubt be willing to vouch for us. We were becoming seriously affected by the cold and wet; etc., etc. "This is a private hut", said the spokesman of the dry people within, speaking in what we instantly registered as an Oxford accent. "The Rules of the Club say that guests must be accompanied by a Member." One of our difficulties was that we had no very plausible explanation for our presence in Wasdale. We could hardly admit that we had been frustrated in our nefarious plan to occupy Black Sail Hut. In the end we were turned away from the door, back into the rain and darkness. Or rather we took ourselves off, gathering the rags of our dignity around us, resolved to seek shelter in the barn of Wasdale Head Hall, half a mile away.

Our interview at the door of the farm was a good deal shorter. At first we thought we discerned some glimmer of sympathy in the eye of the farmer's wife, but when she saw there were girls in the party her face assumed a rather stony expression and it was thumbs down from then on. Whether she imagined she might be giving licence to romps in the hay, or whether she simply felt that girls needed better accommodation than a barn, was not disclosed, but it made no difference. We had the choice, she said, between Brackenclose (half a mile), the hotel (two miles) and the Youth Hostel (four miles).

She found it easier no doubt than the climbers to refuse us. There is a certain kinship among climbers, even between respectable club members and those beyond the pale. For them, turning us away must have felt a little like turning away poor relations. But to her we were visitants from another planet, part of that strange alien tide of townspeople that lapped intermittently round the boundaries of the farm.

We went back to Brackenclose to report our failure. This time we pushed the girls well to the fore. They hardly looked like sex symbols with their blue faces and bedraggled hair, but perhaps in those days chivalry was less dead than it is now. The climbers, moreover, had had half an hour and more to listen to the rain beating on the windows and to compare their lot with ours as they sat toasting their toes before a roaring fire, mugs of tea in hand.

They relented, and our troubles were over. Some brave and kindly soul must have entered his name in the book as the member responsible for us. (I wish I knew who he was, to be able to thank him again after all these years). We paid up, we crept obsequiously around keeping out of people's way and cooking our soggy food. The girls, stripping off wet clothes and combing out their dripping hair, revealed themselves to be more girl shaped than might at first have been thought and made themselves exceedingly pleasant to the company at the fireside. On the whole our intrusion did no one much harm and some perhaps a bit of good. It was only years later, however, that I realised fully the nature of the dilemma we put those people in.

But the point of this story, if it is has a point, and the culmination of the whole incident and the thing that has made it stay in my memory when so much else has faded, was climbing into that top corner of the three-tier bunkhouse, close under the sloping dry timbers of the roof, to be cradled in the total luxury of dry blankets, and to hear the rain furiously pattering and hissing on the slates a few inches above me. I was at one with all animals, in all dens, all over the world.

GOING WALKABOUT IN THE ALPS

As Burns pointed out, the best-laid schemes of mice and men gang aft agley. There was, for example, the time we laid siege to the Brenva Face of Mt Blanc in the poor summer of 1954. I had read Graham Brown on the subject, and weighed the hazards of the Route Major, the Sentinelle Rouge and the Old Brenva. I had found someone with his sights on the same goal. His name was Desmond Stevens, and since he had cut off all the margins of his Mt Blanc guidebook to reduce its weight I deemed him a man with a good grasp of essentials. We agreed that what we needed for the Brenva was a rock-solid spell of fine weather. Instead of spending ourselves on lesser objectives, we decided to lie in wait, harbouring our strength, until the time was ripe.

We were in Entrèves, camped close to, in fact practically under, a huge notice board that bore the words Vietato Campeggio–Defense de Camper–Camping Not Allowed. We had arrived there some time earlier down the Val Ferret from Switzerland and we had found the site occupied by a large party from Manchester Grammar School. The master in charge told us that they had camped there every summer for several years, and on finding this year that the site was no longer available they had been granted a dispensation. "When we leave tomorrow," he said, "they will turn everybody off."

They left but we stayed. A couple of days went by without incident; then a policeman appeared, drawing our attention to the notice board. He was young and polite, and as we were preparing our evening meal we asked his advice about the best way to cook spaghetti. He discoursed on this subject at length and with enthusiasm. When he left he bade us 'buon apetito' and made another apologetic reference to the notice board.

The weather was changeable for several days. We became familiar figures in the charming little village and frequent customers at the village shop. Every so often the policeman would come by to do his duty of warning us off. We gave him to understand that it was only the unsettled weather that delayed our departure, and that we fully accepted the illegality of our presence on the site. Language difficulties of course did much to cloud the preciseness both of our promises and his strictures.

A further complication was the arrival one dark and drizzly night of Desmond's wife. Desmond's tent was hardly big enough for the three of us, and the warmth of the married couple's reunion made me feel *de trop*. So next evening I asked the girl in the shop, with whom I was by now on friendly terms, if there was any shed or outhouse I could sleep in, and after speaking to her father she showed me into a storeroom full of pasta: "At least you will not starve to death" she said. It was ideal; it had a bed and its window looked right on to the mountain.

As darkness fell I had more to look at than the mountainside, for the mother and father of all thunderstorms started. I sat at the open window, luxuriously dry, enjoying the magnificence of the lightning strikes, the crackling reverberations of the thunder and the rattle of rain on roofs and pavements. I spared a thought of course for Desmond and his wife, but reflected that at least they had each other.

The mountains were now covered with fresh snow and would be out of condition for days, so the Brenva project came to nothing. The Stevens proposed we all went to Chamonix in the hope of better things, but I had been there and wanted something new. They were rather relieved, no doubt, to get me out of their tent. We left the Vietato Campeggio in opposite directions, they on foot up the Val Ferret, I on the back of a scooter, bound for the Gran Paradiso.

I had made the acquaintance of an Italian family, the Arneris. Signor Alberto Arneri was a long-distance swimmer with the physique of a sea-elephant. Though new to mountaineering, he expressed an interest in joining me, and since he had transport I eagerly encouraged him. The vehicle in question was a 125 cc Lambretta on which he sat like Dumbo. With me on the pillion we set off for the Valsavaranche, and each time the courageous little bike panted to a standstill on a hill I would jump off and walk while my friend goaded it up to easier gradients. The Gran Paradiso was a far cry from the Brenva Face but at least it was a four-thousander.

We climbed it next day, having spent the night at the Rifugio Vittorio Emmanuelle. Unfortunately my friend Alberto became so unwell that our brief mountaineering partnership came to an abrupt end and he went back to his family.

Left on my own in the Valsavaranche I now wonder what to do. I have nearly two weeks before I am to meet another friend in Martigny. I think I might cross over to the south of the Paradiso, and accordingly set off uphill on a zigzag path through the forest. It is already late in the day and I am looking for somewhere to bivouac. I need to find water, but the path is up a steep spur and at no point crosses a stream. The slope is unrelenting and the forest dense. In the end I leave my rucksack on the path and traverse through the trees until I come to a gully with running water. I fill my water bottle, return to my rucksack, light a tiny fire and brew up. I then spread my light-weight sleeping bag on the most nearly level part of the path and get into it. It is already dusk.

Sometime later, after dark, I am astonished to hear voices up above, and then the crunching of boots on gravel. Two men are pounding their way down the path, and moving fast. Fearing they might tread on me, I wait until they are close and say "Buona sera" from almost under their feet, at which they leap into the air, but carry on without breaking step, their voices taking on a higher and more animated timbre as they stride on down the zigzags below me. They are hunters carrying guns. Soon the sounds of their passage die away, leaving the world to darkness and to me.

By six-thirty I am on my way again in the pale watery light of the morning, and by nine o'clock reach a broad upland valley. The sun is now warm and I stop by a stream in a fragrant hollow, to brew up on a fire of juniper twigs. It is a place to linger in, and I linger.

At length, after an ascent ending in a long scree slope, I reach the Col Lauzon, 3501 m. The hard work of the day over, I drift pleasantly down the other side, seeing fox, chamois and steinbok. I am in the Gran Paradiso National Park, a beautiful unspoilt mountain region with an abundance of wild flowers and animals. I am tired. My sleeping bag is barely warm enough at night and I have nothing to put under it but my anorak, so I supplement my night's sleep with an afternoon nap. I lie down among the marmots, which crane their necks and whistle all around me, and I snooze in blissful comfort, the sun warming my sleeping bag and the sleeping bag protecting me from the breeze.

Refreshed, I go down past the Rifugio Sella, a rather dismal barrack in a desolate hollow, to Valnontey, where I seek permission from a wizened old crone to sleep in a barn. She refuses me very cordially, with the assurance that it is not going to rain. I take her word for it and sleep out satisfactorily, after making a soup of pemmican and raisins over a wood fire. A staple of my diet on this trip is Mapleton's Nut Pemmican, very cheap, very nourishing and very unpalatable. I make a bed of pine boughs, use a flat stone as the basis of a pillow, and take a hot rock from the fire to bed with me.

The old crone's confidence in the weather, however, is misplaced. At six in the morning it begins to rain. I make a big fire and cook breakfast over it but the weather is getting worse. I make my way down the valley sheltering wherever I can in the heaviest showers. By the time I reach Epinel I am in what turns out to be a steady three-day downpour.

Epinel is an Alpine village which the tourist trade has overlooked entirely. A tight jumble of crazy tumbledown chalets inhabited by gnarled peasants, goats, shy children and a few young men with motorcycles, it is picturesque without being welcoming, but I need a roof, and after some abject pleading, and thanks largely to the fact that Mussolini never succeeded in stopping French from being spoken in the region, I get permission to stay in a hayloft with an open side looking down a narrow lane. It is marvellously dry and for some hours I am content to gloat at the sight of that curtain of rain falling in front of me and not touching me. But on the third day of my being holed up I have had enough. I have nothing to read, my hosts ignore me, and the cat, the only living creature showing any interest in me, runs off with my salami in broad daylight. Expressly forbidden to light a candle I find the nights very long. I am monumentally bored. The odd thing is that in retrospect that long vigil seems a significant episode in my life. It is as though some growth was taking place, though I cannot think what.

As I am at last about to leave, a strange bucolic procession winds down from the hills with the singing of songs and the playing of musical instruments, the women bearing great round cheeses on their heads and the men driving yellow and white cattle. 'To what green altar' I find myself wondering 'leadst thou that heifer lowing to the skies' and 'what little town is emptied of its folk this pious morn'. There is something timeless and classsical about this festive rout. They might well have stepped off a Grecian urn.

I make another long climb out of the valley and brew tea on a fire I get going with difficulty with wet wood. From a lovely high ridge dotted with eidelweiss and other alpine plants I look down on Aosta. Immediately below me is a broad alp from which rises the sound of cow bells. I descend to a group of cow sheds where the cattle, black and white with friendly blunt features, are being driven in for the afternoon milking. I have to discourage the calves from wiping their noses on me.

At a wood fire against the wall of a shed a yellow mixture in a cast-iron cauldron is being stirred and pounded with a smoke-blackened piece of wood. I make the mistake of thinking this is food for the calves but it turns out to be polenta for the men. An ancient patriarch, dignified in spite of dirt and careless buttoning, invites me to taste it. I enter an entirely black hovel, where the polenta, so solid it retains its shape, is tipped out on to a greasy board and cut into slabs with a wire. The old man gives me a large hot handful, together with a piece of mouldy cheese *au petit lait*, and a bowl of curds. I make a substantial and quite delicious meal along with the others, a half-dozen men and boys, who guzzle appreciatively as if round a trough. They are shy and courteous. I give the boys my packet of Rich Tea biscuits.

They stay up there, they tell me, for three months making butter and cheese and living on milk products and maize.

I am reluctant to leave this upland and stay basking in the sun in a meadow full of large flowers and alive with butterflies, before going down into Aosta. There I lodge at the Albergho Gran Paradiso for 300 lire, the cheapest doss in town. All I demand is a room to myself.

It is Sunday night and the place teems with life. I eat in a brawling tavern full of the drunken and licentious *bersaglieri*, looking very raffish in their feathered hats. Wandering the town I fall in with some young people who speak a little English and I become so enamoured of the girls that I promise to meet them at six the next morning for a walk.

On entering my room at the hotel at about midnight I am much displeased to find a thin man lying on one of the beds, fast asleep and snoring. He wears only an off-white singlet and a pair of striped underpants. I sleep badly, and rising exhausted at 5:15 I let myself out, eat bread and cheese (Fontina) and plums in the public gardens, our rendezvous, and await events, hoping no one will turn up.

The first to arrive is a personable girl called Marisa. She offers to have her aunt take care of my rucksack, and also call at the poste restante for my mail.

The others arrive, five in all including a small boy. One, a girl, has perfectly beautiful legs but they are not used to walking and I survive the day largely because she demands so many rests. I am extremely tired and must seem a dull companion. We spend a long afternoon beside a lake, my only contribution being to make a fire. I fall asleep before it, lulled by the young people's incessant chatter.

At seven in the evening we get back to Aosta and say our goodbyes. I then have tea with Marisa, collect my rucksack, have an excellent meal in a Piedmontese restaurant, and at half past nine set off for Switzerland. I walk for some time in moonlight as bright as day and when I am well out in the country, though still on cultivated land, I turn in on a pile of new-mown hay under an apple tree. It is a night of great beauty.

Early in the morning I wake up to find a farmer raking hay a yard or two from me. I start up with apologies but he implores me to remain tranquil and not disturb myself, so I bury my head once more in my sleeping bag.

It is a hot day. I stop a mile or two up the valley and make cocoa on a small fire by the roadside, watched with interest by some women haymakers, who call "Buon apetito" when I begin spooning the hot liquid into my mouth. A peasant woman with amalgam teeth stops on the road to question me, with intelligent curiosity and no trace of inhibition, about myself, my travels, my wife, my age, profession and family, and then passes serenely on. I trudge up the road stealing an occasional apple, and crawl at last into Valpelline, where, in response to a sign promising a ristorante in 50 metres, I slump into a seat under a striped sunshade. A waitress with a kindly eye brings me two fried eggs which I eat avidly with a large quantity of bread, and a measure of red wine. Then, thinking it a pity to spoil the ship for a ha'porth of tar, I order a second course of steak, asparagus and salad and make a really excellent meal, its sauce the sympathetic presence of my waitress. Everybody along the road has asked the same question, "Are you all alone?" To the gregarious Italians this is incomprehensible. And so many have asked me if I am not afraid that I begin to wonder whether the Col Fenêtre is in bandit country.

The road is now steeply uphill but it is cooler and I begin to emerge from my fatigue. In the little village of Ollomont, two inns and a shop, I drink a glass of marsala and buy provisions with my remaining Italian money. I then walk up the road clear of the village and bivouac in a little meadow among trees.

For some reason this is not a satisfactory camp. I make careful preparations, springy boughs to lie on, stone pillow, hot rocks etc. yet I am vaguely ill at ease. The glow of the fire, I feel, is showing me up while concealing in deeper darkness any watcher of my movements. Once turned in I cannot get comfortable; I am overtired. I should never have spent the day out with those young Italians.

It is nevertheless a perfectly lovely moonlit night. There is a heavy dew and consequently a chilly dawn. I rise early, light a fire to warm up and dry out, then turn in again and doze until the sun is well up. My progress up toward the Col Fenêtre is very slow. The day is windless and hot. I browse on wild raspberries, and at a waterfall I stop and shave. Shaving on this trip I find is good for me; it brings a sense of well-being, persuading me I am coping with things, and keeping on top.

I begin to think I might look for another bivouac before I reach the col and when I top the rise which brings me into the final hanging valley I find a little group of cowsheds. No people. This is By. I wander around it but finding all the habitable places locked I move on. Eventually, further up the valley I come to a long cowshed with a little living-hut at one end, up steps. It is open. Outside, a metal pipe discharges a jet of pure mountain water into a trough. In the hut there are box beds, one with straw; a neat pile of wood lies outside. The time is four in the afternoon. This clearly is the place for me and finding it does much to temper the forlorn aspect of the bare, deserted valley.

Before settling in however I go over to a clean grassy knoll beside a beck, strip off all my clothes and inspect every inch of them in the bright sunlight, in pursuit of the fleas that I have brought from the Albergho Gran Paradiso. When I find them I crack them between the backs of my thumbnails. It proves an entirely successful campaign. Any I miss must have fled for their lives.

My satisfaction at finding the hut is even greater when the skies darken and the rain comes. The storm, however, brings in three Italian alpinists who were bound for the Chanrion Hut over the border, with a view to climbing La Ruinette. They are a married couple and a seventy-two year old man, all pretty wet. I make a fire and prepare a thick soup of nut pemmican, pasta and onions followed by tea with lemon and biscuits. The Italians, pecking at patent mountain foods, are impressed. The married couple commandeer the bed with the straw. As they have no sleeping bags I can hardly complain. I share the other box with the old man. As soon as we are quiet the rats begin rustling about, but the main night noise is the drumming of rain on the roof. Each heavy shower wakes me, but the gratification of being safe, warm and dry in such weather compensates for the lack of sleep. The old man lies so still and silent throughout the night that I begin to wonder if he has died.

In the morning I join forces with the Italians for breakfast. My pot, their coffee. The weather is clearer, the rain off. There is new snow on all the rock summits. My friends abandon their climb and make for Ollomont, no doubt to sleep in some hotel. I plod stolidly off for the col.

Further up there is yet another cowshed and this one is in use. I go in and am offered a one-legged milking stool, a bowl of the steaming liquid from which the cheese is made, and another bowl of cold white curds like junket. With this and a lump of cold polenta I make a good second breakfast. My host, a wizened little man with a tremendous jutting moustache, tells me he was in the maquis, and, captured by the Germans, was taken to forced labour in Germany. It is odd to think of someone like him being dragged into a world war. His cheese steams in a huge cauldron of copper over a pine wood fire. He puts in a sort of home-made vinegar from a local shrub. Pulling the cauldron off the fire by means of a great wooden crane he dredges its contents with a cloth held between his two hands and his teeth. Later he takes lumps of butter from a churn and squeezing it dry in his hands plasters it onto a huge egg-shaped mass standing on a board. He has charge of a hundred and ten cows; ten are his own. His Ollomont house is let for the summer to a schoolmaster on holiday. The delicious appearance of the produce contrasts strongly with the smoke-blackened dairy, the mud on the floor, the spitting of the dairyman, and his rough bed in the corner, of hay, blankets and sheepskins.

This is my last impression of Italy. I go through the now snow-covered Col Fenêtre and before me lie the jumbled glaciated mountains of the Valais. I start down a bleak narrow valley; it is all downhill now and at Martigny I can expect letters from home. I make soup on a juniper fire and journey on down the long valley over a remarkable little twelfth-century stone bridge where the river is squeezed into a deep ravine.

Further down a new sound, harsher than the sound of glacial torrents, makes itself heard and I come upon a scene of intense activity. The valley bed is being excavated by mechanical shovels feeding a constant procession of roaring trucks. The river churns along a channel well above the level of the excavation. This turns out to be the Mauvoisin ten-year hydroelectric project in its third year. Everyone wears helmets, even the young executives in lounge suits and big boots, the officer class. Strange that the only place I have before seen this kind of all-out effort, this excitement and concentration, has been in war. The Swiss seem to love moving mountains. Some half-dozen engineering firms are here collaborating in the building of a *barrage voûté* eight hundred feet high. Cable railways, rock tunnels, mushroom villages for the workers, are all part of the fun. At one place the broiling river, unwanted for the time being, has been pushed raging into a rock tunnel to appear further down, writhing with terrifying vigour down a smooth concrete trough.

I reach a point where a notice says: *Danger de Mort Pietons et Touristes Attendez ici s.v.p. pour la voiture.* I wait and am joined by two Swiss alpinists. After an hour we are taken through electric-lit tunnels in a powerful car to emerge at Mauvoisin. The driver, a young engineer in a tin hat, has an RAC badge on the front of his car. With a certain modest instinct for self-advertisement I say thank you in English as I get out. The result is that a few minutes later as I swing down the road beyond the barrage he overtakes me, pulls up and offers me a lift down to Fionnay.

By the time I reached Martigny I had come full circle because it was from there that I had walked through the Val Ferret to the foot of the Brenva. I had exchanged the thrills and achievement of a climb on that formidable face for a rambling, solitary journey through the mountains. I was never again to get to the Brenva, but the days and nights of solitude in the hills made a lasting impression upon me, and I recall them now, after forty-five years, with a kind of gratitude. At that time of my life I came to the Alps to get to summits, to scare myself to death on rocks and glaciers, and tick off mountaineering achievements. After the Brenva disappointment it was only the fact that I had arranged to meet another climbing companion later that caused me to go walkabout as I did. Yet in drifting through the Gran Paradiso National Park and over the Pennine Alps into the Rhône Valley I found riches I'd not expected, in the vagaries of the weather, the vicissitudes of travel, the charm of fresh woods and pastures new, and 'the silence that is in the starry skies, the sleep that is among the lonely hills.' I witnessed the whole pageantry of each day from the pale misty dawn to the chill of the evening and became attuned to all the little sounds that contribute to the silence of the natural world at night. And I feasted on light and colour.

I was often tired, occasionally despondent. I could have done without the rope and crampons that I humped over all those hills; and I missed my wife. It was not all pleasure. But I would do it all again.

MORE RAINY DAYS IN 1954

After wandering alone in the mountains for several days, I meet a former pupil of mine, Harry Stephenson, off the train at Martigny. He is an undergraduate of Nottingham University on his first visit to the Alps.

We go by train to Sion, then by bus to Les Haudères, where, in heavy rain, after inspecting some caves with a view to sleeping in one of them, we think better of it and hire an upper room in an old wooden house, for 2fr50. Very satisfactory, except that the roof leaks during the night and soaks the foot of my sleeping bag.

The poor summer of 1954 continues, with new snow down to 1800 m. The rain keeps falling, and we are glad to be under a roof, however leaky. Being holed up in bad weather is something I quite enjoy. It is a time for reflection, for make and mend; and rain is in itself not unattractive when it isn't actually running down your neck. We buy provisions at the general store in the village, and invent an almost too-efficient alcohol stove out of empty food cans. On it we manage to cook in our room without setting the place on fire.

The following day it is not actually raining, so with characteristic English optimism about the weather we pack, victual up, and take the track to Arolla. The sun comes out and the air is cold and invigorating. We continue with renewed hope beyond the village, up a bare, stony valley, until the next spell of rain and cloud arrives. This causes us to abandon any idea of going further, especially as we have come across a dilapidated cheese-maker's hut with gaping cracks in its walls and piles of snow under its eaves.

All afternoon is spent making this unpromising place habitable. We gather a large stock of firewood, and make a thick, aromatic mattress of larch boughs to sleep on. There is no chimney, but such an abundance of holes in roof and walls that the smoke gets away easily. We pass a pleasant evening and a supremely comfortable night. I generally seem to sleep better when I have not paid for the accommodation.

The weather is still cold, cloudy and unsettled next day, but feeling we must do something, we leave our pleasant woodland hideout and head off for the Pas de Chèvres. We are soon up into the snow, which obscures the path, but there are footmarks to follow and we find our way to the col, in spite of blizzard conditions. Here two iron ladders lead down a cliff to a waste of snow and boulders and somewhere across this expanse lies the Val des Dix Hut. We are lucky enough to catch an occasional glimpse of it, as the mist swirls about, but for the most part we flounder dangerously in a white-out among moraines choked with soft snow, and then across the glacier itself, until we reach it.

This is all very far from our idealised vision of the Alps as a place of dazzling beauty, blue skies and burning sun. It is comfortless and cold, and our feet are wet. At the hut we find an English party, who make tea and depart without paying for the wood they burn. No *gardien*. A dead rat in the water bucket. We spend a chilly evening and a rather poor night. In the small hours the sky comes clear and starry, but by daylight the normal state of affairs, snowfall and mist, prevails once more. We turn tail.

Going down into the Val des Dix, we can find no path and make extremely painful going over snow covered moraines, plunging and slipping into unseen holes, and stumbling on hidden boulders. At length we come out of the mist, find a track, and trudge in a drizzle of sleet down an interminable muddy valley to a dismal, pale-green lake, which we cannot help but compare unfavourably with ours at home.

As we approach the dam at the end of the lake the valley walls narrow and steepen. The track is now cut into the rock, and in the shelter of an overhang we make a brew of tea, using a broken plank for fuel. We continue, somewhat cheered, but with sodden boots now beginning to chafe our feet. We take a wrong turning up steep zigzags, and have to come down again. The proper path, we find, goes through rock tunnels. Here we meet a string of peasants coming up laden with bulging loads of hay for the cattle, whose grazing in the upper valley is snow-covered. We run the gauntlet of an olive-green cascade of water to enter a dim, muddy tunnel, and on coming to a sign saying "Route barrée, Danger de Mort," diverge to the right into the open air, and down a big iron ladder on to the top of the old dam.

In front of this barrage another is being constructed, and vast works are in progress. A metal prefab hotel six storeys high houses some of the two thousand workers. One téléférique brings great buckets of gravel from the mountainside, while another delivers tubs of cement from the Rhône valley. These are being tipped into the caissons of the new barrage and sprayed from hosepipes.

We now go down countless zigzags into a typical alpine valley, green and pleasant, but dominated by the inexorable procession of cement buckets marching overhead between tall red pylons. We find a lodging with a cheerful, hospitable old man who has come up to do a day or two's mowing. We use his stove for cooking and drink his wine as an aperitif. He cordially offers us one of the big beds that lie at the opposite end of the room. This unexpected kindness and hospitality is a solace to us and we accept thankfully. But the chalet is so warm we sleep badly.

We continue by road round to Les Haudères, a long, footsore, weary slog. Waiting there for the post office to open in the afternoon, we meet a lanky, angular young Englishman who has been camping near the village since the beginning of May. He and his friend have given up their jobs in a printing works, made their own down sleeping bags (tog 30+, I should judge, warm enough for the South Pole), patched up an old motorbike-and-sidecar, and made for the Alps with a view to becoming mountaineers. The motorbike-and-sidecar, he tells us, fell to pieces at Zurich and was scrapped. Having had no previous climbing experience at all, they have paid for a guided ascent of Mont Collon, and on the strength of that equipped themselves with rope, axes and crampons.

We learn all this over tea in the cafe, then hire our same old leaky room, and that evening go for supper with the campers. A faint improvement in the weather leads us to plan a joint glacier trip next day.

Their camp is a model of cleanliness and order. Laurie Bertrand is a quiet intelligent humorous man of few words. Ray West, the tall one, his high-pitched Cockney voice perpetually raised in cheerful complaint, is more outgoing, and quite at home speaking French, taking incredible liberties with the pronunciation.

It is fine next morning and the four of us set off for the Cabane Bertol, 3300 m., sending our rucksacks up to Arolla by jeep for one franc each. Halfway up to the Col Bertol we stop to brew mint tea in the tiny military barrack, and watch a tremendous avalanche, which covers the whole face of Mont Collon in a cloud of snow. We press on up through the snow and reach the col in the gloomiest possible weather. Leaving our axes there we climb the chain to the cabin, panting a little. That evening we look out from our lofty perch upon what seems to us the abomination of desolation, snow, darkness, precipices, glaciers.

At four a.m. the *gardien* is heard growling something about clear skies and the need to hurry before bad weather comes in again. Now, we look out, in the feeble morning light, upon a marvellous serenity of sky and snowfield. We breakfast by candlelight, Harry and I watching with astonishment and impatience as our two friends go through a full English breakfast of corn flakes, eggs and bacon and toast and marmalade.

The chain is extremely cold to handle at this time of the morning, and my damp boots have frozen immediately into hard clogs. Under a glowing orange sky we set off across an immaculate, scintillating, diamond-studded plain of snow. The surface is breakable crust, for everyone, that is, except me, for I am light enough not to go through. This highly satisfactory state of affairs does not last, however, and as we head towards the Tête Blanche I find myself in front, stamping out a track in deep snow. At each step the snow lets the foot down slowly and deliberately, like a hydraulic lift.

We stop for a long time on the Tête Blanche, long enough for me to take off my boots and let the sun warm my feet. It is a wonderful viewpoint for the Matterhorn, the Dent d'Herens, the Dent Blanche, Monte Rosa, etc. This is what we came for.

Travelling on, we have hardly gone more than a couple of hundred yards before three of us put legs down a crevasse. There is absolutely no other indication of its existence. We proceed now with tight ropes and no little anxiety, but arrive safely on top of the icefall next to the Stockji. Unable to see a way down, we slog back and try the other side of this *rognon*. Since fresh snow has hidden the promised path we follow the rock ridge until we can descend a steep snow slope, which brings us to the bottom of the icefall. From here it is plain sailing to the Schönbuhl Hut.

This hut is a pleasant place to be around, with green grass, friendly goats, and pretty girls up from Zermatt for the day. Being in the mountains has always intensified my admiration of the opposite sex. It is Saturday evening, we are the only people staying, and the *gardien*, after deliberation, tells us he is going down for the night.

Next day we spend the whole morning lounging in the sun outside the hut. Life seems very sweet, what with desultory conversation, the remote rumble of avalanches, the benison of hot sun striking through crisp air, and the inspiring sight of the Zmutt Arête and the hanging glaciers of the Dent d'Hérens. But advancing inexorably towards us are the pedestrians from Zermatt, and we leave at midday as the first of them arrive.

In Zermatt we enjoy the holiday atmosphere, and find it impossible to pass the patisserie without ruinous expenditure on pastries. We make a wonderful midday meal in a meadow, and find our night's accommodation next door to the Bahnhof Hotel, in a little barn standing on stilts. Water is available from a horse trough across the road, and the station itself provides sanitation. We put our own price on this lodging, paying H. Petrik Casas fifty cents each. The big hotels send their diligences, postillions and all, jingling down to the station to meet the trains.

In the morning we victual up and make for the Rothorn Hut. Two tread-mill hours bring us to Trift, where clear streams, moorland and rocky out-crops give a Cumbrian look to the area. Here we take a long rest on a delectable grassy bank, surrounded by running water, whose murmuring is like a positive silence, muffling the sound of conversation and other distractions.

Our path after this zigzags upwards over glacial debris. The hut, at 3117 m., is brand new and not yet shown on the map. Our thoughts now turn to the Zinal Rothorn, thought to be out of condition owing to recent snow; but hearing one party has climbed it this morning we make a reconnaissance of the start. (Having failed on the Grandes Jorasses once through getting lost in the dark of the early morning, I am anxious not to rely too heavily on our candle lanterns.)

We make the acquaintance of a tough young Edinburgh climber called Bill Wallace, who has come up alone, hoping to find someone to climb with, his companion having fallen by the wayside by getting frostbitten and snow-blind on Monte Rosa. Wallace lives on glucose tablets and spaghetti, and views with astonishment the Bertrand/West breakfast of cornflakes, tinned pears, tea, bread and butter and marmalade.

Starting at five a.m. we cross the glacier and gain a broad ridge which we climb using the giant footsteps of the descending party of the previous day. There follows a rock arête, then a fine easy snow ridge, the Schneegrat. We can now see our peak. The way leads across a steep face of snow and rock, then by a snow couloir to the W. Ridge. From the top of this couloir we take only one axe. At first we are on easy, firm rocks, but soon are pushed off the ridge line along a slabby traverse, liberally daubed with snow, and up beside a rib in an exposed position. My rubber-soled foot

slips on snow-covered ice, giving me a fright. It is a potentially dangerous place, and we are glad to make use of a piton we find planted. On another traverse we are held up for a few minutes to allow a guided Englishman to pass on the descent. He fumbles urgently, put off his stroke perhaps by our presence, by almost dislodging a rock while stepping round an exposed corner, and by the constant urgings of the guide, a gnarled old mountain man with huge hands and a couple only of big yellow teeth. He wears four point heel crampons.

A very exposed bit of descending snow arête is followed by an airy step or two along a ledge, off balance but with perfect handholds, and now the summit is within reach, a beautiful little snow platform high in the air. We sit on it as on a magic carpet, devouring that most delicious of mountain foods, sardines. The weather is perfect, the time just after nine.

The descent seems to require more care than the ascent, and takes us longer, though this is because we have to wait for the two Londoners to catch up. We are back at the hut by two p.m., to spend the afternoon drinking mint tea and basking in the sun.

Just as the Matterhorn dominates the Zermatt landscape, especially in picture post cards, so it dominates our thoughts during the evening. Harry Stephenson, in particular, cannot get the Hörnli Ridge out of his head. I can, for I think it still has too much fresh snow on it to be suitable for our party. On the principle of wait and see I suggest an easy day on the Wellenkuppe; the Ober Gabelhorn, beyond it, seems too ambitious a goal. And next day this is what we do, except for Bill Wallace, who has gone down to Zermatt to look for more adventurous companions. We have a delightful mountain day, and it says much for putting enjoyment of the hills before ambition. Easy rock scrambling and a snow arête take us up to our summit, from which we survey a mountain landscape of exceptional grandeur. Later we linger all afternoon by the babbling streams near Trift, and, back in Zermatt, have a long candlelit feast in our barn, the velvety night sky lit by frequent summer lightning.

By morning it is raining again.

We now abandon all hope of getting up the Matterhorn. One or two guided parties, we hear, went up the previous day, but no guide would take more than one client. Our friend Wallace, shouldering a large pack, strides off on the twenty-mile walk to Visp, refusing to pay the sixteen francs rail fare. Our plan now is to go back over the cols to Les Haudères, and we go up to the Gandegg Hut, taking two and a half hours, against the guidebook time of four. Our original intention of staying here the night is altered on learning it costs six francs. We push on in cloud, following footmarks in the snow, to the Theodul Pass, and go down wetly into Italy. We reach Breuil, at the head of the Valtournanche – a half-finished ski resort, later to be called Cervinia – at the end of the day, and are unable to find any barn to sleep in. We are so tired and hungry we postpone the search until we have had a meal in an unsatisfactory pensione, from which we emerge, in the dark, with no idea of where to go. We have to stay near Breuil, as it is probably the only place we can buy food on our proposed route. We are now off our map and relying on my recollections of a panoramic picture map I looked at weeks ago in a tourist office in Aosta. All we know is that there is a col between the Valtournanche and Prarayer, and that from Prarayer we can cross the Col Collon to Arolla.

These uncertainties, however, seem more supportable as a result of our being on the right side of a good deal of red wine and spaghetti, and a similar optimism with regard to the weather, mingled with increased drowsiness, induces me to suggest sleeping out. It is a suggestion the Londoners receive with horror. However, having wandered fruitlessly about for some time in the dark, and blundered into an electric fence, I settle arguments by unrolling my sleeping bag and getting into it on the dewy grass. There is an empty house nearby with a covered porch, in case of rain, and I am anxious to go to sleep before the comforting effects of the meal wear off. The Londoners prefer to go off and pay 400 l. for a mattress in the Fior di Roccia. Harry and I, having drowsily arranged to see them at 7 a.m., pull our balaclavas over our ears and sleep.

At some point in the night I become aware of Harry's saying something about rain, but it seems an oddly irrelevant remark, and I go to sleep again.

The dawn is chilly with a slight breeze, which, increasing the evaporation of the dew – or rain – on our sleeping bags, brings down the temperature inside to a marked degree. We stick it out until six, then get up, to find we are on a golf course; the empty house is the pavilion. We pull up a small stake and, with feelings more of vindictive satisfaction than compunction, split it up with a knife and make a very serviceable little fire on the back wall of the clubhouse. By the time Laurie and Ray arrive there is hot cocoa for all.

We buy two days provisions and get some vague directions on how to reach the Col de Valcorneri. Once we have got clear of Breuil we find the Valtournanche very attractive, and we follow clear little trout streams and woodlands, making for a white rock, under which, we have been told, we shall pick up our track. It is hard work after an indifferent night's sleep, and the absence of any path apart from innumerable cattle trails leading from one bit of pasture to the next, causes some despondency about our route.

We traverse the valley side for two or three kilometres, then, having passed the white rock, turn a corner and head up a broad grassy combe towards a col. Ray is sure this is the Col Valcorneri, but I find it hard to believe we can be already approaching 3,000 m. Travelling in the hills without a map gives one an interesting insight into what it was like for the first explorers. Our day is filled with hopes, conjectures, and disappointments.

Arrived at the col, we look down in dismay at a large reservoir about a thousand feet below. From it an important-looking trail leads up into a great range of cloud-capped mountains. Clearly we have hardly yet begun our day's walk.

We go down past the reservoir and slowly regain the height we have lost, until we reach a higher combe in which cattle are grazing. Here the path bifurcates; one trail, much braided, goes off towards a saddle to the left, the other makes a frontal attack on the mountain mass ahead. The track ahead looks difficult, but it is strait and narrow, and appeals to our virtuous spirits more than the broad and primrose way that may lead, for all we know, back into the Valtournanche, instead of the Valpelline.

We go up steeply beside a great cascade and come to a rocky hollow, wild and trackless, and another lake. Through the mists we can now discern a deep saddle which must be on the main ridge. Passing the lake we climb a long scree slope and make our way over snow and rock to this col. It is broad and roomy, with a little harmless-looking glacier going down the other side at an easy angle. Far below we can see a narrow bottomless valley. The Valpelline. It has to be.

The glacier has an awkward snout, and we are compelled to stay on it, as the rocks containing it are smooth and steep. It is seamed with small crevasses and covered in parts with rocks fallen from its sides. We get down by moving from embedded stone to embedded stone, cutting steps where necessary in between, and sometimes using boulder-filled crevasses. Ankle-breaking glacial debris then leads us to the lip of the hanging valley. We can see no track down into the Valpelline, so go directly downhill, mostly by way of a streambed to avoid the vegetation. Though steep it makes quite pleasant going, and there is only one climbing pitch. Once down we find a cattle trail through woods and across a bridge to Prarayer. It is hardly a village, just a large, gaunt hotel and a dairy farm. The farm hands are the wild and woolly types we expected, but they refer us to a disconcertingly well-groomed woman who offers us rooms at 800 l. per person and treats with disdain our request for simpler accommodation. Tired as we are, and with the time now six in the evening, we shoulder our packs again and take the zigzag path up to the Val D'Oren, to look for cowsheds, and, if we do not find them, to continue, sleepwalking, very likely, over the Col Collon.

In half an hour a ramshackle chalet comes into view. Entering its upper floor by way of a sort of veranda, we find hay-beds, a fireplace, table, bench, and any amount of fresh air. Below is the byre, with a stream running through it. Articles dropped on the floor are apt to roll through cracks in the floorboards and disappear into this underground waterway. Nevertheless we are elated at finding such an ideal bivouac. Soon we have a bright fire of resinous wood going, with our pot-au-feu hanging over it from a huge gallus, and the table covered with good food. From outside the hut we can see the narrow defile of the Valpelline plunging down in mists and darkness towards Aosta. It is a lovely out-of-the-way spot.

After an excellent sleep in the haybox close under the roof I rise in the sweet morning air and look out – by the simple expedient of putting my head through a gap in the roof – upon a misty day with the hills still in cloud. But we are now once again on the map, and by seven we are walking again, and climbing through the usual sequence of high pastures, moraines and glacier. After some interesting scrambling up by a waterfall we attain a waste of debris and old ice, which gives way to gentle névés. Perched on the left is the Rifugio Principessa di Piemonte, a rudimentary wooden hut. We wonder whether the princess would be flattered to have it named after her, yet these remote Italian huts are to be preferred to places like the Rothorn Hutte with its hotel atmosphere.

We walk doggedly up the snow slopes, each given up to his own thoughts. One of the best things in Alpine travel is the way one can ruminate in privacy while going uphill. Shortage of breath precludes random conversation, and the monotony of the exercise somehow frees the mind.

It is cold and cloudy on the Col, and the glaciers look sad and soiled. How much, I think, sunshine contributes to alpine scenery. We put on long trousers over our shorts, and wrapped in sweaters and windproofs make a hasty shivering meal, eating with gloves on. We rope up, and crossing the gentle slopes of the saddle make our way easily down the broad highway of the glacier, under the great rocks of the Mont Collon. There is some fresh snow; otherwise the glacier is dry. An hour's walk sees us among the moraines, where we traverse off to the side to a construction site, from which we think there must be a track down. But it turns out to be just the entrance to a tunnel. We get down ice-smoothed rocks to the lower glacier, and then warily down slippery bare ice. Lower down it gets too steep and we have to escape on to the lateral moraine. We are learning that the snouts of glaciers are seldom easy.

At the Mont Collon Hotel all they have left is some mineral water, for they are taking down curtains and preparing to close up at the end of the season. Les Haudères is now only four or five miles away down a good mule track. The sun comes out and we stride out in the increasingly hot afternoon like horses heading for the stable door, and we are there by about three.

We get a handshake from the postmaster and salutations from the village women, all looking very neat in their native Sunday best. It makes us feel we belong here, as in fact the Londoners do, since they have been here for four months, and have paid local taxes, rent for their campsite, and a further charge for loss of hay. The villagers scold us for not telling them we were going away, and though it is Sunday the postmaster opens up to give us our letters.

It has been a long three-day walk back from Zermatt but this is a satisfactory finish.

Harry and I install ourselves in the same old upper room, then go up for supper at the Londoners' camp. The bad summer has one last crack at us, and we get very wet as, by torchlight, in torrential rain, we slither down the muddy track into the village.

I kept in touch with the Londoners for some time, and for years I had, in a frame on my wall, a large photograph Ray West sent me of the Ober Gabelhorn from the Wellenkuppe.

It was a long trail home in those days. Harry and I had a wait of several hours in Lausanne. Lac Leman, as always, lay dreaming in a misty sunshine, and the city seemed distressingly full of beautiful women and handsome cars. We took the night train to Paris. I quote from my diary:

Catch our train at 10 p.m. No difficulty. Find seats to spare.But what of the night ahead? Eight hours have to be endured.

Will the schoolgirls whose voices carry from the next compartment eventually get tired of telling the world what a dreadful au pair experience they have been through? What causes that deafening, rasping noise which is so common on French railroads yet rare on British? Do the jutting headpieces separating the seats serve any other purpose than preventing lovers from putting their heads together? Is it really more restful pretending to be asleep, or would it be just as good to dismiss sleep from one's mind altogether? What is the good of longing ardently for the dawn when all the dawn will bring is Paris and the necessity of struggling through the warrens of the Metro? How much does this incessant shaking and jiggling about contribute to the total fatigue of the journey? The good of how many days in the Alps does a journey like this undo?

And so to Paris, dead on time, six a.m. Join the hordes of sallow workers who run competitively down the metro's burrows, or stand passively breathing their small allowance of air between stations.

Paris at this hour of the morning has little to offer a traveller who has sat up in a third class carriage all night. Go therefore to the waiting room at the Gare St. Lazare and prepare to sit it out for a couple of hours. Life is to be seen even here. A harassed official turns out homeless loafers repeatedly, notably a little sparrow of a woman who curls up on a wooden bench and tries to sleep. A black man is arrested and in the brief struggle a jungle ferocity takes possession of his face. We go out into the city separately and come back with our purchases of wine, spirits etc.

On the crossing from Dieppe to Newhaven go down into the bowels of the ship and spend the whole trip in the bunks.

At London we make straight for the bus station, book seats on the 8.30 p.m. bus, and have nice time for a meal before starting. The bus is not full and I manage to lie down all night along the seat, fairly comfortable in spite of the intense vibro-massage. Stops are frequent. We dawdle north, and arrive at Warrington just before six. Alight here, say goodbye to Harry, stand for a few minutes in the chill, clean morning twilight and get a bus to Liverpool. Home just after seven. My mother says I look as if I have been living among the apes. A bath, shave and shoeshine brings about a remarkable improvement.

At 3.30 p.m. leave to hitchhike to Workington (only bus arrives at 11 p.m. Too late.) Lifts from Roman Catholic priest, van driver, commercial traveller, elderly couple, Shropshire farmer and wife in a new Velox, Lakeland holiday maker, Whitehaven tradesman, and, after dark, a local haulage contractor. Arrive shortly after eight.

After being so long away I felt a strange reluctance to arrive at my house. I was shy of meeting my young wife, and nervous about how I would be received.

But it was all right. A homecoming to remember.

TRAINING FOR THE HAUTE ROUTE

"Great," said Dick Cook when Eric Arnison and I arrived at Zermatt with one day to spare before starting on the Haute Route, "We've got a good training day laid on for tomorrow." The rest of the party had already been out five days, lost their northern pallor, and found their ski-legs. We on the other hand were still tired from pushing our way through the various obstacles that in those days separated the English third-class traveller from his destination in the Alps, viz: the discrimination shown by Southern Railway staff against anyone carrying ice-axe or skis; the Customs (Are you carrying more than 25 sterling, sir?); the Channel; Paris, that hostile tract full of sarcastic natives which had to be traversed to the Gare de Lyon, preferably by means of a free bus concealed in a back alley near the station; the French language; and the long night sitting bolt upright on shiny green upholstery, hounded in one's dreams by the thudding of the wheels and that occasional long-drawn-out high-pitched banshee howl emanating from the rails. We lodged in the attic of the Bahnhof Hotel run by an Anglophile Swiss guide called Bernard Biner. Dick Cook's training day hinged on our catching the first lift up to the Schwarzsee at eight o'clock in the morning. The Bahnhof was placed about as far from the start of the Schwarzsee lift as it was possible to be while remaining in the same canton, so the forced march thereto, after a rudimentary breakfast of bread and coffee, made a harsh start to the day.

From the Schwarzsee we made a short but eventful descent on frozen rutty snow to a drag-lift. At the top of the drag-lift a small group of people was gathering round a snow-mobile. We were each supplied with a rope's end from the rear of the snow-mobile, and stood with skis pointing in the direction of the Theodulpass, the Matterhorn looking impassively down upon us. When the machine lurched into motion we all converged upon the same point, fell down, and formed a drogue which eventually brought the snowmobile to a standstill. After one or two such false starts, however, we got the hang of it and rode higher and higher through the splendid alpine morning towards the top rim of the huge snow bowl .

We stood on the Theodulpass, surveying the grandiose scene. Southward we looked into Italy. Breuil lay about a vertical mile below, and who knew how many stem-christies away. We had skied on Ben Lawers and on Cairngorm, but without benefit of lifts, and our stock of expertise was small. First we had to gain access to those huge snow-slopes. A narrow wooden snow-covered ramp had been constructed, with Latin insouciance, slanting downwards across the face of some crags. It had a ramshackle railing on the outside, lined with old striped mattresses so stained with use that one shrank from coming into contact with them. The modern skier would no doubt go down such a place in a series of tiny turns on his four-foot combi skis, but we were simply spat out of the end of it like peas from a pea-shooter on to the broad slopes below. We fought our way down the endless slopes. It was not so bad high up where the snow had never melted, but before long we were in the frozen crust and had to win through that to the granular stuff below, and finally to the resort itself, which was full of girls of a disturbing beauty. So many terrors and excitements had been crowded into the descent that we found it hard to believe it was as yet scarcely mid-day. We sought out the Ristorante Pirovano and Dick asked for the owner. The waitress's gaze held no hint of distaste for our climbing breeches and balaclavas; on the other hand it held no warmth. Piero was not here; he was somewhere on the slopes, she told us.

We ordered a flask of wine. As we took our ease in the hot sunshine of the terrace one of us drifted over to a panel of glossy press photographs that stood in the entrance of the restaurant. They recorded the expedition to Amadablam in which Piero Vano and Dick Cook had taken part.

'Look at this' he exclaimed, and there, in a row of bearded, baggy-trousered expedition men, was unmistakably Dick Cook. Dick took the waitress over to the pictures. 'Mi' he said, stretching his Italian to the limit.

Two minutes later a big, handsome Italian burst on to the terrace, fell upon Dick, and kissed him on both cheeks. Dick turned to us as though wishing to explain, but Piero Vano was already wringing our hands with crippling force. His eye caught our flask of wine.

'What do you drink?' he groaned, in deep mortification. A short burst of Italian and the girl replaced it with new bottles and glasses. He sat among us, laughing and expansive, but with a keen eye for an empty glass, which he instantly filled. He relived the Amadablam expedition with Dick, who kept a wary eye on him at first in case of further kissing on both cheeks, reminisced about Signor Gighlione, introduced us to a bewildering number of his friends, including numerous spectacular girls, and generally caused the midday sunlight to take on a shimmering, unreal and altogether superior quality.

Presently waitresses began removing some of the bottles and shuffling ashtrays to one side. Crusty bread and butter and plates of charcuterie including that finest of all alpine foods, air-dried raw beef sliced paper thin, were brought on. This made an excellent meal in itself but turned out in fact to be only the beginning. Next came two fried eggs on a bed of asparagus tips, dressed with the oils of Italy and spices of the Orient, followed by fillet steak supporting a pat of butter flecked with parsley, with radishes and spinach on the side. Richly garnished salads and cheeses came next, then finally fruit. Bottle after bottle of Chianti helped us through these viands, and at length we sat grossly back in our chairs in the afternoon sun with cigars and Courvoisier three star brandy. At the centre of the feast, surrounded by empty bottles, sat Piero Vano and Dick Cook, in joyous reunion. 'Che contento sono' Piero kept repeating, and 'Eeh! Shoot me while I'm happy' beamed Dick Cook. Every so often, through the golden alcoholic haze, rose the spectre of that high col of the Theodulpass and the long descent to Zermatt; it seemed an impossible task, as in our overfed state we had difficulty in heaving ourselves out of our seats. We would at intervals take Piero's arm and explain with ponderous earnestness that we had to get back to Zermatt to start the Haute Route. He roared with laughter.

As the afternoon wore on we even began to express anxiety about catching the cable-car before it stopped for the day. Piero brushed it all aside.

"I will personally see you back to Zermatt. Have faith. I am a qualified mountain guide."

Dick Cook then insisted on hiring him then and there for the job, at a fee of a quarter of a Swiss franc. This deal called for further drinks to clinch it.

Another of my misgivings was that I had not yet sent a postcard home. It is one thing to be prevented from writing home by the exigencies of ski-mountaineering, but when the silence is caused by silken dalliance in a fashionable resort the conscience is apt to stir. I touched on this to Piero.

'Carte postale' he roared, and the whole postcard stand was trundled our way. Piero distributed postcards: pens appeared. We wrote to everyone on the Amadablam expedition, including Alf Gregory, Gighlione and John Cunningham. We then wrote to any common acquaintance we could discover. Everybody, including the girls who came and went ceaselessly round Piero, signed everything. A mound of cards accumulated on the table among the brandy-glasses and cigar-butts and at Piero's command it was cleared and sent to the post.

As the afternoon shadows lengthened not even Piero could resist the corporate pressure to get back to Zermatt to start the Haute Route. We got heavily to our feet and made our incompetent way to the cable-car, scything passers-by with our skis.

"Mama Mia" they said, and "Piano. Piano".

There was a large queue but at a word from our guide various carabinieri forced it back to make way for us. The immense cablecar filled instantly, the doors clanged and we were swung upwards at high speed to the middle station. We lurched across to a second car, and finally debouched in the thin astringent air of the high mountain, quite disoriented.

We were on a fairly exiguous rocky platform, connected to the Swiss snow-slopes by a narrow and stony bit of piste. We stepped into our rat-trap bindings, feeling that life had suddenly become real and earnest again. But Piero's spirits remained undimmed. He rhapsodised over the immense shining panorama, the valleys already showing dark and vague in the afternoon.

"Bellissima!" he breathed, and launched boldly off down the piste, to fall flat on his ear after ten yards.

If the slope scared us before it terrified us now. But Piero picked himself up with a laugh and swept off in a series of parallel turns, many of which were successful. Occasionally he scooped up a handful of snow to staunch the blood that flowed from his temple.

"It is like a holiday to me", he said. 'Che bella la montagna."

His elation infected us all, and even improved our ski-ing. At the Schwarzsee we stopped for another bottle of wine, laced this time with quantities of water, and on arrival in Zermatt the laws of hospitality seemed to decree that we should take Piero out to dinner in some grander establishment than the Bahnhof. This turned into another party and during it Piero became bent on visiting a certain Mr. Somerfeld, resident at the Schweizerhof. Dog-tired, we went over there.

Mr. Somerfeld was having dinner with a German girl about one third his age. He accepted our intrusion into his tête-à-tête with admirable suavity and cordiality, had chairs brought round his table and pressed us to drink while he continued his dinner. He knew London. In fact he had a flat in Park Lane. He recommended not the Haute Route but the Basse Route which he had completed in one day. It involved making a special arrangement to have the Schwarzsee lift opened early in the morning. One then travelled by sno-cat to the Theodulpass, skied down to Breuil, took a taxi to Entrèves, cable-car to the Col du Géant and skied down the Mer de Glace to Chamonix.

The party continued, given a new boost by Mr. Somerfeld. A flash-photographer was brought in to record our pleasures. We danced with Mr. Somerfeld's companion, who danced divinely. We must finally have said our adieux to Piero and somehow made it back through the snow to the Bahnhof, for that is where we woke up next morning.

We held a meeting to attend to last minute details, but it was not a success as we kept falling asleep in mid-sentence. So we went straight round to Saas Fee and started the Haute Route.

AND SOUTHWARD AYE WE FLED
The South Georgia Survey Expedition 1955-56

The word 'expedition' has, through overuse, lost much of its glamour. But in the days of my youth the golden age of polar travel was still fairly recent and I was brought up on the expeditions of Shackleton, Scott and Amundsen. Going on an expedition spelt high adventure and a heroic dream come true, so when my close friend Keith Warburton, now a doctor, told me about the South Georgia Survey, I was immediately interested. I went to London to see Duncan Carse, the leader, who seemed to assume from the start that I was going. South Georgia, he said, had a wet-cold climate, and ferocious blizzards. The expedition would take about nine months and there would be no pay but no expenses. The aim was to map the island.

Duncan Carse was a household name at that time, for he was Dick Barton, Special Agent, in a radio series which provided fifteen minutes of desperate high-speed adventure every evening at six o'clock. When we were brought together on board SS Southern Opal at South Shields the press, to his irritation, showed more interest in Carse the actor than in Carse the explorer. Some of the dockers even identified me as Snowy, one of Dick Barton's faithful henchmen.

At length, however, we were done with feverish last minute preparations, had said our goodbyes and were moving slowly down river on our great adventure.

Besides Duncan my companions were: Keith Warburton, doctor; Tony Bomford, captain in the Royal Engineers and cartographer; Stan Paterson, mathematician and climber; Louis Baume, Swiss watchmaker and mountaineer; John Cunningham, shipyard worker and climber; George Spenceley, teacher, photographer and climber.

Our voyage out took a month, and this long approach added to our sense of the island's remoteness. The only place we called at for a few hours to refuel was Dakar. We crossed the equator in smooth and glassy seas, flying fish occasionally landing on board. As we steamed through the tropics we spent time assembling our Nansen sledges with rawhide lashings, and adjusting skis. Some of us 'worked out' before breakfast on the foredeck, to the amusement, not to say derision, of the officer of the watch. Travelling out with us were the personnel of a whole whaling enterprise with the exception of the few over-winterers who had remained in South Georgia. Plus one woman, the wife of the new caterer at King Edward Cove. She would appear on deck in a swimsuit, the cynosure of a hundred

eyes. The whole deck seemed charged with electricity on these occasions.

As we rolled south, the seas gradually changed from silvery blue to a restless, hissing grey, and sometimes 'ice, mast high, came floating by, as green as emerald'.

Then one morning, before dawn, the engines stopped. Awakened by the silence we went on deck and saw great snowclad mountains standing out of the sea. We were there.

South Georgia at that time had two whaling stations and a small government base. Among the few buildings at King Edward Point was the most southerly jail in the world, in which we now established ourselves. At the seaward end of the Point stood a large cairn, and in it a bottle containing a list of the ship's company of Shackleton's last voyage. Across the Cove, behind a beach composed entirely of whalebones, was a little church and the graveyard where Shackleton was buried.

Over this scene, squalid enough in its detail and full of muddy tracks, dirty snow and roughly laid railway lines, loomed the vast and precipitous slopes of Mount Paget, 9,500 feet, and unclimbed.

When Cook sighted the island in 1775, he thought he had found the Terra Australis Incognita, but on rounding its southernmost cape he knew he was wrong. That cape is still called Cape Disappointment. Since then the vast majority of the island had been known only from seaward, and much of its detail was inaccurate. For example, we found that two parallel ranges of mountains shown on Admiralty charts were in fact one, and also that King Haakon Bay was badly misplaced.

Our survey was one of the last to be done by triangulation, measured base lines and star sights, for already aerial survey was taking over.

Our greatest difficulty was the capricious nature of the weather. The mountain tops were visible on average for only eight hours a week. We endured nineteen major blizzards while camping in the mountains, the longest lasting eight days. Visibility was reduced not only by precipitation and fog, but by drift, that is snow set in motion by the wind to produce total whiteout. Fine weather was so short-lived that one needed to be poised, in the right place, ready to seize any chance offered for a survey station; consequently brief sorties from base were useless. When we went into the field we went prepared to stay there until we got the sights we wanted. Our first journey lasted eight weeks, seven weeks moving outward taking survey stations, one week high-tailing it for home.

Getting inland in South Georgia was very difficult. Once there, great glacier routes opened up and the going was comparatively easy, but these inner solitudes were hidden behind a coast of remarkable steepness, itself protected by uncharted or ill-charted reefs which showed as angry livid streaks on the dark surface of the sea, or as brown smears of kelp. The usual mode of access was to land on a beach at the side of a glacier snout. Then the problem was to attain surfaces suitable for sledging. Equipment, weighing about three thousand pounds, usually had to be backpacked in the early stages, four or five portages each being needed. The sledges themselves made awkward loads twelve feet long, especially in a stiff breeze, or when carried over ice thinly coated with mud and stones. At the end of the season the glaciers became bare in their lower reaches and miles of heavy crevassing had to be circumvented.

Even the sea passage round to the chosen bay, in a small and lively sealer, had its trials for anyone prone to seasickness. We would then have to transfer to the pram, to be pulled by horny handed seamen to the shore. Carse had provided thigh boots for wading in the surf while we got the equipment onto the beach but we were able to send them back to our base.

Sledging soon became part of our working day. It was only on good surfaces that we could haul all three sledges together. A more usual method of uphill progress was for all eight men to take one sledge on for a mile or two, then return for the others. That gave opportunities for some pleasant ski runs back. Sometimes half loads only could be managed, which meant that the ground had to be covered, in one direction or the other, eleven times; occasionally it was impossible to sledge at all owing to balling up between the runners, and the choice lay between camping until the surface improved, or back-packing. In difficult sledging the enemy was not so much fatigue as ennui. Each hard thrust forward gained perhaps six inches of ground. After half an hour of it, head down, one would glance up at the ice-falls abeam on the side of the glacier. They would seem not to have moved an inch, while the col ahead remained still infinitely remote. With no breath for conversation one had to resort to daydreams, or to reciting poetry in one's head, or even counting.

Sledging down hill on the other hand could be entertaining. It could be like taking a very big dog for a walk, in that you were never quite certain who was in charge, you or the dog. Descent on skis with the sledges was for the most part beyond us, though we tried it often. It entailed no danger as the fallen skiers would act like a drogue behind the sledge and soon stop its headlong career. For steep slopes the sledges were fitted with brakes, short lengths of rope passed underneath the runners, but as they could only be applied when the sledge was at a standstill they were not a means of slowing down. Good judgement was needed to know just when to put a brake on. If it was done too soon you had the mortifying task of hauling downhill; if too late you might not be able to stop to do it at all.

Our sledging was very varied. We hauled over bare ice, over ice encrusted with stones, over patches of snow and mud, through ankle-deep slush, through the heavy blown powder we called Pom, through breakable crust, and new-fallen soft snow. We hauled on ski, on Vibrams and on crampons. And on more than one occasion some of us, in a sort of fury of endeavour, hauled on hands and knees. The sledges, of Scandinavian make, lashed by ourselves with rawhide, were I think the most nearly perfect equipment we had. Their strength lay in their resilience, and to see them sliding sinuously over hummocky surfaces was a delight. One of them, however, misbehaved by running off on its own while we were hauling the others up a hill. When we came back for it all we found were the two parallel lines of its track disappearing into the mist. At the bottom of this slope, as we well knew, was a maze of crevasses, an ice cliff and the sea. We walked down the track the runaway sledge had made, each thinking his own thoughts. After something over two miles we found a rucksack. The tracks were now discontinuous, indicating that the sledge was sometimes airborne in its headlong career. A little later we came across a sprinkling of broken candles, some primus prickers, a flame spreader, shreds of tobacco, and eventually in the great ditch between the glacier and the moraine, the sledge itself, lying undamaged except for a split 'cow-catcher', in a heap of equipment and broken ration boxes. We were lucky, for a sledge, like a ski, will always turn into the fall line, and this time the fall line happened to take it off to the side of the glacier.

We used two-man tents specially made for us by Black's of Greenock. They were wedge-shaped, with poles in sleeves, and tunnel entrances. For making camp each tent had an inside man and an outside man. Together the two would roughly stand the tent up. The inside man would dive inside. The outside man would pass him the two sledge boxes, one containing food, the other stove and utensils. The inside man would then throw out a couple of pans for his companion to fill with snow, assemble the primus stove, and light it. Meanwhile the outside man would be straightening out the tent and fixing the guys and pegs. It was a competition to see who could be drinking hot cocoa first. John Cunningham, who was my tentmate for the first eight-week trip, could pump a primus to such a pitch of fury that it would jump about on the sledge box and boil water in minutes.

We lay on air beds, in down sleeping bags, with the boxes between us serving as tables. In camp there was no comfort except in the sleeping bag, so we spent our indoor lives, and took our meals, reclining like ancient Romans. We wore long-johns, vests, khaki shirts and sweaters, and wind-suits of Ventile. We wore our underwear throughout the eight weeks, never changing it. One may imagine from this that we stank, but all my nose could detect in my sleeping bag was a faint odour reminiscent of the white mice I sometimes kept as a boy.

Bad weather often kept us pinned in our tents reading novels like *War and Peace* and *Anna Karenina*, chosen for their length. No printed word anywhere was left unread, not even advertisements in old newspapers, or the labels on tins. During our first gale the tent guys proved inadequate and we had to go out and sew rawhide replacements with numb fingers. The noise of such storms as they raged and pummelled the tents was like the abusive language of bullies. Sometimes, however, we would be drifted over, and silence would ensue. We soon learned to make a diagram each time we camped of where we had put things. Failure to do this could result in hours of digging for buried equipment.

In some ways we found snow quite agreeable to live with, certainly much preferable to water. We were usually pretty damp, but seldom really wet. Our sleeping bags were pale blue inside when dry, a royal blue when wet. A polite enquiry was, "How much royal blue have you got?". We always had some, usually where hips or shoulders pressed the down flat, but encased in our long underwear we did not feel it. The only drying agent available was body heat, and I regularly dried wet socks by putting them on over the dry ones I was wearing when we turned in for the night.

This may sound a rather dismal and squalid way of life, but in fact it was one of my happiest times. Life was reduced to basics. Our bodies were well fed on oatmeal and pemmican and our spirits nourished by the beauty and sublimity of our surroundings.

Survey stations were usually mountain tops. A team of three would set off on skis, carrying the Tavistock theodolite, its big tripod, binoculars, camera, compass, various notebooks and pencils and, of course, crampons and ice axes. We might spend up to three hours on a mountain top, and it was usually cold work. It was my practice on arrival, sweating, on the summit, to strip to the waist and put on my clothes again in the reverse order, sweater first, underwear last, thus avoiding the misery of cooling off in damp clothing. My job was to take a photographic panorama, and also, with the aid of a compass, to make a drawing in four ninety-degree arcs of what could be seen. I developed a technique of making quite detailed drawings while wearing three pairs of gloves. Keeping my nose from dripping onto the paper was always a problem.

Meanwhile Tony Bomford or Stan Paterson would be taking angles on the theodolite, face left then face right, while the third man wrote down the results. It was important not to disturb the theodolite tripod, and Bomford, a purist in surveying, would always step well clear of the legs when moving round it. On narrow summits over big drops I sometimes felt concerned for his safety. The scale of the triangulation was controlled by a number of base-lines. These were measured on the ground by means of a steel tape. Two measurements were made each time, and unless they were within four inches of each other, over a distance of some five hundred yards, we had to try again. Measuring base-lines was not a popular activity. We measured one such before breakfast, as bad weather could be seen in the valley below and the wind was already increasing and would soon make it impossible to see from one end of the base-line to the other. When, cold and hungry, I returned to our tent after the job had been done, I found I had left the breathing tube open and snow had drifted in forming a perfect cone of powder covering the boxes and sleeping bags.

To place the triangulation accurately on the surface of the globe, we took a number of twelve-star fixes. For these of course we had to wait for cloudless nights, and the observations would take about three hours. Tony would work the theodolite, Louis Baume would handle the chronometers and Stan Paterson write down the angles.

Not all trig stations were on mountain tops. I remember one, on a little headland, which was in the middle of a penguin colony, the legs of the theodolite straddling several nests, the birds crowing and generally getting under the feet of the surveyors.

Inland, the island was an austere world of snow, ice and rock, with nothing living to be seen except for an occasional chough or whalebird. But the coasts teemed with life and the rich colours of mosses, lichens and tussock grass made a striking contrast. A walk through the tussock was like one of those ideal and fictitious nature walks where every ten yards some interesting wild creature is discovered doing something fascinating. As a person before whom all birds and beasts go quietly to ground or freeze into invisibility, and to whom, in consequence, even Whipsnade seems a series of empty pastures, I never ceased to marvel at the profusion of sea elephants, leopard seals, fur seals, penguins, albatross, skuas jostling for space on that narrow littoral. On our eight-week journey we were only once forced by the difficulty of the mountains inland to come down to the coast. In general, coastal travel was not feasible, on account of precipitous headlands, deep bays and fjords and an absence of snow.

One night of particularly ferocious storm, the wind was carrying large plaques of ice over the glacier surface and they were sweeping over the tents in an alarming manner. Suddenly we heard a great shout from Carse, "Tent's gone! We need help."

We leapt into our windproofs and dived out through the tunnel entrance. Carse's tent had a three foot rip in it. We saw the occupants' hands holding the fabric together.

"Hold it while we pack our stuff and get out," shouted Carse.

I went to do so, but at that moment a violent gust of wind kicked me up the backside carrying me right over the tent, which acted as a sort of launching ramp, and I was airborne. For a moment I thought what if I can't find the camp again. But in a few yards I touched down on the snow and fought my way back to the tents.

After the refugees had got out Carse's tent was flattened and secured under food boxes.

Soon afterwards, another suffered the same fate. We ended up with four men in each of the remaining tents, bracing the fabric against gusts that came upon us with the roar of an express train. I found I could brace my portion of the tent roof by pressing the foot of my sleeping bag against it. The damp bag froze onto the tent wall and so eased the strain of keeping my feet up. I dozed, and had the persistent hallucination of being in a huge hall echoing with sound and not in a small crowded tent. It was quite a night. The wind usually came in bouts of fury like the crises in an illness, but in the small hours of the morning there occurred a continuous three-quarters of an hour cataract of raging wind that seemed to go on beyond possibility. And that, I think, was the turning point. Next day we were able to emerge, wet and disordered, to sew up with aching fingers the stricken tents and set the camp to rights.

The wind nagged ceaselessly at this period, frequently changing direction and compelling us, at the height of many a blow, to get out and swing the tents round to present their tapered ends to the weather. We found it was better to be camped right out in the open rather than in the illusory shelter of some ridge or snowbank, where violent gusting seemed more likely.

During the eight-day blizzard which was the longest continuous blow we had, I was sharing with Bomford. One night he woke me and said, "Tom, can you go out and do something?"

I was doped with sleep but gradually became aware that he was sitting bolt upright with his head pressed against the tent roof. The shaking of the tent imparted a kind of palsy to his frame. He pointed to his head.

"A rip started," he said.

I went out into a scene of typical polar desolation. The only incongruous feature was a lock of Bomford's hair sticking through the tent roof and already gathering hoar frost. Crawling about in the high wind, the drift like icy moths beating into my eyes, I broke boxes out of the snow and built a wall up to and above the level of the tear, packing snow all around it. This makeshift repair lasted for the several remaining days of the blizzard.

Towards the end of the expedition, the tents became so abraded by the snow that you could poke a hole through the fabric if you jabbed at it with your fingers. We discouraged such experiments, in much the same way as one discourages a nervous cragsman from shaking a doubtful belay block. We took to building snow walls round our encampments, and could if necessary have lived in igloos. Snow building became quite a sport and sometimes we made ornamental gateposts at the entrance to our walled enclosures.

When in 1915 Shackleton lost his ship in the Weddell Sea, he made an epic small boat voyage to South Georgia and crossed the island with two companions in a thirty-six hour walk. With his book, *South*, in our hands we went over the same ground and identified the features he described. He overestimated the heights of the mountains, we found, but it was for us an unforgettable experience to be in the very place where that extraordinary tour de force took place.

We had three other lengthy journeys and many adventures in South Georgia. Between trips Cunningham and I went out for three days in a whale catcher. In one day the gunner harpooned six fin whales. We would steam along with the whales sounding off all around us, as though our little ship was part of the school. Sorensen, the gunner, would then run along the gangway that joined the bridge to the gun platform and stand waiting for a shot. Whales would rise a few yards away but he would not fire. When I asked him why he said he fired only when the gun platform was not moving, and the only time when that was the case was at the top of a lift or the bottom of a scend. The appearance of a target had to coincide with such a moment. He sometimes waited for an hour but when he did fire he never missed.

During that day he once nearly missed, however. The harpoon went right through the whale near its tail and we heard the grenade at its tip explode in the open air. The whale was hooked but not stunned. It put up a tremendous fight and finally, before it gave up, breached completely, its whole seventy foot length clear of the water. It was then hauled alongside and another harpoon fired into it to kill it.

A whale, once caught, had compressed air blown into it from a long lance, so that it would not sink. A staff with a dan flag and a metal box was then stuck into it and it was cast adrift to be picked up by radar when the hunt was over.

We steamed back to South Georgia with six fin whales pinched against the ship's sides by means of chains passed through hawse holes and round the narrow part of the tail.

Captain Sorensen offered us a drink.

"Gin, whisky, vodka, aquavit, what you like," he said.

Whatever you chose came out of the same bottle of Puro, pure alcohol, ninety-eight percent, from Montevideo, flavoured as appropriate from small bottles of tincture.

On the ship's radio every night the progress of the whaling season was brought up to date. Whaling was a race and a scramble to get the best possible share of the twenty-five thousand international whale units allowed each year. When the total was reached all whaling ceased.

The other big whaling firm was Pesca, from Argentina. They also took elephant seal, having a licence from Britain for six thousand bulls a year. This involved landing in the ill-charted bays of the island. The captain of the little sealing vessel was Captain Haage, a mild man with chronic conjunctivitis. He knew more about the coast than any man alive, and we recorded much of what he knew for future inclusion in Admiralty sailing directions.

The big bull elephants, weighing up to five tons, would be shot with a rifle and the blubber, four to six inches thick, stripped off them on the spot. The carcasses were left for other animals and birds to eat.

There is now a reef named after Haage on the map of South Georgia.

Our survey work all but complete, Carse now felt he could unleash the mountaineers for an attempt on Mount Paget. We planned to travel round to its easy side and tackle it from there. Cunningham and I were to be the first summit party.

Bomford, however, could not resist grabbing one more survey station on the way round. There was some angry discussion about this splitting of objectives and the compromise made was to have the main party continue while Bomford, Paterson and I went off to take the station. We would then catch up. It was a decision that had unfortunate consequences.

As we took observations from our mountaintop, bad weather began to fill the valleys. When we descended, it was into thick drift and high wind. We could not use the skis and in fact had to put on crampons so as not to be blown sideways. All tracks soon disappeared. The likelihood of finding the camp seemed remote, and we had only what we stood up in. I was always very conscious of the dangers of exposure to cold and felt pretty gloomy.

At one point, however, a hole appeared in the drift and for a moment we saw a peak we recognised and took a bearing on it. We now acted upon a

new set of conjectures and set a new course. After some miles during which we grew more and more anxious, cold and despondent, we found a footprint. We spread out and went forward. More footprints appeared, then the tents. We raised a ragged but heartfelt cheer.

The tents were empty.

At first we were amused. But when our companions failed to show up and our investigations showed that they had left without taking ropes, food or extra clothing, we became concerned. The blizzard continued. We three now had a tent each and though we shouted cheerful remarks to one another, we did not voice our real fears, which were that no one could survive such weather without shelter. I went out and placed a long line of ski sticks across the approach to the camp, and we left a torch burning, a pathetic gesture. But no one came.

For my part it was a long and troubled night. For some time I'd been aware that the principal danger we faced was that of failing to find the camp at the end of a survey trip. Even on a broad and apparently level snow field, and in clear weather, it was possible to pass within a couple of hundred yards of the tents without seeing them if they happened to lie in some slight depression or behind some scarcely discernible ridge. Our own anxious search earlier that day had confirmed these fears. I brooded all night about a possible tragic end to our expedition.

In the afternoon of the next day the storm ceased and the sun lit a great plain of smooth and dazzling white with not a mark upon it. Its beauty made a strong impression on me, perhaps because the situation was so serious. We ranged about. I spotted in the distance a dark object and headed towards it with some foreboding. It was in fact quite close and turned out to be a little whale bird, frozen into the surface, its head encased in a transparent globule of ice, just like the body of a helicopter. It was alive. I took it back to the camp feeling quite emotional.

The following day we packed up the survey material and the personal effects of our missing companions, loaded as much as we could haul on two sledges and set off for Grytviken.

The story has a happy ending. The five had gone out to meet us, not intending to go far, but they failed to find their way back to the tents. Their case was getting desperate when Louis Baume fell into a crevasse which, fortunately, was bridged a few feet down. Down there it was out of the wind and felt quite comfortable, so they all got down. Apparently it was like standing in a subway with trains thundering overhead. As snow sifted gently down through the hole they trod it into the bridge. They stood there all night and halfway through the next day. Cunningham found a piece of

Kendal Mint Cake encrusted with lint in the bottom of one of his pockets. That was their only food. Louis, who had spent three years as a Japanese prisoner of war, and had served an apprenticeship in watchmaking, was a long-suffering and patient man. He advocated waiting another night but he was outvoted. When visibility improved slightly they got out and made a dangerous journey without ropes or ice axes through the crevasses back to Grytviken. On the way Cunningham did fall into a crevasse, but managed to climb out. It was lucky it was he and not one of the others, as it is unlikely anyone else could have got up unaided.

That of course put an end to the Mount Paget attempt and brought our survey to a close, though Warburton, Bomford and I went back and brought out most of the equipment we'd left behind.

We sailed in the last ship to leave, the tanker SS Southern Garden. She was very slow but we did not complain as we soaked up the sun of the tropics. She was low in the water, being full of whale products, and it was almost like voyaging on a raft. We fuelled at one of the Cape Verde Islands and toured that parched looking scrap of land with the Shell agent.

Fellow passengers on our voyage home were a number of King penguins, bound for Edinburgh Zoo. Before leaving Britain, we had been given a hundred pounds and a roll of chicken wire by Peter Scott, the ornithologist, with a request to bring back one or two South Georgia teal for Slimbridge. We had captured two or three of these charming little birds but did not succeed in keeping them alive. We returned his hundred pounds.

At Tilbury we found Margaret, my wife and Bomford's wife Elizabeth there to meet us. I had missed my wife and thought about her lovingly throughout the expedition. It is a strange fact, but true that we have always felt warmer towards each other while far apart than when together.

Our map was handed to the Director of Colonial Surveys, who was mightily pleased and settled all the expedition's outstanding debts. Carse gave us all, as promised, a gratuity of a hundred pounds. The Antarctic Place Name Society invited us to name a peak or a glacier. As there was already a Mount Tom Price in Australia, I named the Price Glacier.

The survey, in spite of our rum-doodling at the end, had been a success. Ninety-five percent of the island was now securely mapped, the odd five percent consisting of bits of coastline which could not be seen except from seaward. There are all too few blank spaces left on the map of the world, yet each man kills the thing he loves, and now there was one fewer.

BILL PEASCOD

Though I knew Bill Peascod quite well immediately after the War, I did not often climb with him, as we both had other regular climbing partners. He climbed with Brian Dodson of Carlisle, now a doctor, with George Rushworth, a fellow miner, and with S.B.Beck, a Workington schoolmaster. It was with Beck that he pioneered many new routes in the Buttermere area, and with Rushworth he opened up the crags of Newlands Valley. As a coal miner he was in a reserved occupation, and continued climbing throughout the War. He was 'discovered' by Graham Macphee, who had a talent for singling out gifted lead climbers – Colin Kirkus, for example – and did a number of first ascents with him.

Bill had the sort of physique that in those days was regarded as the optimum for rock-climbing, short, strong and compact; and hewing coal had given him strong hands. He was for those days a good technician and able to contrive sound running belays. He was even experimenting with a harness instead of a bowline round the waist, except that he thought in terms of a chest harness, not a pelvic one.

He was fun to climb with, making light of difficulties, and laughing at one's reactions to them.

He was fond of trying out his new finds on his pals. One such climb he got me to lead was Zigzag on Castle Rock of Triermaine. It was, in fact, one of Jim Birkett's, first done in 1939, but for me in 1949, it was a step into a new kind of steepness and exposure, and the crabwise sidling across the tilted gangway towards the top I found sensational. Another he tried out on me was his own Honister Wall. This was not so hard, but it followed an exciting straight line up Buckstone How, the crag rising out of a scree of quarry waste, on the side of Dale Head. The crux was a neat, exposed traverse out of a corner. Bill gave me no clue as to how to tackle the pitch, and instead of traversing I went straight up the wall. It led disconcertingly to a steep, smooth roof, which I shot up 'like a scalded cat' as he commented with his characteristic chuckle.

That of course all took place in those happy West Cumberland days before he went to Australia. His departure was sudden and unexpected and we were stunned at the loss of this bright star from our little firmament. I never corresponded with him, but bits of news occasionally came through via his Cumbrian wife's family, including the rumour that he was becoming known there as a painter. After he returned and bought Melbeck, a farm house at the back of Skiddaw, we were near neighbours, and he, his new young Japanese wife Etsuko, and their daughter Emma, became family friends of ours. We shared many good days out.

One Christmas our two families arranged to spend the day at Melbeck and have Christmas dinner together. It turned out to be a perfect winter day, one in a thousand, with generous snow cover everywhere, blue skies, not a breath of wind. It was the sort of day that made me feel quite on edge, torn between the urge to go bounding over the mountains and the awareness that I lacked the energy to do so, or had other commitments. Gloriously fine days have always done this to me. So on this occasion, along with the wines and goodies we were contributing to the dinner, I put my skis into the car.

When we unloaded at Melbeck and I proposed to go skiing everybody wanted to come too, and at last we set off, some just to play about on the slope above the house, others for the top of Skiddaw. The day was so beautiful it seemed unreal. The Lake District was turned into a sparkling wonderland, the sky cloudless and blue, the air a pleasure to breathe and more like spring than winter. By the time we reached the summit the short December day was already showing signs of declining; the distant hills and the sky above them were taking on a delicate purple hue and the valleys were becoming canyons of grey gloom. But we at three thousand feet were still 'apparelled in celestial light, the glory and the freshness of a dream'. We lingered as long as we could in the warmth of our upland world and finally descended in long easy traverses, the downhill men faring better than the langlauf skiers, until we were gliding smoothly and effortlessly down the final intakes to the farmhouse. It was a Christmas Day I hope I shall never forget.

Bill re-entered the climbing scene with all the enthusiasm of a young man, though it had been a heart attack that had caused him to come home from Australia. He was ambitious, and sought in spite of his age and shaky health to be among those at the forefront of climbing. Unlike Jack Carswell, who though still strong and active in the hills, would have nothing to do with modern climbing equipment and consequently said goodbye to the rocks, Bill eagerly embraced the new technology and acquired a 'rack' as comprehensive as that of the modern rock man. He still hankered after getting his name among the first ascents, and combed even the northern fells, which are of friable Skiddaw slates, for possible new routes, however scrappy. With my son he put up a couple of new climbs on the shattered crag beyond Buckstone How. On one of them Bill 'came off' on a traverse and did a spectacular pendulum. My son, who as leader had the prerogative to name the route, called this one The Swinging Sixties. I secretly rather disapproved of these excursions as I knew Bill's health was not sound and feared his enthusiasm might kill the two of them.

Bill was an optimist. He had taken his pension in the form of a lump sum and bought the farmhouse with it. He expected to make a living from his painting and from teaching in Further Education. In fact he had rather the same attitude to finance as Mr. Micawber, ever hopeful that something would turn up, and the last thing he was prepared to do was draw his horns in. His life style was generous and expansive and though he lurched from one financial crisis to another he rebounded every time with a buoyancy one had to admire. "This, I think, is the Big One" was a favourite expression of his as he outlined some ambitious project to achieve wealth and fame. His optimism even extended to the elaborate barbecue he brought back from Australia. In the whole five years that he spent back in Cumbria he did not lose the conviction that it was possible to hold a barbecue party at the back of Skiddaw. It never worked; we always had to retreat into the house out of the rain.

This persistent cheerfulness and zest for life made him a very likeable character, and he was popular wherever he went. He was particularly courageous about his health. Perhaps what made him such a good climber was that he would not acknowledge defeat. I sometimes went on the fells with him. He was terribly slow uphill, but on rocks, though he was now too heavy for strenuous pull-ups, his old form seemed to come back. I remember we did one of Paul Ross's routes, Adam, together, leading through, and I was amazed at the salutary effect steep rock had upon him.

I think throughout his life he climbed on his nerves. When he was young and at the peak of his form he once or twice froze on a climb and required a top rope. And there was a time when he and Bert Beck went to Pillar from Wasdale Head and found a young climber lying dead at the foot of the North Climb. He had fallen off the Nose. For some considerable time, Bill said, it destroyed his confidence.

He had occasion to do Eagle Front again when he took part in a series of rock-climbing films arranged for TV by Chris Bonington. He and Chris were to climb in the same gear as was used on the first ascent in 1940. The weather was not good, the rocks greasy, and Bill's language as he fought his way up became a source of scandalised delight to many of the climbers who watched him on TV. On the day the film was to be shown Bill, who always had a great sense of occasion, arranged for us to climb Honister Wall and then repair to his home to watch the film and have a dinner in celebration. The climbing party consisted of Bill and me, with Ronnie Faux, northern correspondent of the Times, and his wife Frances. We climbed in two ropes of two; it was a fine day, and all went well. Ronnie Faux was carrying a small rucksack and when we finished and were sitting, pleased and expansive on the top, he produced from it a bottle of Bollinger champagne, a gift from Rupert Murdoch to his staff to mark the paper's hundredth birthday. The cork was fired into space over Honister Pass, and we drank Bill's health, and our own health, and perhaps even Murdoch's, from plastic cups. There are times when alcohol really comes into its own and this was one of them.

The trouble with Honister Wall is that the way off is just about as desperate as the climb, and we had to be very careful as we descended. We were almost late for the film, arriving with only two minutes to spare. After it there was the further treat of Etsu's inspired cooking. She prepared food with the greatest care and attention to detail; she was the only cook I knew who peeled grapes. It was a most enjoyable day.

Three weeks later Bill died.

He was on the first pitch of Great Slab on Clogwyn Du'r Arddu, with Bill Birkett and Don Whillans, when the heart attack that had been lying in wait for him for the last five years at last struck. I was the first to know, as Birkett phoned me to ask if I would break the news to Etsu. It was actually my wife who went round to Melbeck to do so.

Bill Birkett gave me a photograph taken just minutes before Bill died. Whillans is reaching up, his broad hands grasping the edge of a crack, left foot high up on the slab, stomach bulging, cigarette in mouth, cloth cap on head. Bill is belayed below him, back to the camera, wearing his old marmalade-coloured fleece jacket and his off-white peaked cap. It is a photograph which now has a portentous significance, for it was only a week or two later that Don Whillans also died.

Bill was buried in Bassenthwaite churchyard, a quiet spot lying at the foot of the long ridge which rises to Ullock Pike. Some days later a memorial service was held at the little chapel beside Bassenthwaite Lake, near the place where Tennyson conceived the Morte d'Arthur. Chris Bonington and I both spoke. I quote part of what I said:

Here today we cannot help but be moved when we think of him and of the finality of death. We grieve for him. But our grief is really mostly on our own account because we have lost his bright and sanguine presence among us. As far as he is concerned, we can echo Milton's words and say, 'Nothing is here for tears, nothing to wail and knock the breast'. Bill died at a time when he was full of hope, full of plans, full of his former adventurous spirit. He had somehow contrived to reach the age of sixty-five without at all growing old except in experience and wisdom. He was not jaded, nor disillusioned, nor world-weary. Life was still fresh and exciting to him. He lived generously, with warmth and with style. He loved people, and he was delighted when his achievements were recognised. Bill was a tough, practical man but with the heart of a poet. It was his creative impulse, springing from a keen appreciation of the gift of life, that made him a climber, a painter and a writer. I can imagine him thinking the thoughts of old Ulysses in Tennyson's poem:

> How dull it is to pause, to make an end,
> To rust unburnished, not to shine in use.

Bill shone in use to the last minute of his life, and for that, and for the richness of his sojourn on earth, we can feel gratitude rather than grief.

THE ESKDALE MOUNTAIN RESCUE TEAM

One of Kurt Hahn's precepts was to inculcate in young people the spirit of service, and consequently each Outward Bound school provided a rescue team, either on the hills or at sea. We at Eskdale only occasionally had to rescue our own students, but call-outs to assist the general public were frequent. I picked up more dead people during my seven years as a mountain rescue team leader than I did in six years of active war service.

The best known and most experienced rescue teams in the Lake District at that time were Langdale and Keswick. The Langdale team was led by Sid Cross, the busy landlord of the Old Dungeon Ghyll Hotel. He was an extremely efficient rescuer who got injured climbers and walkers off the mountain in a remarkably short time, and with a minimum of fuss. During the Easter holidays of 1965 he was called out nine times in eight days. He was direct and practical, and he had no time for red tape or for making a meal out of the task. He received a well-merited M.B.E. for his services. George Fisher, too, was a most able and sensible team leader who, backed by the then president, Colonel Rusty Westmorland, built up the Keswick team and made it the best equipped and most wealthy in the district. They had a keen and devoted Dr. Lyth, who stoutly maintained, against the prevailing wisdom of the time, that a good slug of whisky did more for the morale of an injured climber than most other treatment. George had been a member of the original staff of the Ullswater Outward Bound school, but foreseeing the growth of the outdoor recreation industry he set up a climbing equipment shop and was extremely successful. He had a flair for management and expansion, and applied these talents both to his business and to mountain rescue. He too was awarded the M.B.E. The other teams were Cockermouth, Patterdale and the Outward Bound schools at Eskdale and Ullswater. All were recognised by the Mountain Rescue Committee of the British Mountaineering Council.

Rescue areas naturally overlapped. The team leaders formed a panel which met periodically to discuss rescue matters, the usual venue being the Lake Hotel opposite George Fisher's shop in Keswick. In these meetings we would sit around behind pints of beer, except that Sid Cross invariably had a pint of milk. Panel meetings were looked forward to as social occasions as well as business meetings, and were useful in reducing the sort of friction that could occur between teams if, for example, one was felt to be 'poaching' on another's territory.

When a search for a missing person produced no early result all the teams would join in, and occasionally even bring other groups from Lancashire and Yorkshire. Lester Davies, the Ullswater Outward Bound warden, who as an ex-RAF regular always retained the title Squadron Leader, had considerable organising ability and devised a system for dealing with big searches which gained general acceptance. The team leader in whose area the search had started would remain the organiser, but Lester would bring to the base of operations his small caravan, a big map and a huge notice board on which could be recorded the various search groups, the numbers in each group, and where and when they were out searching. Sometimes hundreds of searchers would be deployed. Before this organisation was set up a very lengthy but unorganised search had taken place, when a young man named Nicholas Hawkins had gone missing from Langdale. The search went on sporadically for several weeks and was at last abandoned. His body was found months later, entirely by accident, in Eskdale near Brotherilkeld.

A characteristic of the rescue teams was that they showed eagerness rather than reluctance to be called out, to the extent that one or two cynical observers described mountain rescue as a sport in its own right rather than a service. Opinions certainly differed on what the criteria should be for going out. Some felt one should never decline an appeal for help; others demanded firm evidence of genuine need before being prepared to move. Thirty years later this question has acquired a new cogency with the advent of mobile phones. Fell walkers can now phone for help if lost or anxious, or even if they're getting a little cold and tired. Of course the ultimate responsibility was with the police and it was they who would normally alert the rescue teams. They were not the experts however and would consult a team leader by telephone, day or night, however trivial the matter seemed; and though telephone calls late at night were no great trouble to a duty officer in the police station, and perhaps even did something to relieve the tedium of the night hours, they could be a trial to someone who had been at work all day and was now trying to get some sleep.

On this question of whether or not to take action there was one occasion when I came in for criticism from several people, including one or two of my own team. A climber came down one evening out of Upper Eskdale to say that a companion, who was as it happened a former Outward Bound instructor, had had a fall on Esk Buttress and probably broken his ankle. The party were camped near the buttress and the injured man said he was quite all right but would be glad if we could carry him down next day at our convenience as he could not walk. He was sorry to put us to such trouble but could see no alternative. I sent the message back that we would be glad to help and hoped he would have a comfortable night. When taken to task over this I said I was doing exactly what the man had requested; to do more was to make a fuss, when that was the last thing he probably wanted and would only add to his loss of face at having to be rescued. My critics however said he had a painful night and should have been brought out immediately. I still think I was right.

A long term resident at the Woolpack Inn in Eskdale was a retired army officer and occasional short story writer called Dudley Hoys. He was always ready to make a drama out of a guest's non-appearance at dinner and would ring me up proposing a search party. After some tactful discussion of the pros and cons I would recommend that we wait until midnight and then decide whether to take action or not. The missing people invariably turned up in the next hour or two.

It was searches for missing persons that on the whole caused most trouble. For one thing one could seldom be certain that they really were missing; there were cases where a missing person had come down in another valley and told no one, or had gone home and was warm in bed while a rescue team was out scouring the fells. It was possible, too, to pass close to a body without seeing it and then to assume that that area had been exhaustively searched. I remember one such search for a Blackpool doctor whose wife reported him missing from Wasdale Head. His plan had been to climb Scafell by Lord's Rake, following the instructions in Wainwright's guide. It was fine summer weather but since the tops had been misty, two or three of us went up during the night and walked around the Scafells in case he should be injured and shouting for help. We planned to start a larger search next morning. At dawn I was on Mickledore with a search dog Hamish McInnes had given me. I shouted and listened but heard nothing except the echoes of my own voice on the still morning air.

I now alerted other rescue teams and set up a search HQ in Wasdale Head. I put the most experienced teams on the most difficult areas. Keswick Mountain Rescue were allocated the steep ground round the beetling north and east faces of Scafell. Others ranged over the tops of the Scafells and into Upper Eskdale. In the afternoon of the first day the weather changed and it became wet and stormy. There was still no sign of the doctor. As the days went by the search area was extended, and the most obvious places were searched a second time. Still no result. I found it quite trying dealing with such large numbers of people, keeping track of their movements and collating the reports of their searching. As it happened my brother was visiting me from Canada after an absence of twenty years, and each morning of his one-week visit I left home at six and returned late in the evening. At the end of a week of fruitless searching the police, having delved into the doctor's private life, questioned whether he really had gone on the fells as he said, and called the search off. The wife, I may say, found these aspersions particularly distressing. Three weeks later a party from Brathay Hall, led by a temporary instructor, was traversing from Mickledore to the Foxes Tarn path up Scafell. They got too high and found themselves on steeper ground than they had bargained for. In stepping across a small gully the last student in the group glanced down and saw a body some twenty feet below. It was the doctor.

When I asked the group how it was that only one of them had spotted the body, they said they were so worried about the exposure that they were trying not to look down.

Having once before been criticized for moving a corpse before the police had seen it I took the Eskdale constable up with us when we recovered the doctor's body. At the inquest we learned that the main injuries had been a broken jaw and broken wrist. The head-down position in which he was found, and the growth of beard since his last shave indicated that he had not regained consciousness. I thought back to that beautiful still dawn at the beginning of the search, when I stood with my dog on Mickledore, listening for any cry of help. I had been quite close to him and he may have been still alive.

It was not difficult to reconstruct what had happened. In the mist he had mistaken the steep scree up to Mickledore for Lord's Rake. His Wainwright told him that he must on reaching the top of Lord's Rake go down a short distance, then up over a rise until it was possible to break out onto the summit plateau. He had accordingly crossed Mickledore, descended a little towards Eskdale, then traversed the steep ground under the bulging crag of the East Buttress where, in attempting to cross a little gully, he came to grief. The Wainwright guides are very attractive picture books, but they can give a false sense of security to the uninitiated, and are no substitute for map and compass or for experience in the hills. The coroner at the inquest more or less compelled me to state that people should not go alone in the hills, nor wear drab colours, two things I have been guilty of all my life.

At the Outward Bound School we did some experimenting with search techniques, using small walkie-talkies to co-ordinate the groups. One such exercise, near Devoke Water, was enlivened by interruptions, loud and clear, from an amateur radio enthusiast in America. We also tried line searching, with parties advancing across open fellside some fifteen feet apart, looking for people or dummies lying in what scant cover there was. The limits of each sweep were marked by sprinkling dry whiting on the ground. On one such exercise I lay tucked in the lee of a bank about a foot high in the turf, hidden as one approached, but plainly visible as one passed. The line went over me without seeing me, and indeed I thought one man was going to step on my head. The reason for this was not so much carelessness as the fact that the eye is constantly selecting what to notice and normally it is something ahead, not at one's feet. Again, movement of any kind will draw the eye's attention, and in focusing momentarily on a bird or even on a moving blade of grass, something motionless can be missed. For the same reason searches by helicopter give one the illusion that nothing can escape one's notice, but this is not the case. True enough, anything brightly coloured or anything moving will easily be seen, but when a helicopter traverses a felltop sheep will run, drawing one's eye away, and in the second or so that it takes to bring one's attention back to the ground, the helicopter will have moved several feet forward and a small area will have been left unseen. The Lake District fells are not extensive and the tops are bare and empty, yet it is surprising how a body can remain undiscovered in them, even after days of searching.

Hamish McInnes was a keen advocate of the use of dogs for search and rescue and introduced into Great Britain a system of training and certification similar to that used in the Alps. He had some working Alsatians whose ears did not stand straight up but stuck out sideways like wings. He gave me one of these dogs on the understanding that I would train it for searching. In my family we already had one dog, so in accordance with the old Cumbrian numerical system we called this one Tan. Except for the ears she was a very handsome dog and good tempered. Unfortunately she was not safe with sheep, and though I went to some length to curb this fault, including having her penned up with Mr. Stagg's tups at his Mitredale farm, she worried a lamb and had to be put down.

One serious occasion when I took her out on a search was in a period of wet weather in the summer when, in spite of heavy rain, it was remarkably warm. We were called out to look for two Bangor University students who were doing the three peaks, Snowdon, Scafell Pike and Ben Nevis, in twenty-four hours. They had already climbed Snowdon in the rain and had set off from Wasdale to do Scafell Pike and be picked up at Seathwaite in Borrowdale. By dark they had failed to turn up and as they were clad only in running gear and it was still raining hard they were thought to be in trouble. We went out right away, and I took my dog. There was not much we could do in the dark except follow the main paths, and shout occasionally and listen. When daylight came we ranged about above the Corridor Route, and eventually we came across a Keswick team member who had just found the body of one of the missing men. We found the other about a quarter of a mile away. An odd thing was that my dog took not the slightest interest in the dead bodies. They showed no injuries and it seemed they had died of hypothermia compounded by exhaustion. The story went about, unsubstantiated as far as I knew, that they had taken Benzedrine tablets to boost their energy. Our team took them down to Wasdale.

By this time awareness of hypothermia as one of the main dangers to be encountered in the hills was gaining ground. Dr. Griffith Pugh, of the Medical Research Council, himself a mountaineer, had for some time been investigating it with particular reference to long-distance swimming, and had subjected himself and Major Zirghanos, the Channel swimmer, to a number of experiments involving immersion in very cold water. Zirghanos died later while attempting to swim across the Irish Sea. Following the death from hypothermia of an Outward Bound student, Pugh took an interest in wet-cold exposure in the hills, and advised us on how to prevent it. Climbers in those days did not go in for impermeable clothing very much, claiming it made them just about as wet with sweat as the rain. But Pugh pointed out that a Woolworth's plastic raincoat was a cheap and highly effective protection, and the truth of this was dramatically demonstrated on the 1963 Lake District Mountain Trial, which took place in appalling conditions of wind and rain. Out of sixty-two runners only one finished, and he wore a plastic mac over his running gear. His name, appropriately enough, was Brass.

One of our annual commitments as a mountain rescue team was to provide support on the day of the Lake District Mountain Trial. One year, when the event started from Wasdale Head, we had our team on Illgill Head, the last checkpoint on the race. It was again a day of bad weather, cold, wet and misty. We found a competitor wandering aimlessly about the summit area, and after following and observing his random behaviour for some time, we put him in a sleeping bag and took him down on our stretcher to Wasdale Head. On the way down he made a rapid recovery and to this day, I imagine, he will claim that we kidnapped him and prevented him from finishing the race. Perhaps he was right. But irrational behaviour is a symptom of hypothermia and full and rapid recovery from it when treated is also common. All the same, I have often wondered about that incident. There is no doubt that mountain rescuers do sometimes jump in a little too eagerly, lending some weight to a cynical opinion that one purpose of the straps on the Thomas stretcher is to stop the patient from getting off and walking.

Throughout the time I was involved in mountain rescue the techniques were becoming more and more sophisticated and the first-aid training more thorough. The Thomas splint was replaced to some extent by inflatable splinting. Protection and weatherproofing of patients was much improved. A wire cage over the head safeguarded the accident victim on the stretcher from stonefall. Operations at night were better lit. A great standby from earliest times was the Bialaddin, or Tilly pressure lantern which, once hot, defied all attempts by wind and rain to put it out, but high powered search-lights also became common and could direct a long beam over acres of fellside. One helicopter evacuation of an injured climber which took place at night in Hollow Stones, the great rocky combe below the crags of Scafell and Scafell Pike, provided a most impressive and theatrical scene, with the crags on all sides illuminated by the powerful searchlights of the aircraft. Stretcher-bearing, however, still remained hard and sometimes back-break-ing work. Six people would man a Thomas stretcher, two on each side, one on the front handles and one on the rear. Shoulder straps were provided to take some of the strain off the hands. Being on the front had the advantage that you could see where to put your feet. The men at the sides had to stumble along mostly off the path, and those at front and back on the handles often got the impression that the side carriers were using the stretcher more to steady themselves than to bear its weight. The stretcher had sledge-runners, but in my experience these were seldom used with a patient who was still alive, as the terrain was too uneven. We experimented briefly with the Austrian Marriner stretcher which had one central wheel, but it was not found to be any improvement on the Thomas. Lester Davies also invented a motorised stretcher, which he called the Fellbounder, but it too failed to gain acceptance.

I have to say that in seven years of my mountain rescue experience we never had to lower a stretcher down a crag. Climbers either fell to the bottom or were helped off by friends or rescuers. Yet stretcher-lowering down crags was a favourite exercise which we all practised. It required quite elaborate rope-work and bomb-proof belays. Certainly it made an interesting group exercise and provided a spectacular demonstration of rescue techniques on such occasions as the Eskdale Annual Garden Fête, when, with innocent male machismo, we would lower the matron from the top of the Outward Bound School tower. Sadly, it was on a stretcher-lowering exercise that the Cockermouth Rescue Team had a fatal accident owing to a rockfall. .

A stretcher carry could be an ordeal for the patient as well as the stretcher bearers, a bumpy ride increasing the anxiety and shock following an accident.

There was one time when we had to carry two severely injured climbers down from Pillar Rock. They were both experienced mountaineers and had been climbing the Rib and Slab Route. There is a difficult 'open book' pitch on this climb and that is where the leader came off. The second's belay failed and both climbers fell about a hundred feet to the foot of the climb. Pillar is quite a long way from help and by the time we arrived, having driven all the way from Eskdale round to Ennerdale and then climbed up the fellside, they had lain there for about three hours. One, a young woman, had bled a great deal from many injuries. The other, a middle-aged man, appeared to have broken his back. Both were deeply unconscious, the young woman as though dead, the man breathing stertorously. We loaded the man on the stretcher with great care and kept it horizontal as we negotiated the steep and rocky slopes down to the forest and then through the trees to the road. Both casualties were taken to Whitehaven Hospital. They recovered, the woman to full health and strength and an active out-door life, but the man, who had been in training for an expedition to the Himalaya, was left a paraplegic.

Few of our call-outs were as serious and unfortunate as that. One was to a couple stuck on Needle Ridge, an easy climb on Great Gable. A young man was introducing his girlfriend to rock climbing. They were near the top of the climb when she got her knee stuck in a crack. Attempts to free her failed, they shouted for help, and someone ran down to Wasdale Head and called us out. By the time we got there it was quite late in the evening and she had been in this uncomfortable position, half hanging by the trapped leg, for a long time and was crying in fear and frustration. Her knee had become swollen which made it more difficult to release. Someone sug-gested lubricating the joint and a fleet young member of my team ran down to the valley to get oil and grease. Meanwhile another contrived to anchor himself in slings immediately below the girl so that she could sit on his head and thus take the weight off the trapped leg. He remained in this devoted position until the runner came panting back with a selection of butter, margarine and grease. The boyfriend left it until then to mention that he actually had a half pound of butter in his rucksack.

In rescue incidents time goes by remarkably quickly as one struggles with one difficulty after another. It was one o'clock in the morning by the time Miss Witherspoon – that was her name – was finally released. The butter helped and in the cool of the evening the swelling had gone down. It had been such a long ordeal for her that we expected her to be a stretcher case, but she recovered her strength and her composure quickly and walked down bravely and without fuss. We took the pair back to the Outward Bound

School to give them food and drink and a comfortable night's rest. The instructor whose head she had sat on had grown quite fond of her as they chatted through the hours of darkness.

I was already turned in one night when my bedside phone rang. It was the police to say that a climber had just come in to report that his companions were cragfast on Pillar Rock. It was always a good thing to try and speak directly to the person reporting the accident rather than rely on the interpretation of a third party. Luckily the man in question was still with the police and I was able to establish for certain that his pals were stuck under the capstone at the top of Walker's Gully. The exit over the capstone is notoriously difficult, especially for a short man. I also checked that they were in good shape, the weather was mild and they had food. I said I would arrange the rescue as soon after daylight as possible. I then phoned the leader of a Frizington search group and asked if he would go to the top of the Gully and drop a rope down to the chap underneath the capstone. I advised him not to go in the dark. The group was so keen however that they did not wait for daylight but went out so as to arrive at the rock at dawn where they had no difficulty in bringing up the marooned climbers. This was the only time I managed to effect a rescue without getting out of bed.

Many call-outs were to groups of young people qualifying for the Duke of Edinburgh's Award. Rescue teams became so critical of the Scheme that they arranged a meeting with Sir John Hunt, its director, at Ulverston. As a result of this meeting, Sir John undertook to have a book of guidelines produced for his candidates, though to his credit he was reluctant to do so, believing that people learn best by finding out for themselves.

We were often called upon to rescue cragfast sheep. The idea was to leave them on the crag until they were weak. We would then descend upon them on a rope. I found it useful to take a long stick with which to corral a sheep until I could grab it by its wool. We would then lower it to the base of the crag. The best way to do this, we found, was to tie the rope round its neck. Tying it under the legs seemed to injure them, and they were liable to slip out of the noose. This service did something to keep the sheep farmers with whom we shared the fells happy.

There was a surprising variety in the call-outs we had, and in order to illustrate this I quote some random extracts from the reports I had to make to the Board of Directors of the Outward Bound Mountain School at the end of each one-month course.

March 1962. On the way down to Borrowdale at the end of a very cold day on Napes Ridges, a party of us was met by Keswick Rescue Team out to find an injured girl on Scafell Pike. The weather was now becoming so bad I hesitated to take all the students we had with us, but selected the two strongest, the rest being sent on down. Thus we added six to the stretcher party, (including David Floyd, the visiting Australian Warden, and Ernest Tapley, the Chief Instructor of Colorado Outward Bound.) The girl was dead, having slid down the hard snow from the col between Scafell Pike and Broad Crag. For the two boys who took a hand it must have been a memorable experience, especially in such a desolation of snow and foul weather. The visitors too saw an awe-inspiring aspect of English mountaineering. One of the students concerned wrote in his final report: 'I think that the day that will be impossible for me to forget was when I went on a mountain rescue. A blizzard blew up and it was the hardest fight of the course to get up through the wind and the blinding snow, helping with the stretcher, to the wounded woman. The unfortunate part of this was that after getting up to her, she was no longer in need of help – she was dead. I shall never forget how I felt at that moment. Her body was lying with a light covering of snow and the wind was blowing so hard that I could only just stand up. All my feeling of coldness and tiredness left me when I saw the body.'

During the final scheme Ralph Clough was called from his post in Wasdale Head to assist with the rescue of a Cambridge University student who had fallen from Abbey Buttress. He found a party of our students already treating for shock and being generally useful. This was another valuable experience of real service.

May 1962 On Whit Sunday evening we were called on to help fetch down a young man lying with a broken femur in Pier's Ghyll. As there were abundant hands at Wasdale Head we did not rouse the students, but went ourselves with lamps and flares. It was an awkward carry lasting until 2:30 a.m. but the patient did well.

June 1962 On the first Training Scheme in the hills each group stages a rescue operation. This course, however, Watkins Patrol chanced upon the real thing, when before their eyes a climber fell down Kern Knotts Buttress and was held, gyrating in space, below an overhang. The patrol instructor, Ben Lyon, retrieved him from this position, led the remainder of the party off the crag and had his group carry out treatment for shock, rope burns, cuts and abrasions.

It was only after the end of the course that we found time to go for a ewe, fast on Raven Crag, Hardknott. She had been a month on the same grass ledge but was still lively. She was lowered successfully to the bottom.

July 1962 The Mickledore stretcher at last arrived and was taken up by a First Scheme patrol.

A party of Boy Scouts led by a headmaster were making an unroped descent of Broad Stand on Scafell when the first boy, having been lowered down the bad step by hand, fell the rest of the way. Fortunately there were some strangers at the bottom to look after him while the rest of the party went round by a safer route. Our connection with the affair was that the boy was brought into the school late the same evening and thence taken to hospital with a cut wrist and suspected internal injuries.

Two weeks later a party of three Boy Scouts was reported missing from a camp in Borrowdale. Keswick Mountain Rescue conducted a night search without success. At 9:30 a.m. one of the party appeared in Eskdale, seeking help for his two companions, one of whom 'couldn't be woken up'.

John Lawrence went off up Eskdale on the rescue motorcycle while Ben Lyon took a stretcher party from Wasdale Head. Unfortunately the messenger mistakenly reported the casualty to be near Esk Hause when in fact he was near Ore Gap. With the aid of Final Scheme students picked up on the hills the stretcher was eventually taken down to Langdale, its occupant alive but very ill. It was a great experience for our students. It also confirmed us in our view that the rescue bike (a Matchless 350 cc trials machine) is a useful piece of equipment but too heavy for the job.

August 1962 On the first Saturday evening of the course with the coop-eration of an old boy who acted as patient, we staged a search and rescue lasting well after dark. The lights of the stretcher party in Blea Tarn made a vivid and picturesque impression and the whole operation was done with such realism that most students left at the end of the course convinced of its authenticity. We felt sure of the value but rather confused about the ethics of such a deception.

A local farmer, Mr. Cooke of Fold End, offered his services on our mountain rescue team. A former Highland shepherd and stalker, he should be an asset.

May 1963 On the eve of the course newly arrived instructors were called straight out to the aid of a climber who had fallen on Esk Buttress. He fractured his coccyx but was able to walk.

On the busy last evening of the course we learned that a Liverpool

University student had fallen from Eagle's Nest Arête on Great Gable, sustaining a fractured femur. Two patrols were dispatched to his assistance, and the rest of the course had to make do with the Warden's final talk and the award of badges.

March 1963 During the First Scheme Shackleton Patrol had scarcely made camp at the summit of Scafell Pike when one of its members, a fourteen stone Borstal boy, complained of violent stomach pains and shortly afterwards collapsed. With the aid of the stretcher from Mickledore he was carried down to the Landrover. As he seemed to be sinking into a coma, we drove him straight to Gosforth, and knocked up Dr. Loudon. He diagnosed hysteria, but being unable to rule out the possibility of poison, advised us to continue to the West Cumberland Hospital.

The whole incident put a great strain on Shackleton Patrol and one student through sheer fatigue became a prey to the conviction that the boy had died and his death hushed up. Happily we were able to produce him, grossly incarnate, after two days in hospital, and he completed the course satisfactorily.

On the eve of the Final Scheme we were called upon to search for two thirteen-year-old Boy Scouts lost on Burnmoor. Small parties searched during the night, and in the early morning the entire course was deployed. Within half an hour the boys were met walking down, and the search called off by means of rocket signals. The whole course returned to school and immediately commenced the Final Scheme with only a couple of hours delay. The little boys were lucky as the night was fine and still and mild. In sending them out their master had broken about half a dozen of our most basic safety rules.

June 1963 On the first Sunday we were called upon to bring down a sixteen-year-old boy found dead at the foot of Heron Crag. He had run away from home and was on the police list of missing persons. We came straight from this solemn task into our chapel service, which had been postponed half an hour, and the whole evening made a memorable impression upon the two patrols involved.

In the third week, while climbing on Dow Crag, we were called to the assistance of a group of young climbers whose leader had fallen thirty feet into a gully, sustaining head injuries and general contusions. We made an awkward and potentially dangerous carry amid rolling scree, using the stretcher bed from a nearby hut, but all went well and the patient was eventually slid into a waiting ambulance. The police thanked us, and we made our way back up to Blind Tarn, very late but buoyed up by the mild euphoria peculiar to the end of a rescue.

August 1964 On three occasions parties of our students out on their own were involved in rescue work. The first group came upon a couple, seated, the girl in tears, and instead of passing by with gaze averted they asked if they could help. The girl had an injured knee, so they carried her down piggyback, in relays, in exact accordance with their rescue training. She wrote a grateful letter, which was read out during the end of course ceremonies.

The second group joined Keswick Mountain Rescue Team in the transportation of a girl with severe back injuries following the failure of an abseil. Their energy and knowledge were commended by the team leader.

The third came upon an incompetent party on a steep slope, with a young woman completely panic-stricken. They finally calmed her and induced her to move, then escorted the party right down to the road.

October 1964 Whitehaven police made a request for help in searching for a girl believed missing in Ennerdale. The duty rescue patrol and a number of instructors went out, but it proved an annoying false alarm. It was not the girl who was to blame, but the police for not making one or two obvious checks; or rather myself for not checking up on the police.

We also staged a search exercise. Six dummy bodies were planted in a large area of rough fell, each containing a dozen bars of chocolate as an incentive to the searchers.

December 1964 On the first Saturday we were called out to the aid of a youth who had disappeared head first down a convex slope of hard snow on Scafell. Our assistance was however hardly required, since a strong party, walking on the hills, had found the boy and were already bringing him down unconscious, on the Mickledore stretcher. This stretcher has proved to be extremely well placed for do-it-yourself rescues. To us falls the less glorious task of taking it back after each emergency.

Early next morning, Sunday, we were called out again to help search for an eighteen-year-old girl lost on Bowfell. Conditions were dangerous and there were at least two casualties among the searchers. Our duty rescue patrol searched below the snow line on the remote chance that the girl had strayed into Eskdale, while several instructors, wearing crampons, quartered the steep snow slopes. She was eventually found dead, having slid down the craggy fellside. The search, or rather the call-off, was greatly facilitated by the use of radios.

Two emergencies arose during our Final Scheme. One boy fell on his face near the top of Green Gable. All concerned acted exactly according to instructions, sending two messengers down for help, and tending the patient with the greatest care. Their only mistake was in their diagnosis of serious head injuries, which turned out to be merely a bloody nose. The other accident was more serious but caused much less stir. A boy slipped on some ice and fractured his wrist. He was however spotted by a roving instructor, rescued from the exposed position he landed in, brought down on foot and dispatched to hospital. The hazard of hard snow slopes is a real one, even to students initiated into the use of the ice axe. But it is not in my view serious enough to rule out the high fells in winter conditions.

April 1965   During the Easter period we were called out three times. The first was to Pier's Ghyll into which a young climber had fallen. Owing to an error on the part of the police we were not immediately told of this emergency and the first attempt at rescue, which used up all the daylight, was made by a party of climbers who happened to be at hand. The next sortie was by Keswick Rescue Team, armed with winch and hawser, but the weather was very bad and they too failed to find the lad, one group being trapped in the ghyll until first light. It was only then that we were called in. By this time the becks were in full spate and the rain and cloud as dense as ever. We succeeded however in finding the climber, who had died instantly, and brought out his body with great difficulty, lashing it up in the casualty bag and arranging various pulley systems, including a pendule across the precipitous side of the ghyll. Being heard from one rope's end to the other was impossible owing to the din of water. It was a daunting and lugubrious place, full of loose rock.

At the end of our first three-day hill walk we were called out to Green Hole to assist an exhausted member of a school party. It was a textbook example of the kind of situation which called the Mountain Leadership Certificate into existence. The master in charge, finding one of his boys going lame, sent him home, alone and without equipment, from Ore Gap to Eskdale. The boy collapsed in less than a mile but was lucky enough to attract the attention of the one walker who passed that way that afternoon. The third rescue operation was one of those trials of patience which teams cannot escape. An ill-disciplined school camping party had lost four thirteen-year-old boys. At midnight they were eventually found comfortably camped on a site of their own choice. The only satisfaction we found in the episode lay in making them strike camp and return immediately to the fold.

June 1965 We were called out to an accident on Pillar Rock, but soon after our advance party had set off, news came that the victim was dead and already being carried down. He was Mike Fearn, a former RAF temp at Eskdale and a member of the RAF Mountain Rescue Team, with whom he was climbing on this occasion. It was yet another instance of an experienced climber falling unaccountably from a climb well within his powers.

A rescue occurred at the end of the first full day of the course. A solitary walker had fallen from Broad Stand, but fortunately there were some climbers about to get help. The duty rescue patrol, tired after the long first day and untrained in the hills, foundered one by one on Brown Tongue, and lay prostrate at intervals over the entire slope, until we brought the stretcher down past them when they eagerly lent a hand. The patient had fallen on his face but was not seriously injured.

Three weeks later another solitary walker fell from the same place, suffering similar injuries, and was evacuated by the same route. This time, however, the rescue patrol was undeterred by the ascent.

January 1965 We received a call for help from a group of Boy Scouts encamped near Esk Hause, who reported one of their number seriously ill. On arrival in the vicinity of the camp we had some difficulty in finding it and there was no response to our calls, as everyone, including the sick boy, was sound asleep. After finding pulse and temperature normal we had no qualms about leaving him where he was, and turned homewards, our annoyance at the fruitless journey alleviated by the relief of having only an empty stretcher to carry back. We got to bed at 5 a.m. The party in question was extremely well-equipped, and the eighteen-year-old leaders well versed in safety matters, but they lacked the experience or the judgement to apply their theory correctly. The duty rescue patrol had been dragged from sleep at 11 p.m. and the only member not to flag was a Home Office boy on probation. He remained a determined walker and stretcher carrier to the very end, no doubt like Samson deriving his strength from his hair, which he wore at shoulder length.

March 1966 Changing over from one course to the next during the Easter weekend had the disadvantage that many of the people who would normally be having accidents at work or in the home were now having them in the Lake District, and consequently our day and a half of report writing, turn-round and recuperation was filled with mountain rescue work. Some time after midnight on the last day of the course I was informed by the police that a seventeen-year-old boy was missing between Buttermere and Ennerdale. He had turned back to retrieve a dropped anorak, saying he would catch his companions up, but had not been seen since. As the weather was good I took no action that night, nor did I feel justified next morning in putting off the dispersal of the course. Five instructors covered the hills in question, and when by midday they had drawn a blank and the weather had turned bad, I asked the police to call in other teams, including the Ullswater Warden and staff, at the same time urging them to continue checking at farms and hostels. At 4 p.m. the youth appeared at Coniston Youth Hostel, having altered his plans without making the least attempt to let his friends know.

The next evening the Whitehaven police again requested our assistance, this time with two canoeists capsized in Wastwater. By the time instructors arrived there with Landrover and dinghy the canoeists were ashore, and were in a tent awaiting an ambulance, conscious but very cold. Hot baths were quickly arranged at the nearest hotel and this treatment brought about a rapid recovery. Dr. Loudon was also called in to examine them.

September 1965 The duty rescue patrol stood by on the day of the Mountain Trial in the region of Stony Tarn, and while they were there responded to a call to the civilian aircraft which had just been discovered crashed and with occupants dead on Esk Hause. They were not needed however in the stretcher parties. At dawn next morning, at the request of the police, John Coates, temporary instructor, guided a constable and a photographer to the scene of the crash.

Early one Monday morning I received a telephone call from the wife of a Seascale climber. Her husband had gone climbing with a companion on Esk Buttress the day before and had not returned. I was impressed by her forbearance in not calling me sooner, and arranged for Martin Sinker and John Dawson to go immediately to the buttress, keeping in wireless contact. But it appeared this chap had rather a reputation for being benighted on rock climbs, and sure enough he was found returning home in good order, having escaped from the crag at daybreak.

November 1966 The weekend of the Board Meeting was so busy that when I received a sheep rescue request from Ennerdale I telephoned the newly formed and consequently very keen Egremont Search Team. I explained that two ewes were stuck on Angler's Crag, that we were very busy but they ought to be got off before the weekend was over, as they had already been there ten days. The leader set his callout machinery in motion with great alacrity thinking I had said "two youths". No doubt he thought a certain callousness was to be expected in an Outward Bound Warden.

In the third week we had three rescue calls in four days. The first was for two newlyweds who got lost in heavy rain and spent the honeyed middle of the night in the top of Great Gully on the Wastwater Screes. They were found next day by Robin Shaw, near to collapse, especially the man, but responded rapidly to being warmed up on the spot in an Outward Bound tent. The man was carried down, the woman walked.

The next rescue interrupted our cross-country. A party from the Imperial College started a small avalanche of snow near the summit of Scafell Pike. Several were involved in the fall but only one received serious injury, a fractured skull.

The next night two climbers were reported missing. They had become detached from the rest of their party on descending from Great End. Keswick team searched Esk Hause during the night. We rose at 5.00 am and went up Eskdale. At 8:30 we found the two men on the summit of Silvery Bield. They were well equipped and had lasted out the night quite satisfactorily.

Our mountain rescue log book records twenty-one incidents so far this year, not counting sheep. We have carried down seven dead or dying. The time spent on rescues of people other than our own students is something in the region of seven hundred instructor hours, including attendances at inquests etcetera.

February 1967 One patrol demolished a porcelain toilet, which had been cemented in place on the summit cairn of Scafell Pike as part of a university rag.

June 1967 On the Saturday before we started the course an accident occurred on Yew Crag, Eskdale. A leader fell, and as the second was tied only to a loose block, he fell too. The leader of a second rope who had also tied onto the same loose block joined in the general debâcle. Fortunately no one was badly injured but as one man had been unconscious for some minutes we sent all three to hospital.

July 1967 A thirteen-year-old Girl Guide was bitten by an adder while trying to photograph it. Jim Davis took her to hospital.

One Sunday evening we were called to an accident in Pier's Ghyll. A young man had plunged head first down a waterfall and broken his wrists. He was carried piggyback some 140 feet up the precipitous side of the ghyll by the stalwart Don Beckitt, assisted by a rope hauled in by the duty rescue patrol. He was then transported by stretcher to a waiting ambulance.

Sheep rescues were very frequent this course. The grass is always greener on the more inaccessible ledges.

A donation of fifty pounds to the school rescue fund was made by Mrs. Millard, whose husband lost his life on Scafell a year ago and was not found until three weeks later.

August 1967 Basic training for the course was upset by our participation in a widespread search for a missing fellwalker. After two days of fruitless searching, involving long tedious journeys by lorry to Langdale, and very late nights, I withdrew the school from the search but offered to take over myself as search controller. Fortunately the man's body was found on this third day. He had gone astray in a thunderstorm and fallen over a crag. Such searches are very tiring and nerve-wracking to be in charge of and set one back terribly in one's ordinary work but in the early stages I did have the unexpected pleasure of sitting in the open doorway of a helicopter, soaring effortlessly up hillsides on which, on so many previous occasions, I had expended innumerable foot pounds of energy. The students did well. Local people expressed admiration at the purposeful way they worked, and we had an appreciative letter from the Chief Constable.

September 1967 The evening the students arrived we had a rescue call. None of them took part, only myself and such temps as could be spared. The casualty had made the classic fall down Broad Stand on Scafell, and had already been reached and put on a stretcher by a convivial party of climbers from the bar of the Wastwater Hotel. Though he had in fact fractured two vertebrae, he did not seem seriously injured, and the descent had more of the character of a fête champêtre than an act of public service. When I ventured to enquire after the patient's health his jocund bearers said he was ready to get off and walk. Unfortunately this outing lost us one of our police temps as he twisted a knee in the dark and had to go home.

March 1968 At the beginning of the first hill expedition we were called out to rescue a schoolboy alleged to have slid down Deep Ghyll on the snow and disappeared from sight. Fortunately the party were not at Deep Ghyll, as they thought, but at Mickledore. The youth picked himself up after a descent of about two hundred feet and walked down to Wasdale. He was taken to hospital with bruised ribs and some shock. With the aid of wireless sets, patrols were able to clear up the confusion and still proceed to their campsites before dark. On the same day another party from the same school had a boy die of exposure.

Many of these incidents I had forgotten but a few remain vividly in my memory, even if time has distorted the facts. One involved a scuba diver who had got into difficulties in Wastwater. We were asked if we could supply a rowboat, and this we did, as fast as we possibly could. A diving group had been making a descent to the depth of one hundred feet and one of them, a young French girl, had got into trouble. Her partner had come up to give the alarm. The shore party had taken cross bearings of the spot where she had gone down and under their instructions we took the boat out to the place and anchored it by means of a big rock tied to the end of a climbing rope. Divers then went down the rope to try and locate the girl. Looking down from the boat and seeing the rope stretching down through the clear, cold water until it disappeared in the gloomy depths gave me a feeling exactly like that of exposure on a rock face. After two unsuccessful dives had been made there was some doubt as to the exact placement of the boat and we moved it a few yards. It was getting late in the day and the light was failing down below, the chief diver said. I remember he had a big tear in his wet suit, revealing a white shoulder. He would go down once more and that would be that.

This time he found the girl. She was dead, having been missing now nearly three hours. As the body in its black wet suit rose to the surface a great wave of pink froth poured from her mouth like candyfloss.

"Don't let's try to get her into the boat," I said. I felt sure that if we capsized I would drown. I held on to the body as we rowed in to the shallows, and there we were able to lift her out onto the bank.

They attributed the accident to 'drunkenness of the depths', but I thought she might have lost her mouthpiece because the cold of the water numbed her lips. She had done most of her scuba diving in the Mediterranean.

Another incident which has somehow stayed in my mind was when an ex-student of the School, trying to find Lord's Rake from the top of Scafell, came to some steep and difficult ground which was clearly not the way. About a hundred feet below him he then spotted what looked like a body, and at considerable risk he managed to scramble down to it. It was a dead man. He continued on down and telephoned us.

We had just run the cross country, but after snatching a cup of tea we went round to Wasdale Head and accompanied the young man up Brown Tongue to the area in question. From below, however, he could not be certain where the body was and we spread out searching over the steep ground to the right of Lord's Rake. It began to get dark and we had the duty rescue patrol of inexperienced students with us. The man was already dead and I saw no reason to add another so we called it off and went home.

The same evening the police informed me that a woman in Langdale had reported her husband missing. They had motored up from the south of England during the night. She had dropped him off in Eskdale and taken the car on to the Old Dungeon Ghyll Hotel where they were to spend the night. This news lent a new urgency to the matter of the dead body so we went back out before dawn. This time two or three of us went straight to the summit of Scafell to climb down the way the young man had gone. We saw the body immediately and descended the difficult and dangerous ground to it. I searched the man's pockets and found in his wallet confirmation that this was the one reported missing. His skull was fractured; he must have died instantly. He was twenty-nine-years old. I felt very sad to think that his love of the hills and his enthusiasm to get on to them without delay had led to this sorry end.

I remember too a very beautiful summer day. We had just finished a meeting of the School Board and were having lunch when the phone rang. One of my staff, climbing on Scafell on his day off, had run down to Wasdale to tell me he had seen a serious accident. We set off immediately. By the time we reached the scene one of the two victims who was still alive was already being carried down on the Mickledore stretcher. He died on the way. I took another stretcher party to the other victim. He was lying under a ground sheet. The pair, students from Liverpool University, had completed a hard route on the overhanging East Buttress of Scafell, and were climbing the easy ground at the end, moving together when they fell. They had fallen three hundred feet and then bounced down the steep ground below the crag. I took the sheet off and revealed an appallingly broken body among a jumbled mass of slings and karabiners. I placed the ground sheet on the stretcher.

"Come on," I said, "Get round. Let's lift him on."

I grasped his shoulders. It was like trying to get hold of a fish, every-thing slimy with blood and lymph. I heard my breath go in with a gasp. On this terrible and macabre scene the sun beat down regardless. It was a beau-tiful summer day. One of the victims, I found out later, had been highly recommended to me as a potential instructor.

A day or two later there was an unpleasant rumour that a small rucksack left at the foot of the climb by these unfortunate young men had gone missing with an expensive camera in it. I went up and found it tucked away behind a rock.

A year or two earlier we had undertaken to put a rescue box and stretcher on Mickledore. The box was constructed in sections of heavyweight marine plywood to be assembled on the spot. On the advice of an expert woodworker we did not paint it but simply treated it with a wood preserving fluid every couple of years. Mickledore must be wet with mist or rain more often than it is dry but the wood of the box remained sound and even outlasted the iron bars with which it was anchored to the ground.

Getting it up was an interesting operation. Every Outward Bound course included an element of service to the community and accordingly we conscripted a group of students to carry the materials up the fell from Wasdale Head. The seven-foot sections of the box were lashed onto pack frames and made impressive loads. Other materials were put in rucksacks. On arrival at Brackenclose in Wasdale Head we lined up these loads on the ground and asked our students to take one each and start up the hill. The eager and the willing came forward immediately and took the big box sections. The less enthusiastic hung back and went for the rucksacks. What they failed to realise was that most of these contained cement and sand and were twice as heavy as the box sections. Even so we got the whole lot onto Mickledore in less than two hours. One of our instructors, Arthur Rogers, was a civil engineer and an expert on concrete. He found a suitable source of clean aggregate nearby, dug holes for the iron bars and cemented them firmly in place. The sections of the box were bolted together, secured to the bars and loaded up with stretcher, sleeping bag and other equipment.

Our most serious mountain rescue I did not take part in, as I was sailing the topsail schooner, Prince Louis, to Norway. At Easter a family party climbed Scafell by Lord's Rake and Deep Ghyll. There was a good deal of old hard snow in the ghyll but they succeeded in getting up it. They descended the same way, but in the meantime it had snowed a little and conditions were more slippery. I have known someone to fall from top to bottom of Deep Ghyll and walk away, but that was in deep new snow. This party slipped, knocked each other down, and fell, hitting rocks and ice all the way down. The father and three children were killed; the mother and one son, though injured, survived.

The father's life was insured for £31,000 but the policy excluded rock climbing and climbing was in fact what they were doing. Fortunately the insurance company's definition of climbing was using such things as ropes and ice axes and at the inquest we were able to confirm that they were not. The irony is that if they had had ice axes they might well have been able to arrest their fall.

An elderly Alpinist who happened to be about at the time spent some hours helping with the injured while stretcher parties arrived. She was Professor Rosalind Hill of London University, a relative of Sir Roland Hill who established postage stamps. For years afterwards she knitted mitts of

Herdwick wool and gave them to George Fisher of Keswick to sell in his shop, the proceeds to go to mountain rescue.

The evacuation of the dead and dying down the snow-covered screes and on into Wasdale in wintry weather conditions was difficult. Down in the valley a large assembly of police, ambulance men, reporters and onlookers lay in wait.

Mountain disasters were always newsworthy, and reporters had their informants and bush telegraphs. They would hover like vultures over a kill and rescuers coming down tired and distraught from some harrowing accident usually felt hostile to them and unwilling to answer questions. But if facts were not available to them from the people who knew, they would be sought from bystanders or hangers on, and this led to much inaccurate reporting. For example, if a climber had fallen fifty feet on the Napes Ridges of Great Gable, the headline might be: CLIMBER PLUNGES FROM 2,900 FOOT LAKELAND CRAG.

I thought it best to keep the press accurately informed, and on any serious rescue incident I would appoint one person as the spokesman, to whom all inquirers were to be directed. He would be instructed to give facts only, and to decline to express opinions, or apportion blame, or admit liability, or to gossip about the background of the victims. This did not always prevent incorrect or sensational accounts from appearing in the papers but it helped.

An incident I will not forget was when a farmer was reported missing on the fells by his family. We searched all day, taking the search wider and wider, without result. It seemed impossible he would go missing on his own land.

A neighbouring farmer asked me if we searched the barns and outbuildings. This should have given me a clue but the family, who were old friends of mine from my schooldays, expressed nothing but bewilderment and had no theory to offer as to what might have happened, though I am now sure they had a good idea. It was in fact the neighbour who found him. He was in a small scrubby wood, which straggled up the fellside, and he was hanged.

With Ken Ledward and the missing man's brother I went up the steep wooded slope. The brother soon said he would drop back as he could not keep up. The truth was, I think, that he could not face what we were going to find. Ken and I next saw two curved and hobnailed shepherd's boots floating some eighteen inches off the ground, and above them the long, lean body of the farmer, hanged by the neck with red baling twine, his tongue protruding grotesquely from his mouth. Behind him was a twisted branch, which had provided him with a seat while he arranged the noose.

At the farm house, in order to get the stretcher up the stairs we went in through the front door which was hardly ever used. By now the policeman was present. "I have to examine the body," he said to the family, "and I should have a relative with me." The brother looked so stricken that I said, "Will I do?" and they agreed.

In the bedroom we stripped off all his clothes and the policeman noted contents of pockets etcetera. Underneath the long underwear the body was waxy white, stringy and muscular. The scrotum was enormously swollen and to this day I do not know whether this was the result of the hanging or of some affliction that had caused him to do it. He was an old bachelor, and a terrible stammerer, and all his life he had worked hard and ferociously at digging and delving. I had always liked him. This 'rescue' affected me more than most. For a long time I saw the hills of the Lake District as they were portrayed in the dark, doom-laden paintings of Sheila Fell rather than the pure and shining landscapes of William Heaton Cooper. It was not the gruesome horror of the hanged man that troubled me. It was why he did it. I tried and tried to imagine the frame of mind that would lead to such a thing.

In mountain rescue one has to cultivate a certain detachment and try not to get too upset by the pain and suffering one witnesses. I did not find this difficult to do; what was harder to deal with was the question of whether one had done one's best, or taken a right course of action. It was always disturbing to find someone dead, but what impressed me most about a dead body was its chilling insignificance. It was like a castoff garment, or an empty sack, and quite different and somehow more shrunken than it had been with life in it. This made me reflect less upon the meaning of death than upon the nature of life and how wonderful and mysterious it was. There seemed to me nothing mysterious about death; it was just negation, emptiness, a void. What was miraculous, and strange, and passing all understanding, was life. It was at once precarious and enduring. One walked a tightrope between oblivion and the inestimable riches of being in the land of the living. There was a time when I imagined I would prefer to be dead than to be incapacitated, but now I would choose life, I think, whatever the conditions.

One or two rescue team leaders have been inclined to lay down the law about what one should do and not do on the hills, and to cite inadequate clothing and footgear as the cause of accidents. Well-meaning it may be, but I deplore it on several counts. First, if you rescue someone only to get at him for being such a fool, or for causing so much trouble, it would perhaps be better not to rescue him at all but leave it to someone more charitable. After all no one forces rescue teams to operate; they do it of their own free will. Secondly, to blame accidents on unsuitable equipment or the failure to observe rules is to cloud the real and only important issue, which is that it is lack of care that causes most accidents. The fault is not in our stars but in ourselves that we are stretcher cases. In my view people should make their own rules, for what will be reasonable for one person might be suicidal for another. Safety in the hills depends more upon stability of personality than upon good boots, and more on foresight and imagination than upon following rules. Those two early Alpine Club members Hope and Kirkpatrick climbed in the Alps every summer for twenty years, doing many adventurous ascents and traverses, with minimal equipment and making their own rules, one of which was to put the rope on for glaciers but to take it off to climb rocks. They were often benighted but they never came to harm.

Of course no one is altogether proof against accident. And as my mother used to say: a little help is worth a deal of pity. The proper, and I am pleased to say most common attitude of a rescuer, is to be glad that people are still adventurous enough to lift up their eyes to the hills.

ON OUTWARD BOUND

I first heard of Outward Bound in 1947, when I attended a lecture in Liverpool at the Wayfarers' Club. The speaker was Freddie Spencer Chapman, the author of *The Jungle is Neutral*, and he gave a vivid account of his adventures behind the Japanese lines in Burma. I remember him saying that so long as it was not uphill, there was no limit to the distance a sick, starving, exhausted man could walk; it was all in the mind. He also told us he had contracted three fatal diseases during his time in the jungle. The lecture, he said, was in aid of the Outward Bound Trust, whose aim it was to establish a mountain school in the Lake District. This school, he said, would devote itself to 'character training' by demonstrating that there was in the human spirit a huge untapped resource of strength and stamina.

I made a mental note to steer well clear of it. The idea of having my character trained or otherwise tampered with did not appeal. I loved the mountains, climbed, walked and camped in them extensively, but I preferred to do it my own way.

Ten years or more later, I happened to go with Robin Hodgkin to Eskdale to visit Eric Shipton. Shipton, hero and role model to so many climbers, including me, was at this time Warden of the Outward Bound Mountain School, Eskdale. We went for a climb on a local crag. Shipton did not say much. His pale blue eyes gazed at me in an abstracted sort of way, as though his mind was still in Tashkent. I little thought I would follow him as Warden.

I owe my involvement with Outward Bound to a snowstorm. Just after Christmas in 1960 my friend George Spenceley invited me to a climbers' dinner he was arranging at Coniston for a few of his friends. Unfortunately, or fortunately as it turned out, it snowed and I had to leave my car some miles out of Coniston and walk to the dinner. So I stayed the night at the hotel and next morning at breakfast I overheard someone at the next table to mine say: "I wonder who'll get the wardenship of Eskdale Outward Bound." But for that dinner and that snowstorm I would never have known the job was going.

My attitude to Outward Bound had been modified to some extent by a recent experience of taking a group of boys from the school I taught in on a cross-country camping trip from Dalwhinnie to Fort William. I had done it reluctantly, out of a feeling of obligation to my headmaster, who had been kind enough to keep my job open for me during my nine month absence in South Georgia. These youngsters, volunteers for the trip, who were something of a pain in the classroom, proved such sterling fellows in the hills that I was ready to see some educational merit in the outdoor life. I was also ready for a change. I was forty-two, and had been casting the pearls of English literature before the pupils of Workington Grammar School for twelve years.

I got the job and it opened up a whole new world for me. From being for several years an anonymous educational hack, labouring to put boys and girls through O and A levels, in a profession renowned for its niggard-liness, I now enjoyed a freedom and a lifestyle which made me feel like the laird of Eskdale Green. My windows looked out over a tree- fringed tarn, across Eskdale to the inspiring skyline of Harter Fell, Green Crag and Crook Crag. Our estate comprised several acres of hillside, landscaped with Victorian exuberance as a 'natural' wild terrain with fine trees, rocks and waterfalls. You walked from our grounds directly on to the fells, and could stay on them to the summit of Scafell and beyond. I had responsibilities of course, but the financial ones I was happy to leave to the bursar, and to the chairman of the board of directors, Harry Spilsbury, a retired income tax inspector and prominent climbing clubman. My chief concern was in the selection of instructors, and the safe running of a programme which sought to lead the field in being adventurous, and ran year round, whatever the weather. As a teacher I had divided my life into work and private time. What I had now was not a job, more a way of life.

What came as a surprise to me was what enormous fun it was to be part of this vigorous and enthusiastic group. It was especially so compared with the common-room atmosphere I had left behind. As schools went, my grammar school was a reasonably happy one, but the staff lived their own separate lives, and there was always an undercurrent of discontent in the profession owing to its poor remuneration and lack of status in the public mind. At the Outward Bound Mountain School, by contrast, people felt they were an elite body. I never in seven years had to advertise for instruc-tors; they kept on applying. Some even came as temporary instructors, for little more than their keep, in the hope of being taken on to the permanent staff. The pay was small but the accommodation and living was free and quite lavish. And of course everybody was young. At forty-two I was the sage old man of the establishment. Most of the staff were under thirty and could range about the hills like deer. We also had a system whereby staff could be seconded to us, normally for one or two courses at a time, from such bodies as the armed forces, the police, the fire service, and even the Church. This provided an influx of new blood, new ideas and fresh talent.

The Parachute Regiment, for example, lent us Chay Blyth, who a month or two later rowed across the Atlantic.

Another attraction for instructors was that this was the period when Outward Bound was being started in other parts of the world and opportunities existed for my staff to go and help set up new schools. Some came back. Some stayed abroad and soon found themselves in senior positions.

And what of the students, for whom the whole Trust was established? A few came privately, paying the fee themselves, or at their parents' expense. The majority were sent by the firms that employed them, or the schools or Services they belonged to. Consequently for every volunteer there were likely to be two or three pressed men. Outward Bound as a result came in for some criticism from mountaineers for filling the hills with people who did not wish to be there. Occasionally a student would quit and go home. Many stuck it out mainly for the sake of their jobs or their own self-esteem. The majority, however, ended by liking it in spite of its rigours, and almost no one, at the end of the course, said he wished he had never come. Former students frequently came far out of their way to call at the school, to let us know that it was an experience they would never forget, and remember as one of the most important and formative times of their lives. They would then bore us with a detailed account of their course with all its ups and downs. It was for them an adventure which they had survived and in which they had not been found wanting. At Outward Bound almost every student was successful, and even the ones that did not do well would have something to learn from their mistakes. One group, I remember, doing their final three day journey in a heat wave, colluded with their leader in spending the whole time sunbathing in that delectable spot Mitredale Combe, a place of greensward and running water, and using their maps to invent a fictitious itinerary all over the central fells. They were found out in their debriefing. I had to concede that the ringleader showed powers of leadership.

The social mix was valuable. A group might comprise bank clerks, factory operatives, public schoolboys, police cadets and sometimes a Borstal prisoner qualifying for release. For each student the course meant something different, and we tried to recognise this and value people as individuals. Extravagant claims were made, especially by the Trust's P.R. man, Val Lunnon, whose selling line sometimes made me squirm with embarrassment, but there was no doubt that the course was a broadening and enlarging experience for most, and the influence of instructors who had personally opted for quality of life rather than advancement in some tedious job, and who had known insecurity and survived their own misadventures, played no small part in its success.

It was sometimes said – and perhaps with some truth – that the instructors got more out of Outward Bound by way of personal development than the students. In those days it was not seen as a job for life; in fact it was not seen as a job at all, but as an escape from the humdrum world of work into a sort of utopian existence which, while it made more demands than most jobs, enabled one to live in the hills and climb the rocks winter and summer. Three years was a typical length of service before returning, played out, to the real world. So in some ways it was like having another period of university education. (Except that several of my staff had not been in higher education. They were appointed not on paper qualifications but on account of their experience in the hills and their personal qualities. On the other hand some had very high qualifications.) Hahn's views were tested in the field and hotly debated, interpretations of what we were trying to achieve varied considerably, and our enthusiasm for the work was tempered by a healthy scepticism.

My predecessor, Eric Shipton, had introduced a feature into the course which was so effective that it has remained for forty years virtually unchanged. Like Moses, we used to say, he went up into the mountains, and came down with the Three Day Scheme. This was the self supporting wilderness journey without instructors that was the culmination of the month's training. To have a hundred or so students at large on the fells in small groups for three days, winter or summer, whatever the weather, was a heavy responsibility.

This was 1961, the start of the swinging sixties. Much has been made of the cultural changes that took place, but it was also a decade which saw an explosion in mountain walking and outdoor education. Soon after I got into Outward Bound, a conference was held at Plas y Brenin, the national centre for outdoor pursuits, bringing together the various bodies involved in outdoor education. It was chaired by Sir Jack Longland, the Chief Education Officer for Derbyshire. Two resolutions came from that conference. One was to form an Association of Wardens of Mountain Centres. The other was to devise a national training scheme for those taking young people into the mountains, and to consider the question of certification.

The Association of Wardens was a small exclusive body, for apart from the national centres in Wales and Scotland, the Outward Bound Mountain Schools, Brathay Hall and the Army Outward Bound School, there were only about half a dozen centres set up by local education authorities in the whole country, the longest established of these being White Hall in Derbyshire. The Association was the little acorn from which a spreading tree of bureaucracy was to develop, and this in spite of the fact that its members

were all climbers and mountaineers who had grown up in a sport untram-
melled by rules and regulations, and had gained their expertise more by
surviving their mistakes than from courses of training. John Jackson and I
were given the task of producing a training scheme. We agreed on a one-
week course covering the basic skills needed for taking the uninitiated on
hill walking and camping excursions, in other than winter conditions. Where
we disagreed was on a proposal to follow up this course with a second
week called an assessment course, on the successful conclusion of which a
Mountain Leadership Certificate would be awarded. I strongly contended
that our duty was simply to inform people, not presume to judge how they
were going to use the information. I never departed from this view, and
fought a long rearguard battle, but defeat was inevitable. People like
certificates. Even some climbers like certificates. And most of the mountain centres were keen to have as many courses as possible. Business is
business.

So the Mountain Leadership Training Board was created, and I was a
member of it in spite of my reservations.

In the sixties, as Jack Longland used to point out, interest in hill walking and climbing grew at a rate which outstripped that of every other
recreational activity. With it came a boom in the equipment trade. Just after
the war you could count the walking and climbing equipment retailers on
the fingers of one hand. There was Robert Lawrie, the London bootmaker
who invested the making of climbing boots with a hallowed mystique. There
was Camtors, purveyors of high quality lightweight camping equipment.
There was Benjamin Edgington and there was Black's of Greenock. And
there was Ellis Brigham who manufactured Brigham Plates, Manchester's
answer to Switzerland's Tricouni. And that was about all. British Ropes
produced four thicknesses of white hawser-laid nylon rope. Climbers made
their own nuts and wedges. Army surplus stores provided a good deal of
the equipment you saw in the hills, and a favourite garment for climbers
was the cut-down gabardine raincoat. But all that was changing at a
remarkable speed. George Fisher, in at the start as an instructor at Ullswater
Outward Bound School, soon saw the light and left to open a climbing
shop in Keswick, an enterprise from which he never looked back.

It is interesting to see how climbing has moved from being a minority
interest, little understood and much criticised, deplored even by Queen
Victoria after the Matterhorn disaster, the private passion of a few well-to-
do men and a handful of women, to become the interest of a large and
rather exclusive elite, and finally a world-wide recreational activity
offering sport for all.

This growth occurred on two fronts. One was the recreational and sporting side, led by increased leisure and mobility, and given a boost by all those survivors of the war who had tasted a bit of travel and outdoor adventure. And the other was the trend to regard education as personal growth and not merely as a means of academic achievement. Kurt Hahn, the German Jew who had defied Hitler and escaped to Scotland to set up Gordonstoun School was influential in this field, especially as he had the ear of one of his important pupils, the Duke of Edinburgh. He was a kind of latterday Baden-Powell, presenting scouting and guiding in a new guise which came to be called the Duke of Edinburgh's Award Scheme. Kurt Hahn loved certificates and badges. Outward Bound began largely as an attempt to get his award scheme off the ground, but it soon grew into an organisation in its own right, backed by people like Lawrence Holt, G. M. Trevelyan and Geoffrey Winthrop Young.

Before long the sporting and educational interests came into conflict as far as mountaineering was concerned. Education was earnest and respectable; climbing was wild, iconoclastic and irreverent. Education was for the good of society; climbing was for the delectation and aggrandisement of the individual. Education demanded safety; climbers wanted to be free to kill themselves in their own way. No one was more strongly aware of this dichotomy than Ken Wilson, the owner and editor of *Mountain* magazine. To him climbing was a bit like bull fighting, a question of skill, courage and style in the face of danger. It was not sport so much as drama. Educational programmes demanded the elimination of risk and this, according to Ken Wilson, impoverished climbing and indeed sowed the seeds of its destruction.

I tended to agree with him. When I looked into my own motivation for rock climbing, I had to concede that my most rewarding days on the crags were those on which I had come closest to that boundary beyond which lay fear and paralysis of the will. I've always been a cautious person, and at the heart of my interest in climbing was the excitement of tinkering with my margins of safety. It was a form of exploration. And exploration is driven by romanticism.

Naturally enough the romantic view of climbing as a personal adventure and the courting of risk was hard to reconcile with the idea of training programmes and certification, but among the growing number of people who were now seeking to earn a living out of it, it was becoming more acceptable. The Mountain Leadership Certificate was followed by the Mountain Leadership Winter Certificate, the Mountaineering Instructor's Certificate, and the Mountaineering Instructor's Advanced Certificate.

In creating this world of certificates and qualifications we had the embarrassment of having to acknowledge that we, who were proposing to lay down the standards, run the courses and assess the candidates, had no relevant pieces of paper ourselves. We were not even, most of us, physical education specialists. We were just climbers who had somehow got into outdoor education. We solved this problem by the simple device of awarding ourselves the Mountaineering Instructor's Advanced Certificate. After all we had to start somewhere.

In looking back over the seven years I spent as Warden at Eskdale and trying to assess what, if anything, I contributed to Outward Bound, I think it was to encourage a more tentative and self-critical approach to the movement's claims, and to include a contemplative element among the benefits of outdoor life and adventurous pursuits.

I have always been, and still am, unable to keep up with the relentless hunger for more activity, more gear, more information, more photographs and visual aids, that so many of my associates in the outdoor education world have habitually shown. My love of the mountains has not waned after more than sixty years of going into them and suffering the consequences. However it is not in doing more and more that I have found riches, but in having time to absorb the experience, and in being able to strip life of its busy-ness, its getting and spending, and reduce it to its fundamentals. Water, food and shelter are often quoted as life's essentials, but even more basic than these is partaking of life itself, being part of the natural world as other animals are, seeing, hearing, smelling and feeling. And even thinking.

Outward Bound life in the sixties was spartan for financial as well as philosophical reasons. We slept out, except in winter, under seven foot square waterproof sheets, one to two students; in winter in tents without flysheets. We issued no waterproofs until well into the sixties, relying on army surplus cotton anoraks that had been supplied to paratroopers. Eric Shipton, chafing at how long groups would take getting ready in the morning after a bivouac, found that much time was wasted in careful packing of equipment in order to cram it into the rucksacks provided. He devised a new type of rucksack, a huge, shapeless bag, into which all one's equipment could be fed in two minutes. He then averred that thirty-five minutes was all that was needed between waking up in the morning and being on the march.

I fell in with these simple approaches quite readily, and seldom spent my time, as many other centre wardens did, in badgering the board of directors for improvements. But the march of progress was inevitable, and participants in outdoor education have become more and more insulated and protected from the natural world. Though personal development is the declared aim of outdoor education, technology takes over and displaces so many personal skills and initiatives that the wilderness dwindles, the mountains get smaller, and the person shrinks.

One aspect of the outdoor centre world that surprised and pleased me was the warmth and hospitality one met everywhere. Centres seemed to vie with each other in welcoming guests, whether on business or pleasure, and parties and celebrations were entered into with enormous vigour, generosity and enthusiasm. It was a consequence I dare say of the youthfulness and good health of the people concerned, and also the awareness of shared interests. One could always bank on getting a bed, food and entertainment when passing through. This applied not only to Outward Bound schools but to the outdoor education world as a whole. At Eskdale particularly the staff were like a big family, and members kept in touch with each other long after they had left. Even now, thirty years later, I still see several old colleagues quite often, and correspond with, or have news of, many more. It was part of the ethos of the place to do one's best and spare no effort. Even the naturally idle subscribed to it, in theory if not in practice. This thoroughness extended not only to work but to play, and to making people welcome. It was sometimes said that what made life in Outward Bound so tough was not the work, nor the mountain rescue, but the parties.

The one month courses we ran – and I ran seventy-one in succession – in spite of their informality and fun, had a kind of intensity which drew people together. Each one was a shared adventure, with ups and downs and minor – sometimes major – crises. Speaking for myself, and I am sure for most of my colleagues, work at Outward Bound was something to be remembered for the rest of one's life.

THE STRANGLEMENTS

One of the delights of the Outward Bound School at Eskdale was what we called the Ropes Course. My grandmother would have called it 'the stranglements', a term she always used for swings, roundabouts, rope ladders and Tarzan slides. When I spoke of it to my uncle-in-law, a master plasterer who had been a sergeant in the Tank Regiment during the War, he at first looked puzzled and then, as light dawned, said, "Oh, yes, I know. We did it in the Army. Playing silly buggers in the trees."

We were always on the lookout for new tests for nerve and agility, and when John Dawson came up with his parachute jump idea we felt we were breaking new ground. A small platform was constructed forty feet up a tall tree, with a vertical ladder to reach it. There you put on a parachute harness, from the shoulder straps of which climbing ropes went up round pulleys, and down to the ground, where they were attached to a huge ship's anchor chain. When you jumped off the platform you at first fell like a stone, and felt your viscera surging up against your thorax, but as the anchor chain was lifted you were slowed down, to land painlessly on a soft mattress. Stepping off the platform for the first time took a bit of doing.

When I reported this new device to the Board of Directors one of them, Jim Hogan, Deputy Chief Education Officer of the West Riding, said he would check out the apparatus, and his way of doing so was to get Sir Jack Longland, a fellow board member, to try the jump. Unfortunately Sir Jack landed awkwardly, spraining an ankle, and was limping for the next two weeks.

The Parachute Jump naturally enough led us to talk about real parachuting, and half a dozen of us said we were ready to have a go. However, when John Dawson pursued the matter and came up with an offer of temporary membership of the Manchester Sky Divers' Club, the only people to take it up when it came to the pinch were John and myself.

As a middle-aged man I was required to produce a medical certificate, which my friend Tony Drummond was prepared to sign, having rolled my neck around on my shoulders a bit and declared the crepitations merely due to fair wear and tear. The Manchester Sky Divers at first wanted us to attend several fitness sessions, but on hearing we were Outward Bound instructors agreed to settle for one afternoon of training. The fee for the jump was ten pounds.

So off we go in John Dawson's home-made fibreglass sports car, which he has never quite completed. It has as yet no fuel tank, but petrol is delivered to the engine from a five gallon drum propped in the space for an eventual back seat. The car performs well, and when, as occasionally happens, something goes wrong, John knows exactly what it is and fixes it quickly, using the tools and spares that litter the rear end.

The plan is to spend the afternoon at the Skydivers' Club in Manchester, then sleep for the night at the flat of my secretary's sister, at 129A Barlow Moor Road.

At the Skydivers' we are surprised to learn that parachuting is not simply a matter of achieving the degree of abandonment needed to throw oneself out of an aeroplane. We have what seem to me quite heavy responsibilities, such as assuming a spread eagle posture, with arms, legs and head craned back and stomach protruding, and shouting 'A hundred and one, a hundred and two' up to a hundred and six, in order to determine, in an emergency, whether it is time to pull the reserve parachute ripcord. Even pulling the cord of the reserve parachute has to be done properly. Both arms have to be brought in to the body together, to avoid going into a spin and getting entangled in the 'chute as it opens. The idea of having to keep our wits about us while we plummet earthwards is new and disconcerting.

After jumping to the ground a few times from a six-foot high platform our training is complete, and we are told to show up next day at ten o'clock, at Ha'penny Green airfield, near Wolverhampton.

All we have to do now is to find Barlow Moor Road and the promised flat. This, too, is not as easy as it seems. It is Saturday on a weekend of public holiday and the streets are almost deserted. The citizens of Manchester are either driving about in cars, or have got out of town. Eventually we do find Barlow Moor Road but 129 A completely eludes us. Most of the buildings are shops and offices, and few of them display a street number. We are forced to consider other possibilities. We have sleeping bags but no other camping equipment. To look for a hotel or bed-and-breakfast house would constitute a defeat we are not prepared even to contemplate. In the end Dawson digs up from boyhood memories a relative who lives in the suburbs of Manchester, and he thinks he still remembers the address. At least, he says, he would recognise the place if he saw it. We drive for some time through empty streets which in the summer evening sunshine have the slightly eerie atmosphere of a Hitchcock film, and come at length to a silent housing estate, where, in a cul-de-sac, Dawson declares that this is the place. We knock on the door. There is no answer. We knock harder. We peer through the letterbox then go round and explore the back of the house. Clearly there is no one at home.

We sit outside in the home-made sports car wondering what to do.

"Let's get something to eat," I say. "Fish and chips. Then get out of this town. Nearer to Ha'penny Green."

We do it. The food makes us feel better, and looking at the sky with the optimism that comes of a full belly, we think it is unlikely to rain. We will go to within striking distance of Keele Service Station on the M6, and sleep out under a hedge, repairing to the service station for breakfast.

It is like other forced bivouacs, a question of sticking it out until the dawn. We sleep, off and on, and at least it is quiet, apart from the stirrings and rustlings of the little creatures of the night whose environment we have intruded upon. We rise, dew-besprent, very early and, arriving at the service station, we confirm from the mirrors of the washroom, that we look just about as haggard as we feel. But food, as I have often noticed, is a substitute for sleep, (and vice versa), and a good breakfast repairs much of the damage. We get to the airfield too early, which gives us plenty of time to brood upon our fateful plunge into space.

We are required to pack our own parachutes, so that only we will be to blame if they fail to open. We might do two jumps, but the pilot of the aircraft is not happy about the wind speed and the morning goes by without any action, but plenty of rumours. We are now going to be lucky to get one jump each.

There are five static line parachutists, including Dawson and me, destined to jump from four thousand feet, and several experienced people, who, having done their obligatory eight static line descents, are to free-fall from ten thousand.

Finally our 'moment of truth' arrives, and, quite heavily laden with parachute packs on back and chest, we file into the Rapide, a biplane with its door opening on to the lower wing. Modest and courteous as always, I go in last, not realising this means I go out first.

Not that that matters. My mind by this time is at rest. The moment of decision for me is not in leaving the aircraft but in getting into it. The die is cast. From now on I am on automatic pilot, preordained, not to say foredoomed.

When the aircraft has climbed to the required height, the instructor ties the end of a long nylon string to the back of a seat, the other end of the string being attached to my ripcord. I climb out of the door on to the lower wing, and, holding on to the struts, move out to about halfway along it, battered by the rush of air and cocooned in the noise of engine and rigging. It is nonetheless a wonderful thing, which I never expected to experience, to be standing on the wing of an aeroplane in flight. The few seconds I spend there are well worth the ten pounds we have blown on this venture.

Then the instructor gives me the thumbs up, and I let go, urgently assuming the splayed out posture I have been thinking about all night under the hedge. It brings about a sudden and remarkable change, silence and weightlessness instead of sound and fury. I do not fall, but the aircraft shoots up and out of sight. I am counting 'A hundred and one, a hundred and two, a hundred and three' as though my life depended upon it, but no word issues from my mouth. The next moment the parachute blossoms above me and I find myself suspended, in astonishing comfort, floating motionless, or so it seems, in the air. By pulling on the wooden toggles that are conveniently to hand I can alter the direction I am facing and gradually I deduce from the fact that the landscape is getting closer, that I am actually descending, though it does not feel like it.

The landing we have been warned about. The ground comes up and hits you harder than you expect. I do as instructed and crumple sideways, hurting my knee a bit.

We stay and watch the free fall jumpers who take the next flight. They fall like stooping hawks for seven thousand feet and at three thousand their parachutes open with a crack like a gunshot.

Before we jumped we were treated with a certain amount of reserve by the regular club members, but on our return to earth their attitude changed and they welcomed us warmly into the fold. We got only one jump but we'd done what we wanted.

On the way home we gave a lift to a young woman – I squatted on the sleeping bags beside the five gallon drum – who was just about to qualify for free-fall. She had been reluctantly dragged into the game by an enthusiastic boyfriend, but he had lost interest while she had become totally committed.

When we got back the Eskdale police constable came to see us. He was following up a report that two dubious characters in cloth caps had been loitering round a housing estate in south Manchester and a watchful neighbour had taken down the number of a red sports car of unknown make which they were using.

LOOK NO BOOTS

If you are old enough you may remember the joke about the small boy riding round the block on his bicycle, shouting "Look! No hands!" Before long, however, it was "Look! No teeth!"

You may have noticed, on the fells, that when you meet a fellow-walker his eyes drift to your feet. "By their boots ye shall know them," he seems to be thinking, and by seeing what kind of boots you are wearing he can assess what kind of fellow he is passing the time of day with.

When you pick up a book on fell-walking it is ten pounds to a penny that it will recommend, without qualification, that you should wear stout boots, usually with two pairs of socks. For years I have shrugged off this rather uncompromising statement, but seeing the extent to which it tyrannises the hill-walking world, it is perhaps time it was challenged.

Millican Dalton, the educated recluse who lived in a cave in Borrowdale, used to walk the fells barefoot or in boots without socks. Every summer, as the date of the Vaux Mountain Trial draws near, you are liable to be run down on the hills by stringy characters in shorts and light running shoes. Of all the hundred or so people who have completed the Bob Graham Round, of some sixty miles of Lakeland peaks in twenty-four hours, how many have worn boots?

Then there is my own modest case. I like going on the fells, but I can ill afford boots. There was a time when I got an annual tax-free allowance for mountain equipment. Before leaving the mountain centre that carried this perquisite, I spent part of my last allowance on a pair of Galibier climbing boots which had been specially blessed and rendered holy by Rene Desmaison, and a pair of flat-soled climbing sneakers similarly sanctified by Pierre Allain. Thus, equipped with R.D.'s and P.A.'s, I felt I could face the hard world outside.

I remember I paid a staggering £14 for the R.D.'s, Since then I have been unable to bring myself to buy any equipment, the prices have seemed so exorbitant. Yet I have continued to go on the fells, and I have found that you can do so quite enjoyably without first going through the hoop of getting all kitted out at enormous expense. I would in fact go so far as to say I have enjoyed it more this way. It is such a relief, for example, to escape the tentacles of that Velcro, which sprouts like sticky burrs all over modern outdoor clothing, and no longer to feel like a walking Christmas tree in fluorescent rip-stop nylon. I have rediscovered what the Army discovered in the Boer War, that bright uniforms may make you look good and ferocious, but in drab and khaki you can slip by unnoticed if you happen to be trespassing in enemy country. So it's the local Oxfam shop for me, rather than Ultimate Equipment.

But to return to footgear. I have found that easily the most versatile footgear for Lake District hills is a kind of suede 'desert boot' with a smooth sole of micro-cellular rubber, made in Czechoslovakia or Poland, and costing at present about £10. The micro-cellular rubber is extremely light and extremely hard-wearing. You feel as though you are in plimsolls, except that they don't come off when you inadvertently step into a bog. On dry rocks they are a delight. And this matter of weight is really quite important. The average day's walk involves, say, 3000 feet of ascent. If you reduce the weight of each boot by one pound, you immediately decrease your energy requirement by 6000 foot-pounds. But that is not all. Even on the flat you have to lift your feet to walk, and if you lift them only half an inch each step, a ten-mile walk is going to involve at least 20,000 lifts which means approximately another thousand foot-pounds. Seven thousand foot-pounds a day! I wonder what that is expressed in Mars Bars per annum!

As I have pranced over the hills, executing an occasional entre-chat, my heart has bled for all those dupes of the equipment racket who, unused to anything but light city shoes, have been induced to hang a crippling weight on each foot by wearing two pairs of socks and big boots on the hills. (Big boots, by the way, seldom fit, and that is why two pairs of socks are recommended; they disguise the fact.) So deeply entrenched is the big-boot canon that in one school party I was once concerned with there was a girl so young and small that none of the Centre's boots would fit her. She accordingly went out wearing boots with plimsolls on inside them! On another occasion with a large party doing the Lyke Wake Walk, one member, a man in his late fifties, and not a regular walker, had put on his oldest and most comfortable shoes, which were thin town shoes with pointed toes not made of leather but of some plastic that simulated glacé kid. He said if he could dance in them all night he should be able to walk in them. At one point, in the pale light of dawn, he stepped in a bog and lost them. We recovered them after some anxious probing, but then a faction in the group forced the poor man into a pair of strong boots. In less than a mile he announced that either he must drop out of the walk, or be allowed to put his old shoes on again. He managed to get them back from his scandalised companions, who could be observed crossing themselves and throwing their eyes up to heaven, and he finished the walk in fine style.

Of course, desert boots are not all that suitable in wet weather. But what boots are? Quite a good cheap outfit would be desert boots for the dry and wellingtons for the wet. Caught out in wet weather with only desert boots you can put plastic bags on over your socks and inside your boots. Your feet will then keep warm, if not much drier. Last winter I went up High Seat, normally Lakeland's wettest fell, in my desert boots. The bogs were all frozen and the snow dry. My feet were dry and warm throughout. I also wore them on a recent walk over Grisedale Pike when I thought it wise to take an ice-axe as well. I figured there might be places where ice or hard snow made the going a bit hazardous in smooth flexible soles, but the axe would look after that. And it did. Of course there are situations in the mountains for which I'm glad to dig out my old climbing boots, but the point I'm making is that for a large range of excursions in the hills they are unnecessarily heavy, unnecessarily stiff-soled, and unnecessarily expensive.

There is a widespread belief that big boots protect you from twisting your ankles, but an examination of how the heel is kept in place by its ligaments shows that the most effective support for the ankle is *below* the ankle bone. Ice hockey players, whose ankles need massive support, wear boots that come only just up to the ankle bone. A snug fit round the heel, and the avoidance of wide welts, make for better protection than the crude splinting effect of a big boot. It is true, however, that with light footgear there is a bigger risk of painful knocks on the ankles on stony ground and screes.

Another advantage of desert boots is that you can go anywhere in them. They look quite acceptable with your best suit, and that can hardly be said for climbing boots. In the same desert boots I have been up the Napes ridges, made a long canoe trip in N. Ontario, and attended a reception at Buckingham Palace. They would also be possible for langlauf ski-ing, but I have not tried that.

To look for a moment at the wider issue. The hill-walker is the victim, if he does not watch out, of propaganda from two directions. One is commerce, the other is education. Both are good and desirable forces; they make the world go round. But they both have designs on you and me. They know what's good for us. Commerce wants us to buy, buy, buy. Education wants us to be told. And the rescue teams get caught up in the same movement, often against their inclination, but compelled by the need to make broad recommendations to the general public. You are advised to wear bright orange gear so they can find you more easily when you finally sink exhausted to the ground under the vast load of equipment you have been advised to carry. The professionals in the outdoor world, the teachers, advisers, rescuers, etc., have a symbiotic relationship with a vast industry, and at the centre of it are you and I, the consumers.

We have, over the years, been conditioned to believe that a tent with half a dozen poles, a built in ground-sheet, and a fly-sheet, all bristling with Velcro and weighing eight pounds, is still a 'lightweight tent'. We not only have to pay all that money. We have to carry the stuff as well. Yet over fifty years ago, J. Langdon & Sons, of Duke St., Liverpool, were selling a tent weighing $2^1/_2$lbs. complete, while T. H. Holding, of Maddox St., London, was producing one of Japanese silk that weighed 13 oz., to which, however, one had to add poles and pegs. In those days, according to Horace Kephart, a full camping outfit for two, exclusive of personal gear, but including a tent 6ft. x 5ft. 9ins. x 5ft. 9ins., a primus stove, canteen, cutlery, candlestick and candle, weighed 6lb. 4ozs. Add personal gear, and Mr. Holding, regarded in England as an authority on these matters, reckoned that each hike-camper would be carrying 10lbs. Why have we allowed modern technology to increase our loads on the hills instead of reducing them?

In any field of human interest and endeavour there is apt to grow up an accepted canon of belief, based upon the pronouncements of its pundits. Somehow the game seems more significant when we are subject to these stern imperatives. We are relieved, too, of the responsibility for our own actions and our own safety; we do not have to think so much. Finally, none of us is proof against superstition; we need our taboos and conformities.

It may be that as a consequence of saying "Look! No boots" some rescue team is going to look down upon my body one day and say " Look! No pulse !" But think of the money I shall have saved!

BRIDGING THE GAP
Addressing the B.M.C. National Safety Conference
at Leeds University March 1973

I hope you won't be disappointed with what I have to say. With a title like 'Bridging the Gap' you may be expecting something like how to set up a Tyrolean Traverse, or the employment of the Schermuly line-shooting pistol in climbing. But what·I have been instructed to say something about is two kinds of gap, which may turn out to be two aspects of the same gap.

I mean, first the gap that is felt to exist between the person who has taken up mountain leadership as another teaching skill, and the ordinary sporting mountaineer and club member;   and second, the question why comparatively few youngsters, introduced to mountaineering by education, continue the interest and join mountaineering clubs.

The first thing I asked myself was: "Is the teaching mountaineer really any different from the sporting mountaineer?" And my first cautious reply was: "He doesn't have to be." I could think of people from courses of training who have become devotees of mountaineering indistinguishable in their outlook from those whose introduction to the sport had been a keen personal interest leading to membership of a club. It's like members of the Establishment, often surprising where they have come from.

I suppose the truth is that once the spark is kindled, it matters little how it was first ignited;   the result is a mountaineer, an enthusiast.

Nevertheless, all too often one can see a difference, and when one does it is basically a difference of attitude. I can well recall the time when I myself became a teaching mountaineer, after many years of private climbing and fell walking and club membership. It was when I became Warden of a mountain centre. My friends were very generous about it;   they made allowances, they conceded that everyone has to earn a living somehow, and that no-one could be blamed for wanting to go and live in Eskdale, but few of them really approved of what I was doing, and one or two said as much. I felt they had the same kind of reservations as the contemporaries of the Abraham brothers must have had when they went into the postcard business. I was no longer quite pure.

So perhaps there is a gap. And if there is it is one of outlook. Crudely stated, the difference is that educators care about people, while climbers care about mountains. I don't mean, of course that mountaineers, by caring for mountains, do not care for people, nor do I suggest that the educator, by caring for people, is thereby indifferent to mountains. They are not incompatibles: on the contrary, most mountaineers are highly gregarious, and for many, good companionship is one of the greatest joys of the hills. It's simply that the mountaineer per se and the teacher-mountaineer have different preoccupations and often a quite different outlook. For example, the mountaineer does not climb for the good of his health; that it is on the whole a health-giving pursuit is a mere fringe benefit. In fact the mountaineer is likely to persist with his sport to the detriment of his health, laying up for himself who knows what stores of arthritis, haemorrhoids and the like. The educator on the other hand does tend to climb for the good of his health, or rather his pupils' health. He deliberately uses the mountain environment to improve his pupils' physical, and spiritual health. Contrast this with the mountaineer who will sell his soul to the Devil so long as he is not kept off the hills.

One can pursue this difference of outlook into the realm of safety. Sporting mountaineers, one cannot but admit, are on the whole a bit dangerous. It is only when they turn professional that they become concerned and preoccupied about safety. What keeps them alive is a certain sensitivity to danger, and unconscious judgement, born of a long succession of near misses. In a sense, all mountaineers are survivors. This difference of approach is illustrated for me by the recollection that as an experienced private climber my idea of introducing four sixteen-year old novices to rock-climbing was to take them up Scafell Pinnacle by Slingsby's Chimney on a greasy November day. Later, as a teacher-climber, I would have objected to this on at least two important counts: one, that four novices was too many for one instructor, and two, that the instructor had no colleague in the vicinity to help him in an emergency. The sporting mountaineer is certainly much more inclined to travel hopefully than the teacher-mountaineer. I would like to bet, for example, that if you made a raid into the hills one Sunday, and pulled in two or three hundred club mountaineers, and frisked them, it would be a scandal how few orange survival bags you would find on them.

The fact is that the sporting mountaineer sees climbing as a slightly anti-authoritarian activity, or at the very least as an assertion of personal idiosyncrasy. It was particularly so when I was first taking to climbing, for at that time the general public saw it as a perverse and irresponsible activity. People were hostile to the sight of a rope, and would tell you off on railway stations. The teacher-mountaineer on the other hand is necessarily a responsible chap, on the side of society rather than against it or outside it. So to join a University climbing club is quite a different thing from doing mountain-leadership as part of a main PE course.

It might be worth taking this thought further, as it might throw some light on the question asked by some members of the BMC Committee: "Where do all the young people introduced at school to climbing disappear to ? Why do they not appear in greater numbers in the climbing clubs ?" Well, it may be that the inclusion of climbing as a school subject has the effect of putting them off. Education has in the past done a magnificent job in putting people off poetry, for example.

It is too simple, however, to blame this kind of thing on the schools and the teachers. It is really an aspect of the fundamental distinction we make in our society between work and play. There was a time when work was man's chief concern and chief fulfilment. For some it still is the case, notably for the old hill-farmer who looks without full comprehension at the weekend climbers. And of course for people with a vocation. But for the majority work is dull, necessary, repetitive, its chief justification the fact that it earns money. And school counts as work.

This is one of the reasons why many people feel so uneasy at the thought of children enjoying themselves at school, and so inclined to place the onus for disciplining children upon the schools rather than upon themselves. Ideas about the severity of work and education are frequently attributed to puritanical attitudes in our culture, unjustly in my view. The puritans were in fact much concerned with human happiness, the word 'joy' was prominent in their vocabulary, and at their best they showed a keen appreciation of the privilege of being alive and a readiness to praise the Lord for it. What makes education sometimes such a dreary business is not puritanism but something much more recent, what Matthew Arnold, the first Inspector of Schools, called middle- class Philistinism. It is the attitude that insists that pleasure shall always be frivolous, and serious enterprises always dull. It is inveterately status seeking, and has given a new and deplorable meaning to the word 'respectable'. It has turned education into a device for claiming superiority, and this in its turn has led to an insincerity, which has estranged poetry and art and devalued popular culture. Whatever it embraces becomes solemn, pretentious, exclusive, and dull.

I think many mountaineers are intuitively aware of the menace of Philistinism. Perhaps that is what makes some top climbers feel compelled to be gratuitously coarse and anti-heroic in their public lectures. And there is a long British tradition of not training for mountaineering feats. Foreign mountaineers prepare for a major ascent in the gym, British mountaineers in the pub. Or so they pretend ! So maybe the best way for a school to produce future members of the Groupe de Haute Montagne would be to make a climbing wall of one side of the building and then forbid anyone to go near it.

The teacher-mountaineer is likely to be, and certainly ought to be, a mature, well-balanced person fully aware of his aims and fully aware of his responsibilities. The sporting mountaineer, on the other hand, is inclined to be determinedly immature. After all, climbing, even the climbing of Everest, is fundamentally a boyish prank writ large. Mallory's random remark "Because it is there" has been given undue prominence in our explanations of why we climb. I'm pretty sure Mallory said it only in order to close the tiresome subject. A more carefully considered explanation was given at a club dinner by André Roch just after the Swiss attempt on Everest. He said, apropos of the nationalism which was so apt to creep into the sport, that the only reason for climbing was that it was 'fun'. He was speaking in English, in which he had no great facility, and it was clear that by 'fun' he implied a great deal more than he was able to put into words. He was suggesting, I believe, what the Archbishop of Dublin was suggesting when he said: "Happiness is no laughing matter." I think that by that simple unassuming word 'fun' he was even perhaps asserting the primacy of the things of the spirit. And that is, surely, where the educator and the mountaineer can be reconciled, where the spirit of joyous independence and personal fulfilment can be linked with the spirit of purposeful and responsible concern for young people's development.

With these reflections in mind I would make, for discussion, the following suggestions about the way in which mountain education might move.

1. Bring a bigger element of voluntariness into it.
2. Discourage in some way the 'closed shop' attitude to qualifications.

ADVENTURE BY NUMBERS

The idea of adventure is now widely accepted in education, yet when one comes to think of it, it is extraordinary that something that is by its very nature so fortuitous and uncertain of outcome should be harnessed and brought into the service of educational programmes. I sometimes wonder, indeed, how adventurous adventure courses really are, for as soon as one becomes a deliberate purveyor of adventure, one is in danger of losing much that is fundamental to it. It becomes a package deal, with something false about it, like the packages described by Jeremy Sandford and Roger Law in their book, *Synthetic Fun:* 'Synthetic fun is the smile, on the face of the holiday camp fun people, this Friday as every Friday, as they are ritually thrown into the blue, blue swimming pool'.

Synthetic fun is for people who are too tired, or too busy, or too timid or too pusillanimous to go in for real fun. Similarly, painting by numbers is for people who are unwilling to take on the agony and ecstasy of original composition. And it is all too easy, I should think, to deal in synthetic adventure; or adventure by numbers: in other words to methodize it out of existence.

We are, of course, inclined to want to have our cake and eat it. We say: "Give our children thrilling adventures and make absolutely certain nothing untoward happens". This suggests a curious misuse of the word adventure, and I prefer the thinking of the Army commander who said in briefing a party for a landing by canoe on the enemy coast, to be followed by the surprise and abduction of a senior officer from a heavily-guarded headquarters "And remember, men, we want no adventures".

There is no need to pursue tediously the meaning of the word. It is a common one that everybody knows. But it is worthwhile making the observation that how people use it reflects their outlook and is as variable as people's outlooks are.

Anyone who has been mixed up in outdoor activities in the hills has come across ill-experienced and naively adventurous individuals leading parties of youngsters. We have all seen the difficulty with which they conceal their elation at having the rescue teams out, and the peculiarly injured way they receive their chastisement. I've always had a soft spot for such fellows, exasperating though they are at the time, for, however inept they may be, they are genuine adventurers, with something pure and quixotic about them that the MIC holders lack.

I think there is no question that much of what we describe as adventure is not adventure at all, and it is my view that if that is the case we should stop calling it adventure. Young people find adult thought processes confusing enough as it is, and we only add to the confusion when we describe walking on an empty, rounded hill, laden with emergency equipment, as an adventure (whereas, for example, making gunpowder, or cycling two feet behind a bus to take advantage of its slip stream, is condemned as irresponsible). We pay lip service to adventure, but what we mostly teach is prudence, and the importance of being comprehensively insured. As a middle-aged family man I find nothing much wrong with this, but why can't we acknowledge it!

But, of course, it is too narrow a view of adventure to equate it simply with taking risks. After all those who earn their living by dangerous jobs don't find them adventurous except perhaps at first. Once they have mastered the work they find it demanding and exacting, perhaps, but not adventurous. In fact, dangerous work is often described as tedious, because it demands such endless painstaking routines and precautions. Many a lad goes to sea in expectation of a life of adventure, but pretty soon finds himself tied to the interminable tasks of watch-keeping, log-reading, safety-checking, measuring, recording and dead-reckoning. People who climb for a living have much the same experience. Though they may derive some satisfaction from the awareness that other people regard their job as adventurous, to them it is just work. The only difference between it and more ordinary work is that it demands perpetual care and discipline.

Nor is the scale of an adventure so significant. I have heard an ascent of the Old West Route on Pillar represented as the ultimate in cliff-hanging, and who is to say that, in truth, it was less of an adventure than, say, an Extreme done by a party of experts. The truth is that in one important sense, adventure, however much it may be concerned with physical conflict and danger, is really of the mind. What is an adventure to some may be, to others of more prosaic nature, an ordeal, or an imposition, or a nuisance, or a calamity, or even simply a bore. For just as beauty is in the eye of the beholder, adventure is in the mind and spirit of the adventurer. It is not risks and desperate situations that make adventure so much as adventurousness.

It makes more sense, therefore, to consider the spirit of adventure, rather than adventure. Some people have it in greater measure than others. Some appear not to have it at all, and that, perhaps, is the mark of complete maturity. For adventurousness is a peculiarly youthful quality. Maturity is held up as a desirable educational goal, and it is often claimed that outdoor pursuits bring young people to maturity. It might equally be claimed, however, that they keep people young. Certainly one of the most attractive things about outdoor pursuits instructors or teachers is their youthfulness, their refusal completely to grow up and abandon "the heaven that lies about us in our infancy." It is odd the esteem in which maturity is held, considering how close it can be to over-ripeness. The truth is, of course, and in education we neglect it at our peril, that each stage of life is equally valuable for its own sake. The practice of regarding one stage as nothing more than a training ground for a later one leads to a squandering of the precious gift of life. Furthermore it is cruel and untrue to suggest, by valuing maturity too much, that the old and doddering are of no account. We can turn to R. L. Stevenson, whose essay on Crabbed Age and Youth has much to say on this subject, for a wise and kindly comment on the process of maturing: 'To love playthings well as a child, to lead an adventurous and honourable youth, and to settle when the time arrives to a green and smiling age, is to be a good artist in life, and deserves well of yourself and your neighbour'.

That word 'honourable' reminds us that adventure is strongly linked to romance. Now romanticism has two sides to it. It may be condemned as illusory and false, but on the other hand it has its noble side, visionary and idealistic, raising man from the commonplace and trivial to the heights of aspiration, transcending his finite nature and looking towards the infinite and the sublime, 'the eternal spirit of the chainless mind'. It is romantic aspiration and vision that can turn a long hard plod over the Pennine Way into a real adventure. There is a kind of poeticism shared by all who love the hills which is expressed not in words but in physical effort, in technical competence, and in good companionship.

What is so valuable and formative in an adventure is the commitment it invariably calls for in one way or another. There is always, somewhere, a point for girding up one's loins, taking a deep breath, and making a step into the unknown. It is a giving of oneself, a spending of oneself without which, paradoxically, there can be no personal integration and consolidation. How often in accounts of adventures we hear expressions like: 'Well, for better or for worse, here goes'; 'It was now or never'; 'This was the moment of truth'. It is a breaking of the insurance barrier, at which the spirit experiences a kind of sonic boom. It calls for faith, even if it is only faith in a rope or a compass, or an instructor's assurance. And having faith in things, and people, is an aspect of having faith in oneself, and that is the self-confidence we're always claiming adventurous pursuits confer.

This willingness to step into the unknown, into new experience, is not to be confused with mere recklessness. There is about recklessness a certain lack of commitment, a damping down, for kicks, of foresight and imagination. It is essentially frivolous, whereas adventurousness, at its best, is entirely serious. And because a thing is serious it does not mean that it is less exciting or less fun. On the contrary. The reason why children can enjoy themselves more intensely than most adults is that they are so serious, that is, so wholehearted. They have not yet adopted the outlook which equates fun with frivolity, and seriousness with an absence of joie de vivre. The true adventurer takes life so seriously that he cannot bear to fritter it away on mere comfort and safety and respectability.

But perhaps the most valuable element in the spirit of adventure is that most precious attribute of childhood, from which the aspirations of youth and the serenity of age develop, a sense of wonder. The traveller who, gazing upon new vistas, is not struck by a feeling of wonder and wild surmise, will soon settle down and cease his adventuring. Darwin's voyage in the Beagle stimulated him to such a sense of wonder that its impetus carried him through thirty years of dedicated toil, a life-long adventure of the mind. It is a childlike quality, but it can be possessed alike by Einstein or by Wordsworth's 'Idiot Boy' for it is not a question of intelligence. It is a kind of extreme mental health. The total absence of it I suppose is acute depression.One of the great tasks of education is to sustain this childlike sense of wonder into adulthood, and if possible throughout life.

So in outdoor education we should not altogether neglect the life contemplative. Excursions and short courses out of doors tend to be packed with activity, to ensure people get their money's worth. But often there is more value in 'a wise passiveness'.

From an acceptance that adventure, however physical, is fundamentally of the mind and spirit, it is not far to the proposition that learning is itself an adventure. The common elements are venturing, in faith, into the unknown, and the sense of wonder as understanding dawns. It is well for the teacher to bear this in mind, for it is all too easy to produce the impression that there is nothing left to discover. The more we can let people do it themselves, the more valuable the experience will be.

There are snags of course. One is that left to their own devices, some will do nothing at all and be bored for want of leadership. Others will find adventure that spoils the environment and annoys local people. And some, of course, will kill themselves. The special expertise of an outdoor centre should consist in contriving to provide against these snags in such a way as not to nip true adventure in the bud.

Outdoor education, like any other education, can easily be too directed, with the result that what might be an adventure becomes merely an activity. So much is known, and the information so assiduously promulgated, about equipment, for example, that a whole area for adventurous experimentation has been put out of use. Imagine the reception R. L. Stevenson's plan for his travels with a donkey would have had if he had proposed it to an assessment panel for a Duke of Edinburgh Gold Expedition. His crazy sleeping bag would have been rejected out of hand, and his association with the immortal Modestine would have been judged quite unnecessary since a high-loading rucksack and a kit weighing less than a third of his body weight would have rendered her superfluous. Yet what a loss not only to literature, but also to Stevenson himself, if he had been properly trained.

Like many campers, I expect, I am prone to lie awake on the hard ground designing in imagination the perfect tent. From such designs I have only occasionally proceeded to actual experiment, but the first tent I ever had was home-made. It was forty years ago, but 1 still remember vividly the long adventure which produced it – small, simple, badly finished, 'a poor thing, but mine own'. The making of it had most of the hallmarks of a great adventure: the initial vision, the build-up of conviction that it could be done and the determination to do it, the scepticism of others, the absorption in practical considerations, the stamina and endurance to sew those interminable seams, the disappointments and mistakes, and the starting again. It was extremely light and had a door at each end. The first trial was a genuine one, far from home, in a singularly unattractive sad soggy field with cowpats and thistles, nasty looking mushrooms, and no view. It was November, and I endured such a chilly and draughty night and returned home so pale and staring-eyed with fatigue, that pretty soon l sewed up one the doors, and added a nine-inch ground cloth, and be damned to the weight. My proudest time with that tent was when it was the sole survivor of an Easter camp below the gullies of Ben Nevis. With its multi-coloured cottons representing every part-used reel in my mother's sewing basket it lasted some twenty years, and finally disintegrated in an instant, like the One Hoss Shay, on the shore of Loch Coruisk. A pity that the time has gone by for that sort of improvisation and we must give way to a new style of adventure exploring the Aladdin's caves of the equipment shops.

In watching children play, it is surprising how often they prefer to use equipment for some purpose quite other than what it was intended for. They play cricket, for example, with the wrong side of the bat, cycle with no hands, and walk on the hands instead of the feet. Similarly it is almost always more interesting to climb on things not meant to be climbed on, such as rocks, than on purpose-made apparatus. The key to making a good climbing wall is somehow to create the illusion by a thoroughly inconsiderate placing and shaping of the holds, that no-one was intended to get up it. It is thrilling to have a beautifully designed efficient sailing machine to handle, but there is another kind of absorption, and perhaps a deeper one, in being afloat on something that is not a boat and in sailing something, like a canoe, which was not meant to be sailed. It is good to see, as one does, an occasional bathtub and crude coracle in the fleet of an outdoor centre.

Rock-climbing is an activity in which it is easy to over-instruct. The reason for this is usually rooted in confusion about the exact aim of the exercise. If the aim is to attain the maximum skill in the shortest time, then intensive instruction is appropriate. If the aim is adventure, with its wonderment, its delight in discovery, its feeling of 'boldly going where no man has gone before', as it says in Star Trek, then perhaps a good deal of messing about on rocks is more suitable as a start. But with climbing one has to be so careful, and this illustrates the odd truth that, as far as educational situations are concerned, at any rate, the more hazardous the activity the less opportunity there is for adventure. Really hazardous activities call for close control and discipline and the decisions cannot be left to the pupil. Yet there is considerable pressure, in all sorts of ways, to proceed as though the more advanced and technical the activity, and the more costly to equip it and provide for it, the greater the adventure, and the greater the educational pay-off. It is simply not so. If it were, the upper Himalaya would be a better place for a centre than the Lake District.

Perhaps the real truth of the matter is that we make too much of the adventure idea when that is not the essence of what we are about at all in outdoor education. The real core of the business is the enrichment through exposure to experiences and through various feasts of the senses; not least the kinaesthetic sense. That great and unpopular poet Wordsworth who knew hardly anything about nature study and even less about climbing, (though he did walk over 100,000 miles, so they say) has nevertheless more to say for outdoor education than any writer I know, and as recommended reading I would give him higher priority even than *Safety on Mountains*.

The eye it cannot choose but see
We cannot bid the ear be still
Our bodies feel, where'er they be
Against or with our will.
Think you midst all this mighty sum
Of things for ever speaking
That nothing of itself will come
But we must still be seeking.

You cannot plan adventures. The best one can do is allow them to happen.

BINGLEY COLLEGE

Bingley College, founded in 1911, was built on an elevated site between the Aire valley and Ilkley Moor. Its imposing gritstone buildings, including five massive halls of residence, were originally designed to accommodate two hundred and fifty women students, but by the 1960s it had become co-educational with an intake of about a thousand.

I joined in 1973 as Dean of Students. At that time all freshers were required to take a three-month induction course of outdoor activities. This programme was managed very ably by a tubby, not to say spherical, man called Wally Keay, senior lecturer in the P.E. department. He told me one day that one of his students, asked how he had enjoyed his summer vacation, had mentioned in an off-hand way that he had climbed a big wall in Norway. This turned out to be the second ascent of the Troll Wall, and the student in question was Peter Livesey. The first ascent had taken the Norwegians three days, but Livesey, with John Sheard, had done it in one.

Peter Livesey had been in the forefront of British kayaking, and was in line for inclusion in the Olympic slalom team, but the competitive demands of that sport were so time consuming that he turned his attention to climbing. His academic work, in spite of the enormous amount of climbing he did, was of high standard and he completed the course with honours. A year or two later he applied for a post in the College's P.E. department. The head of department was a woman and her chief interest was Dance. She had her own nominee for the post, and in any case had not much liked Livesey when he was a student. According to Wally Keay, she was opposing his appointment.

I have never been much inclined towards politics and lobbying but something moved me to take the Principal aside and make sure he knew that Livesey was by this time a top performer in the climbing world. To get him on our staff, I said, would be akin to getting Nureyev in one's ballet company. He listened to me and Livesey was appointed, though not without a struggle.

Bingley College did in consequence attract a number of very good climbers. Of course it was also well placed geographically, within reach of many gritstone outcrops and not far from the Lake District. But largely it was that birds of a feather flock together. John Sheard was never a member of the College but he was often to be seen in the Union, and another rising star arrived in the elegant shape of Jill Lawrence. She was a 'mature student'; in other words she came to the college not from school but from the world of low-paid work. Pleasantly hard-bitten and street-wise, she spoke with a Liverpool accent and treated pretension of any kind with withering scorn. She had style and with her tall, flat-chested figure crowned by a mass of honey coloured curls she stood out in any gathering. She was elected president of the Students' Union, and though that and her rock-climbing took up much of her time, her college work was consistently excellent. She soon came to be regarded as Britain's leading woman rock-climber.

Another brilliant woman climber and a friend of Jill's was Gill Price. She was small, dark, neat, reserved and self-effacing. When some years later she and Jill Lawrence were included in Chris Bonington's series of films tracing the development of rock-climbing in the Lake District they tried out a climb on the flank of King's How in Borrowdale. It was Nagasaki Grooves, E 4, on Great End Crag, that big rockface that had remained unnoticed until a fire burned the vegetation off it in 1940. I went with them, for Jill kept in touch with me for several years after I left Bingley. When they came to the 6b crux Gill Price got up it but Jill Lawrence could not follow, and after she had made several unsuccessful attempts they abseiled off and turned their attention to a route graded E 3 on Raven Crag, Thirlmere. Jill told me later that when they were being filmed on this climb the adrenalin rush swept them up the rock face with the smooth fluidity of a dream, and they did it so quickly that the film had to include weight-training sequences, etcetera, in order to make up the allotted time.

Gill Price qualified as a teacher but took a job with a French firm specialising in the external inspection of high buildings, using climbing techniques instead of scaffolding. So she became a steeplejack, or a 'steeplejill'.

Peter Gomersall and Andy Jones were also Bingley climbers of note. Jones has worked for several years at the Sunderland Education Authority Centre, Derwent Hill at Portinscale, Cumbria. Gomersall I remember very well as a student I had repeatedly to haul over the coals on account of his absenteeism and his failures in academic work. I found myself defending him time and again against the demands of exasperated tutors to have him thrown out of the college. What I liked about him was his readiness to take the blame and admit his shortcomings. I knew he was a climber, though I did not know how good he was, and I suppose I thought 'there but for the grace of God go I'. For in my youth I too had been all but sent down from Liverpool University for putting climbing before Latin. He seemed almost to hope that he would be thrown out, but somehow he always managed to hang on by his fingernails, resitting every exam and never quite giving up. This tenacity has clearly paid off in his climbing for he became one of the leading performers of his time.

A female climber very different from Jill Lawrence and Gill Price was Bonny Masson, another 'mature student'. Good looking, personable and self-assured, she gave the impression that Bingley College was fortunate in securing her as a student. In climbing, too, she was a bit of a snob, disdaining routes easier than Hard VS and dismissive of those who climbed them. Years later, on the day following a B.M.C. AGM, I remember doing Hope on the Idwal Slabs while she was still moving up and down the same few feet of Suicide Wall or some such desperate climb. Her dedication and persistence in hard climbing, however, led her to improve steadily, and she became a climber of note.

Peter Livesey turned out to be an excellent teacher of climbing and outdoor pursuits, showing a good understanding of ordinary people's difficulties and recognising how quickly or slowly to progress in their tuition. For some time, as a sideline, he ran evening classes for climbers at various gritstone crags in the district, recruiting me as an assistant. He encouraged people to learn by leading, and would minimise the risk by nipping smartly up the climbs placing protection for the beginners to use.

Some years after I left Bingley Jill Lawrence phoned me to say that she, Livesey and Gill Price were planning to climb on Great End and would I care to bring my crampons along and join them. I did so, but Livesey was late in arriving, and the short winter day was well advanced when we at last set off, at a punishing pace, up Grains Gill. He was wearing lightweight footgear resembling trainers, and on arrival at the crag, put crampons on them. Central Gully already had two parties on it, so we took the SE Gully, I with my long ice axe, the others with more modern ice tools. This was a far cry from the days when a winter ascent of Great End without crampons would take us all day. We were up in less than two hours, and while we stopped to eat, and sort out the gear before descending, Livesey went off and made two more solo ascents of the crag by different routes before it got dark.

There was a certain quiet flamboyance about Peter Livesey. One day as I was having lunch in the college refectory he joined me and after a little conversation he said he must be off now as he was climbing that afternoon on Raven. I knew of no Raven Crag anywhere near Bingley and was astonished to learn that he meant Raven Crag, Thirlmere. He was going there in his fast sports car. In this respect he was rather like Hamish MacInnes who used to sweep up to a crag in his E type Jaguar.

He once told me that he was at a lay-by when another car pulled in and the driver emptied a heap of cigarette butts onto the ground and drove off. Livesey scooped them up, gave chase and signalled to speak to him. The man wound his window down and Livesey threw him the butts with the comment, "I think you forgot these."

Another little story he told me was of when he was wanting to sleep out on the side of Wastwater and was persistently harried by a National Park warden. In the end he found what he described as the only place left to hide, which was over the fence and inside the official camping site.

There was one Bingley college climber whom I never got to know, and that was the one who put the Christmas tree on top of the dome of the main building's clock tower. This happened soon after I had been appointed Dean of Students. Seconded by Dennis Gray, who lived nearby at Guiseley, I made the second ascent and took it down, finding the route greasy with industrial grime. I was glad to be able to prise the lightning conductor away sufficiently to get my fingers behind it, and I should certainly not have liked to do it solo, in the dark, even given the Dutch courage of a few pints of beer. I fully expected the name of the culprit to come out sooner or later over the grapevine, but it never did.

AND SOME HAVE GREATNESS THRUST
UPON THEM

Britain is, I think, unique in Europe in not having a national mountaineering club open to everyone. The B.M.C. is the nearest thing to it. But it is not a club, and, in any case, until 1982 the only way to be in it was to get elected to one of the three hundred or so climbing clubs it represented. The major clubs were pretty exclusive, and the doyen of such august bodies was of course the Alpine Club. It even had its own regimental or old school tie – green with a prominent yellow streak as some of its members would laconically point out. Many climbers belonged to several clubs, for membership conveyed status. The B.M.C. was seen as a sometimes tiresome, but probably necessary bureaucratic umbrella organisation. As that mountaineering wit Ian McNaught Davis once put it "The B.M.C. is all right so long as it remains small and inefficient."

On the principal of 'finders is keepers', the feeling was strong among climbers that the mountains really belonged to those who had come to them of their own volition, and there was a reluctance to share them with people herded into the hills by training programmes. As John Hunt delicately put it in the Hunt Report, published 1976:

> Mountaineering is a pastime that most people like to enjoy with a few friends or occasionally alone. Some are more gregarious. But whether they go alone or in smaller or larger groups, all would wish to preserve a sense of remoteness and an element of wilderness in the mountains.

The Sports Council's declared policy of Sport For All did not greatly appeal to club mountaineers. As far as they were concerned the harder it was to get into the halls of the chosen the better.

Nothing, however, could stem the huge expansion of mountaineering activity. From the private passion of a few, it became a growth industry, with fortunes to be made in the equipment business, and a new profession created in teaching mountaineering skills and personal development. Younger climbers did not need clubs. They made informal groupings and met in pubs and campsites, keeping in touch with the climbing world through commercial magazines. With Dennis Gray as General Secretary, the B.M.C. kept up with these new trends and grew dramatically.

Throughout these developments I had taken a stance midway between the interests of the individual mountaineer and the rapidly growing interests of organised mountain training. I had spoken at the B.M.C.'s Safety Conference at Leeds, and struck a note that found favour with that passionate defender of the climber's right to kill himself in his own way, Ken Wilson, editor of *Mountain*. I had also been vice-chairman of the Committee on Mountain Training set up by the then President Alan Blackshaw, and led by John Hunt.

I did not, however, regard my involvement with the B.M.C. as anything more than peripheral, and was very surprised when Dennis Gray asked me if I would stand as President in 1982. Never one to go looking for work, I did not relish the prospect of the three years hard labour that this probably involved, but on the other hand it was difficult to resist the attraction of being numbered among the illustrious band of B.M.C. presidents. I accepted, and was voted into office at a dinner at the Prince of Wales Hotel in Ambleside. Dennis spoiled my meal by saying in an offhand way that he would be calling on me to say a few words, and I spent the next half-hour desperately raking round in my empty brain for an appropriate line of thought. When I got to my feet I told a funny story to lighten the mood, then gave a brief account of my attitude to climbing, and an undertaking to do my best as president. It was well received; in fact Sid Cross told me afterwards that it was the best speech on climbing he could remember; perhaps he meant because it was so short. So I was launched upon this new adventure.

I was anything but a new broom, and my role was that of a cautious adviser and diplomat. The man who really ran the B.M.C. was Dennis Gray. Early honorary secretaries had served for periods ranging from one year to six. Dennis, the first General Secretary, salaried, stayed for fifteen. I never ceased to marvel at his thorough grasp of all the many concerns of the B.M.C. and its numerous committees. In Management Committees he could trot out accurate information on every topic and he was always full of plans and ideas for the future. He was by nature a radical, never afraid of stirring things up. His hero in politics was Tony Benn, whom he always referred to as Wedgie. He never proposed anything without first consulting me, however, and kept me informed of everything that happened. This thoroughness and vigour in administration was matched by his extraordinary energy as a climber, for he climbed regularly and at a high standard, in spite of the exigencies of his job. At one of my A.G.M.s, in Llanberis, he took me off to Tremadoc for the afternoon and we climbed two Very Severes, getting back with two minutes to spare before the start of the meeting. We did not even have time to change out of our climbing gear. On another occasion, after a difficult and controversial meeting in Derbyshire, he took us to a small but repellent cliff at Water-cum-Jolly, and led up a bulging wall at Hard VS. The party comprised the two vice-presidents, George Band and Bill Peascod, myself, and Dennis's seventeen-year-old son. George Band declined to try it, Bill Peascod had to use the taut rope as a handhold, and Dennis's son and I were the only ones who followed unaided, though I for my part was at the limit of my strength. During the three years of my presidency I gained a very favourable impression of Dennis Gray. His pay, based on a modest Civil Service grade, was an inadequate recompense for the work he did and for the abilities he brought to it, but he was too busy to complain and remained lively and cheerful throughout.

Out of the multitude of B.M.C. matters that came before the Management Committee I remember three things that took up a good deal of our time and thought. One was the Sports Council's – or C.C.P.R.'s – management of Plas-y-Brenin, the National Centre, which absorbed something like £300,000 per annum of the grant made for mountaineering, while the B.M.C. received £40,000. Another was the development of climbing walls. Numerous walls were being built without adequate awareness of what was really needed, and in the end Ian Dunn, assisted by Ken Wilson, was employed to advise on this and produce a manual of best practice. The third was the question of the B.M.C. journal. This had started as *Mountaineering*, in 1972 became *Mountain Life* and in 1976 was replaced by *Climber and Rambler*. The deal with *Climber and Rambler* was that the B.M.C. got four pages for its bulletin, and the promise of royalties when the circulation topped a certain figure. The magazine was owned by Rank Magazines and edited by Walt Unsworth. The circulation did rise as a result of this involvement, but when it looked as though it would exceed the agreed limit, Rank brought out another magazine, *The Great Outdoors,* which reduced *Climber and Rambler's* circulation once again. The B.M.C. consequently continued to get very little financial advantage out of the magazine and our frequent conferences with its financial controller never got beyond promises for the future. We became increasingly dissatisfied and an attractive offer from the owners of High magazine caused us to consider making a change. Walt Unsworth, who as editor of *Climber and Rambler* was an ex-officio member of the Management Committee, strongly urged us to stay with it. We had no idea, he said, of the crippling costs of publishing, and he warned us against bankrupting the B.M.C. His tone, however, was so condescending I could see that with every word he was digging his own grave. The Committee, its hackles up, voted almost unanimously for the change.

What was quite impressive was the large amount of voluntary work that was done for the B.M.C., and the devotion so many people showed thereby to climbing. Easily the most colourful character in B.M.C. affairs was Ken Wilson whom I always thought of as the Che Guevara of the climbing world. He had been one of J.E.B. Wright's team of instructors in the Mountaineering Association and later owner and editor of the internationally acclaimed *Mountain* magazine. He equalled Dennis Gray for energy and was a passionate lobbyist on numerous issues. Plain and forthright speaking was a feature of B.M.C. meetings but there was no one to match Ken Wilson in this respect. I well remember an encounter we had with the Sports Council or C.C.P.R. on the subject of Plas-y-Brenin, in which he struck the opposition dumb with shock by the candour of his remarks. He spent much of his life on the telephone, and it was rumoured his phone bill came to £2,000 a year. He and I were frequently at odds and he gave me a hard time with interminable phone calls late at night when he was full of beans and I was at my lowest ebb, but I admired what he basically stood for. When my term of office came to an end he was good enough to come and give me a kind word.

I remember little of the business we conducted in the B.M.C. Most of my recollections are of people. One devoted attender at meetings was Major Charles Marriott, elderly, white-haired and white-bearded like an old-time sea captain. He had in fact sailed with Tilman on several voyages and was much valued by him for the acuity of his eyesight and his patience in adverse conditions. He lived alone and it is said that when he died his house and his car were ready to fall to pieces at the same time, which suggests a sound grasp of economy. Our principal guest at the Llanberis A.G.M. was W.A. Poucher, who, at the age of ninety, drove from London to the Welsh border and there consented to be picked up by one of our members. He made a witty speech, and sitting next to him I was interested to learn that he had started out as a doctor, but his experiences in the Great War put him off surgery for good. As a chemist he invented an emulsifier which made Pond's Cream world famous. In those days, he told me, there were only three groups of people who used cosmetics, prostitutes, actors and royalty.

The Derbyshire town of Buxton was descended upon every other year by a horde of climbers attending the conference of the British Mountaineering Council. According to the B.M.C.'s *The First Fifty Years*, these get togethers 'initially designed as serious debating events, soon evolved into populist jamborees of exotic entertainment, a rich mix of earnest message, political statement, thrilling adventure, slide and film presentations, polemic, panel game, hip-hop, falderal and beerfest.'

I went there in 1984 with Bill Peascod, and on the way we called on

Walt Unsworth at Harmony Hall, Milnthorpe, to pick up copies of Bill's autobiography, *Journey After Dawn*, which had just been published by the Cicerone Press. As president and vice-president, we rated a hotel room for the weekend. We arrived quite late on Friday, and Bill spent the entire night with the light on, reading and rereading his book.

It was a lively, in fact frenetic weekend full of meetings with old friends, drinking and bonhomie. During one carousal, Mo Anthoine, Dennis told me, was chewing up wineglasses. After an interval of thirty years or more Peascod and I renewed acquaintance with old Ronnie Wilkinson, once a reporter on the West Cumberland local newspaper, and the secretary of the short-lived West Cumberland Rock Climbing Club which Bill had been president of before he went to live in Australia. Wilkinson now had a bad heart, which kept him off the hills, but carried away by the excitements of the Conference he drank a good deal, and had an attack on the Saturday night that frightened us into sobriety. It was with relief that we learned next morning that he was still alive and well.

Many famous and notorious characters of the mountaineering world were present and among those contributing to the entertainment were Pat Ament, Andreas Kubin, Eric Jones (with the film of his solo ascent of the Eiger), Jill Lawrence, Ian McNaught Davies, Al Rouse, Don Whillans and Ken Wilson, in fact the whole repertory company of the mountaineering fraternity of those days. But at the top of the bill was Walter Bonatti. Securing his presence at the Conference was quite a coup as he was known to eschew publicity, but he had been persuaded by Mirella Tenderini, who translated his speech into English as he delivered it. To be candid I felt that to have given this speech pre-eminence in the Conference was going to prove a mistake. Listening, for an hour or more, to Bonatti's words being translated sentence by sentence into not very inspired English seemed to me hardly likely to keep hundreds of climbers riveted to their seats. But I was wrong. They listened with awe to the master's utterances and at the end gave him thunderous applause and a standing ovation. I suppose the difficulty with which his message was delivered gave it a special oracular significance.

In his honour and to give the town's blessing to the Conference, the mayor of Buxton held a lunchtime reception, to which as President I was invited. It was a typical cocktail party scene, the animated crowd all holding glasses in their hands and circulating amid a high-pitched barnyard chatter of conversation. Walter Bonatti, however, was sitting neglected in a corner. Since he did not speak English he was simply left out of the party. I went over and asked him if he spoke any French. He brightened immediately and we chatted for some time in spite of the limitations of my French. How we got on to the subject I cannot recall but he told me that he had come to find mountaineering too competitive and too liable to interest the newspapers, and he had taken to making long canoe trips in the North West Territories of Canada, as the great expanses of the Canadian barrens accorded him the same kind of satisfaction as high mountains. This was of great interest to me as I had made a canoe trip in the same region. It was a pleasure to meet a brilliant mountaineer whose values had not been distorted by 'that last infirmity of noble minds', the love of fame. I felt proud to meet Bonatti.

Another distinguished guest was Wanda Rutkiewicz, the Polish high mountaineer. Bill Peascod fell for her immediately. Her personal charm and good looks he might have been proof against but when you added her fame and prowess in the climbing world she was irresistible.

As the conference wound down on Sunday afternoon, and the crowds thinned, and the displays were taken down, and everyday reality once more began to take over, I sat about for two hours waiting for Bill Peascod to show up with his car to take us home. It was rather a sobering experience to be hanging about there witnessing the long diminuendo. At last I was about the only person left, and though I could hardly believe it, I realised that he had gone without me. What he had done, I subsequently learned, was to offer to take the beauteous Wanda Rutkiewicz home with him to meet his wife, and in his excitement at her agreeing, he had completely forgotten that I was dependent on him for a lift. I was annoyed, and being in those days always short of money I stomped off hitch-hiking, no easy task on a Sunday evening as I had to pass through, or get round, the conurbation of Greater Manchester. It was a long road home, with some dreary waits and other frustrations, but also a few remarkable strokes of luck. Hitch-hiking is like gambling; a win, when it comes, makes you feel fortunate and loved. So this journey home was a bit of an adventure in itself and by the time it had reached a successful conclusion a good deal of my hard feeling about Peascod had evaporated.

In the early 1980s the Geneva Section of the Swiss Alpine Club organised an international rock-climbing event. They invited the national body of the sport in each country in Europe to send two expert climbers for a week on the Salève, the big limestone escarpment near Geneva. The S.A.C. would provide meals and accommodation during the meet. André Roch was at that time president of the Geneva Section. He wrote to me saying he thought the two presidents might attend the meet as observers, and he would be glad to have me stay at his house. I accepted, and when Bill Peascod heard of it, he was so keen to come too that I summoned up the courage to ask André if he could be included. Bill had been living in Australia for the last thirty years or more, and returning to this country, and settling in a farmhouse on the northern side of Skiddaw, he had re-entered the climbing scene with the enthusiasm of a young lad, though he was over sixty and had retired early following a heart attack. André of course welcomed him readily.

The British nominees for the event were Ian Parsons, Chris Hamper and Bill Birkett, son of the famous Jim.

The Salève, so accessible from Geneva, was of course covered with rock climbs, and I had on previous occasions climbed there with André and been shown the classic circular routes and traverses, the exposed ledges covered in places with ball-bearing-like pebbles, and the cave pitches. During this meet most of the activity centred on a seemingly blank wall, with numerous bolted routes. Here the formidable gathering of young tigers – and tigresses too, supple, long-haired and painfully attractive – made their leisurely preparations at the tables outside the little café. Like the real big cats, they were relaxed, sleepy and indolent until the time came for the explosive athleticism of the kill. They sprawled about with their feet on the tables, drinking iced lemonade until quite late in the morning. André, Bill and I contented ourselves with watching the climbs through binoculars, and by bouldering on the huge rocks at the foot of the cliff.

One of the Swiss participants, Bernard Weitlisbach, had produced a book for the occasion, Grande Grimpe, a hundred and forty pages of wild cartoons, climbing nightmares, nonsense and in-jokes. There was a draw-ing of a hamburger with an old PA in place of the beef. I mention this book as it reflects the youthful and relaxed spirit of the meet.

On the last day Bill and I had the opportunity of being dragged up a route ironically called Les Pâturages, a mild Extreme. Bill jumped at it. I was sorely tempted after seeing so much activity and doing so little myself, but I felt an obligation to keep André company, for he too must have regretted not being up there with the youngsters.

Bill came back exhausted but jubilant and we prepared for the final event of the meet. This was a banquet at an old castle some miles from Geneva. Fat lambs were to be spit roasted for an al fresco meal. Unfortu-nately it rained heavily and the feast had to take place in the great hall. A pleasing feature of this whole event was that the older members of the S.A.C. hosted it, did all the work of looking after the climbers' wellbeing in makeshift accommodation in the centre of the city, and also prepared and served up the feast. The menu was simple but plentiful, roast lamb with or without garlic – I chose garlic and by garlic they really meant garlic– masses of salad, then strawberries and cream. Wine flowed throughout.

It was a wonderful festive occasion, the great hall resounding with good cheer. There were one or two speeches. André spoke. I got up and, flown with wine, attempted a short speech of thanks in French. No one understood it, I think, and no one cared. Not even I. One of the elderly helpers, M. Tricouni no less, gave everyone present a pin and a medal ribbon from which dangled a shiny No. 1 tricouni.

André had brought as his special guest Lulu Boulaz, a distinguished alpinist now about sixty years old. She was excellent company and sang lustily in the car on the way home. Bill Peascod declared it was the happiest day of his life, and his elation over getting up Les Pâturages caused him to drink so much that after five minutes of singing along with Lulu he fell into a profound sleep and is unlikely to have remembered getting to bed that night.

Another foreign event I attended as president of the B.M.C. was the hundredth anniversary of the Norwegian Alpine Club. After accepting the invitation I was rather mystified, and a little disappointed, to receive through the post an acknowledgement, written in Norwegian, which appeared to tell me the time and place of the celebration, and a station in Oslo from which to take the train. Nothing else. I pictured myself arriving in the airport with the prospect of trying to find somewhere to stay. Fortunately, just as I was setting off, I had a phone call from the secretary of the Club, telling me I had been sent by mistake the standard letter to club members, instead of one explaining that I would be met at the airport and looked after from then on.

I was in due course met by a very pleasant young man, who worked for a climbing magazine, and was looking forward, the next summer, to an attempt on the Eigerwand. He showed me into his studio flat in the middle of Oslo, explained its amenities, invited me to read his books and magazines and to help myself to his food, and arranged to pick me up before the dinner next day. I expressed some concern at putting him out of his flat, but he said no, he was pleased for me to have it, as it gave him a good excuse for moving in with his girlfriend.

The rendezvous for the dinner was a railway station in the city. We arrived there to find a handful of people on the platform, among them a couple of men strolling about with large tanks strapped on their backs, tanks resembling those carried by vineyard workers for spraying the vines. These, however, held hot gluhwein, which was being dispensed to travellers bound for the dinner. The crowd thickened and became quite festive in spite of the cold. Eventually the train came in, filled up, and took us all a few miles uphill to a high point commanding a splendid view of the city and the harbour, where we entered what must be the world's biggest log cabin, a huge restaurant in a prime site. I was introduced to a bewildering number of people, all well-known or famous for one thing or another, and all drinking as though there were no tomorrow. Among many imposing and elderly figures, the club president seemed remarkably young, and he was in fact on temporary leave from prison, having defied the law on some political issue. This was quite a surprise to me, for in all other respects the party had, at this stage at least, an air of formality and respectability. Not that it lacked liveliness, enthusiasm and bonhomie.

Up to this point I had always claimed that the longest meal I had ever had was at a hotel in Trondheim once, on the way back from Arctic Finland, but the Centenary Dinner beat that hollow. It was a wonderful meal, with many courses and as many changes of wine, and it was accompanied by entertainments of all kinds, the guests becoming livelier and more vociferous as the evening progressed. Speeches took place between the courses and sometimes during them. There were speeches in Norwegian and speeches in English. There were songs as well as speeches, and toasts of all kinds. I feared I might be called upon to say something myself, and felt unequal to it, for I have little sense of occasion, and little awareness of the significance of anniversaries and the like. I wondered if I could say something about Cecil Slingsby, which would draw attention to Anglo-Norwegian solidarity without detracting from Norway's own achievements. To my relief however a much more important person than I got up to say something appropriate from the B.M.C. and that was Noel Odell, tall, hale and distinguished, the man who last saw Mallory and Irving alive.

The dinner lasted from about eight until one in the morning. There'd been plenty of help to get people to the event, but there was none to get them home again. After waiting about for some time, trying to keep an eye on my host, the journalist, I found myself boarding a minibus which went downhill into the city and landed us in another party in someone's flat. The people there were mostly in their twenties and thirties, men and women, and although they were all strangers to me, they made me very welcome and I remember talking at some length to a young woman who, had I been more sober, would have struck me dumb with adoration.

This secondary party lasted until about three or four, and I cannot now remember whether I got home to my flat for the rest of the night or was given a place to sleep elsewhere. What I do know is that my journalist friend took me climbing quite early in the morning on a crag at the edge of the city, possibly even in it. It was a pleasant route, of perhaps mild severe, and I was pleased to note that though my mouth was a bit dry, my hands were not shaking and my head was clear. To me now it all has a somewhat dreamlike quality, but I have a photograph of myself grinning as I topped out, so it did happen, and I well remember the wintry sunshine and the sharp, cool air that was keeping me from falling asleep.

Towards the end of the same morning I was invited for drinks at the house of one of the elder statesmen of the Club, where I again met Noel Odell.

The final entertainment offered was to sample the city's langlauf skiing. This may have been on the same crowded day after the dinner, and it may have been the following day. I cannot now remember. It was with the young president of the club, and had its moments of terror. The ski trails wound around through undulating wooded terrain and one's skis ran in quite deep tramlines. There were some long downward slopes where in the absence of any other form of braking I resorted to the craven practice of putting my ski sticks between my legs and sitting on them. But in general it was a pleasant excursion and the president gave me some interesting insights into Norwegian life and politics.

I stayed on in Oslo for a couple of days more, to visit the extraordinary park filled with nude statues celebrating the exuberant health and vigour of a Nordic dreamworld, and to spend hours in the fine museum built for Edvard Munch's paintings.

Mountaineering, it seems to me, is a sport that brings loners together. Though it is a wonderful and healing thing to go alone in the hills, most serious mountain activities require cooperation with others, and the trust and interdependence that comes of sharing dangers and discomforts, as well as triumphs and exhilarations, makes for companionships above the ordinary. In these random reminiscences of my years with the B.M.C. I have mentioned a mere handful of the people I had the pleasure of meeting and working with. As I become older, and people's names increasingly elude me, I still remember with affection many of these characters, Bob Pettigrew, Dave Roberts, Jack Ashcroft, Harold Edwards, Bill Ruthven, Steve Derwin, Al Rouse, Brede Arkless, Alan Blackshaw, John Barry, Vin Machin, George Steele, Charlie Vigano, Audrey Salkeld, Doug Scott, Myrtle Simpson, Alistair McDonald and many more, all remarkable in one way or another. So many associations, fleeting though most of them were, were to me an enrichment. It is one of life's paradoxes that solitude and good fellowship can be equally good for you.

THE ROAD TO MOKHOTLONG

Ever since I'd first looked at the map I had been interested in Mokhotlong up in the mountains, in the far east corner of the country. The name had an outlandish and romantic ring to it like Samarkand or Tamanrasset. I suppose if you live in Samarkand names like Birmingham and Newcastle-upon-Tyne have an outlandish ring to them too. But high romance transcends ordinary logic and these names from distant parts always beckon.

So here we are, on a fine May morning, on a crowded bus from Leribe to Butha-Buthe, heading, we hope, for Mokhotlong.

In the chaotic area of open ground and beaten earth, sprinkled with discarded Coca Cola cans, that is the Butha-Buthe bus station, we stretch our legs, seek out the overworked lavatory and cast about among the truck drivers, street vendors and travellers for someone to tell us where to find our next bus. Within a few minutes we are aboard a very long one for Mokhotlong, feeling lucky as there are only three a week. We begin to be in holiday mood, as are most of the other passengers. Trish, as usual, is the object of a good deal of inoffensive gallantry, and indeed there is a general atmosphere of cheerful camaraderie and mild excitement among the passengers, for it is not every day that people take such a journey. The road winds up a long valley at the end of which rise the Maluti Mountains, a high and formidable barrier. The road here is excellent and the huge bus grinds doggedly upwards round endless successions of hairpin bends to the Moteng Pass. Eventually we reach a high bare upland world, bleak and desolate, with this one road through it to Oxbow Lodge at some 10,000 feet. The Lodge is a somewhat unattractive range of buildings with thatched roofs at the side of the road. The big bus stops and disgorges its passengers who line up eagerly for the toilets. We are leaving it here, for we want to sample this high country and perhaps catch a later bus in a couple of days.

We look at the accommodation at the Oxbow Lodge, but we are not impressed, either by the appearance of the rooms or the cost, 50 Rands per person without meals. We order lunch, and it is just warm enough to have it outside in the little garden; in fact it is warmer there than in the buildings. A group of horsemen is gathered outside drinking beer from cans, a macho swaggering lot, picturesque and dirty, like bandits in a Western.

We decide to walk on and camp out. A few hundred yards beyond the lodge the tarmac gives way to dirt. We soon reach the Malibamatso River and where the road crosses it turn upstream in search of a secluded campsite. The clear cold water runs over great slabs of basalt. There is just enough water to make it difficult to cross to the other bank dryshod. After several attempts we take off our boots and paddle across. We stop in a clean empty place with a bit of level greensward. We could be in Scotland. It is rather dull and comfortless especially when the sun sinks behind the hill, but Trish falls to with her usual competence and we are soon well set up. She is a pleasure to camp with, tidy and ingenious, without fuss. She fishes the pools of the Malibamatso, but catches nothing. Two brindled mongrels have followed us from Oxbow Lodge and we cannot get rid of them. They are, however, very well behaved, make no attempt to get at our food, and are gently submissive without being cringing. They lie quietly by the tent all night. It is cold, but there is a kind of well-being that comes of being just the right side of discomfort, in a small tent, in a desolate place, and especially if one is with the right companion.

In the morning there is hoar frost on the tent, but before long the sunshine works its way down the western hillside and brings its solace to us. We pack up, return to the road and start plodding along it. We are still accompanied by one of the brindled dogs. Traffic on the road is non existent. We are alone in a vast treeless landscape with the lonely dirt road snaking away into the distance.

Not quite alone. A herdboy materialises from the mountainside. He wants to know where we got the dog from. We gladly consign it to his care.

The next event in this long, empty morning is the arrival of a van. In it is a young white man with a black companion. The cargo space is full of assorted equipment. Trish gets in front with the white driver. The black and I stand like postillions with our toes on a narrow metal bar at the back of the vehicle, holding on with our fingers to the small metal channel that runs round the roof. The bar is well under the back of the van body, so it is a considerable strain on the forearms to maintain our position.

"Any problem, just wave," says the driver cheerfully, and gets on his way.

As the gradient of the road steepens we postillions are tilted further backward and the strain on fingers and forearms becomes acute. The van gathers speed and charges up the hill. Soon it is clear to me that I am in no position to wave to the driver as I need both hands to cling to the channel. My arms begin to ache with the effort. I try ignoring them as in yoga. I try shifting position; the relief is momentary and then the ache returns just as bad. I try standing more on tiptoe in order to bring my body nearer the vertical but it is too dangerous, as the road is not smooth and one could be shaken off one's holds. I begin to ask myself what I think I am doing, at the age of seventy-one, clinging on to the back of a van at an altitude of 10,000 feet in a foreign land, six thousand miles from home.

At this point Trish puts her head out of the side window and calls, "Are you all right back there," to which I reply with studied casualness, "Yes, but it's only a matter of time before my arms give out."

The van stops and we try a different system. I sit on Trish's knee and the black sits on the bonnet in front of the windscreen, only partly blocking the driver's view.

They're going only a mile or two further, to what is South Africa's only ski resort, a rather makeshift collection of huts on a south-facing hillside. The driver is making ready for the short but he hopes successful ski season. It looks a bit like the Cairngorm ski area as it was in the 1950s.

We now settle down to some steady walking. As Mokhotlong is some 170 kilometres ahead, we are in no hurry and are walking not so much to get anywhere as for something to do. Nevertheless we put quite a lot of this endless twisting road behind us. We are on top of the Lesotho world, looking down empty valleys which descend out of sight in the distance. We walk well into the afternoon and stop for lunch on a grassy knoll. It is sunny and warm but the air is sharp and bracing. We are hungry.

In mid afternoon a bakkie – South African for pickup – comes along the road. We hear it and see it miles before it reaches us. We give it the Lesotho hitch hiking sign, which is not the raised thumb, but an insistent pointing to a place on the road surface where you hope the vehicle will stop.

It stops, bearing out the hitch-hiker's dictum that the lonelier the road the higher the percentage of drivers willing to give you a lift. The cab is full and there are already two people in the back. He is not going to Mokhotlong, the driver says, but to some place we do not know on the way. O.K., we say. Five Rand, he says. We agree. Each, he says.

Most of the little truck is filled by a tractor tyre. There is also a large plastic oil drum. We climb in.

The driver seems keen to get there. He accelerates fiercely whenever he sees a smooth stretch of road ahead and brakes urgently for the potholes. It is a bumpy ride such as you would pay to go on in a fair ground. There is some slight danger of being bounced off, and a more real and persistent risk of damage to the coccyx. Sitting on the tractor tyre I use my arms as shock absorbers to soften the jarring of my thinly covered pelvic structure. The road climbs through cols, makes contouring sweeps round mountainsides, winds ingeniously down precipitous valleys and up over formidable mountain barriers. It seems endless.

We stop to pick up four herd boys. It is now cold in the late afternoon and we are glad of our windproofs. One of the herd boys, however, wears nothing on his upper body except a couple of bangles and a threadbare blanket drawn carelessly around his shoulder.

We pass a diamond mine with a vast, fresh-looking slag bank and a village of the most wretched houses we've seen, stone-built hovels in a totally bare and worn out terrain in the bleakest of uplands. At last, however, we are beginning to see some changes in the landscape, for we are now going down and down and down, traversing steep slopes, crawling carefully through stream beds and down eventually to a region where there are trees in the streambeds and occasional patches of vegetation.

We stop in a village to off-load the tyre and oil drum. Here the driver collects his fares. The herd boys pay up too, then leap off and disappear, on pleasure bent.

"Stay on," the driver tells us. "We are going further."

He drops us finally at a junction with a few scattered houses. We take the Mokhotlong road. Ahead across a valley is a large building with the word Tiotleng written across its roof in white paint, indicating an airstrip.

We camp the night on the river Senqu, in other words the Orange, orange because of the red silt it brings ceaselessly down out of Lesotho. Here, near its source, it is clean and clear, running shallowly over extensive banks of grey sand. We find a tiny flat place for the tent in a grove of bushes well up river from the road, and inconspicuous from the hillside across the river. Night is falling and we cook in the dark, on a small fire, by the light of Trish's candle lantern made out of a cut down plastic bottle. All night long the river murmurs beside our camp. We are snug and secure, and a good deal warmer than the night before. We talk of earlier camps, of Scotland, Algonquin, of times as far distant as our island camp on Smoothrock Lake in North Ontario. We are contented, if a little hungry.

In the morning we climb a long hill and after an hour or two we are picked up by a big truck. There are already four men sitting on the load, and they help make us comfortable. This is a much superior ride to the one of the day before. We are high up with excellent views all around. It is warm, and the men, grown men, sing in harmony. They begin in a desultory fashion as though from boredom, but on seeing Trish so interested and enthusiastic they warm to the task and go through their whole repertoire. We then do our bit on my harmonica. It is more of a joy-ride than an essay in serious travel. Basothos certainly have a talent for making a hard life tolerable.

Close to Mokhotlong we go by the junction with the road to Sani Pass.

There is a huge notice board warning travellers of the roughness and isolation of the road, and the need to take adequate supplies. Then, about midday, we reach the town that has figured so largely in my imagination.

It is a sprawling, ill-planned – or unplanned – collection of buildings in a broad landscape of bare hill country. There is a post office, a Fraser's, one or two other small supermarkets, and an airport. The place is full of horses. It could be a town in an old western. We see a man in a smart uniform with an arm band saying Stock Theft Officer. We buy provisions and go to the airport. There is a plane scheduled for this afternoon, but it has been cancelled. When can we fly to Maseru, we ask. Come here tomorrow at 0900, the man says, and writes down our names on a list.

We set about finding Mrs. Alina Matubajuba, who once invited me to visit her in Mokhotlong, little thinking, no doubt, that I would actually do so. We eat cheese and biscuits and apples under a tree, receiving friendly comments from all passers by. Inquiries about Mrs. Alina are hampered by language difficulties but we gather from some giggling schoolgirls that she is not now at the school but having a baby at her home village. After a good deal of traipsing around the town we plod off to the mission school where we find the priest in charge, an Anglican from Qachas Nek. He invites us into a comfortably furnished room where his wife serves us with tea. The Reverend Isaiah Seitlheko is a small portly man with a simple faith and a firm grasp of the Christian way of life. His duty, he says, is to help and succour people. His house is therefore at the disposal of travellers. It is not his, he just has the good fortune to live in it. He has fifteen 'outstations' to minister to and needs a horse to get to them. The horses belonging to the mission died last winter of starvation and he is at present without any. He has three daughters whose schooling will cost him dear. We ask if we can camp. Yes, he says, but why don't we use his sitting room. After some demur we accept this kind offer. We cook outside on the stoop, the family showing much interest in our tiny meths stove, which is simply the burner part of a Trangia. The house is wired for electricity but there is as yet no supply. There is however a flushing lavatory. The family retires early and so do we, by candlelight on the floor of the sitting room.

We turn up at the airport (the smart little building donated by the German government in an aid package) as requested at nine o'clock and pay our sixty-seven Rands (about £12), but it is one in the afternoon before we actually fly. This long pointless wait we take with surprising equanimity. Perhaps we are becoming Africanised. We sit and look at the walls. We read the timetables, pure fiction. We watch the handful of other passengers. We doze a little. We wander about outside where it's warm in the sun and eventually we brew tea on the stoop and have a simple lunch. We are oddly content. If the plane fails to come we can sleep at the mission again and take the Sunday bus.

The Twin Otter arrives. It holds about a dozen passengers and the two pilots are visible through an archway. It is the best sixty-seven Rands worth imaginable. We fly over the great tawny mountains drained by the Orange and its tributaries, a network of deeply incised gorges and canyons. The cultivation on slopes and ledges makes patterns that viewed from the air amount to high art. Tiny, remote settlements are laid out beneath us with their packhorse trails winding about the hills. The vast mountain region of the Malutis slowly unfolds, a wide drove road straggling across the highest uplands. The mountains then become more dramatic and we are sailing over great basalt cliffs and peaks which drop away down the western scarps with here and there a trail zigzagging up to a col, and then finally we are over the mesa country with its yellow sandstone cliffs and a multitude of villages and mealie fields.

To our surprise we come to earth at Leribe though there was no mention of it on the timetable. This is close to home for us, but we cannot resist the pleasure of a further flight to Maseru, this time over familiar countryside where I recognise many features.

In Maseru, the capital, we see white people in the streets. They look rather strange and ill formed and out of place compared with blacks.

Romantic sounding places generally fail to live up to their promise. Look at Stornoway. For most of my life Stornoway somehow put me in mind of the ballad of Sir Patrick Spens:

To Noroway, to Noroway to Noroway o'er the faem
The king's daughter of Noroway tis thou must bring her hame.

But when I at last went there and saw the pupils of the grammar school all queueing up for fish and chips at their dinner hour Stornoway seemed no different from Penrith or Wigan.

So I suppose Mokhotlong has lost some of its mystery, but I still think of it with affection. Lesotho is one of the poorest countries in the world, and the Mokhotlong region must be about the poorest part of Lesotho, but it is rich in horses, it has sparkling mountain air, and it lies at the end of that long, empty road. I'm glad we went there.

HA CHARLIE

It is hot. We set off up the dirt road, stirring the yellow dust. We cross a creek of pale brown water, traverse some bare slabs of yellow sandstone and take a path across a tract of mealie-fields. The maize grows six feet high, a rich green. It grows out of red earth, and the trail we follow is the colour of burnt sienna.

We cross another creek, the water a mere wet stain on extensive slabs of waterworn sandstone, and ascend into a pretty village of round thatched houses. "Lumela ntate" and "lumela 'me" we say to the locals. "Eh, bontate" they reply, raising a courteous hand. "Good morny ow are you give me some sweets" say the children, more to display their superior education than in expectation of any reward.

We enter a steep-sided and stony valley, traversing a boulder-strewn slope. We lose the path and follow animal tracks through a zone of bushes, our rucksacks rasping their way through the branches. A stream enters our valley from the left. We descend to it, toil up the other side, climb with some difficulty through a horizontal band of sandstone and gain a small area of cultivation on a sloping ledge of the mountainside. The little valley narrows. The river bed is a chaos of boulders the size of the Bowderstone and overgrown with bushes and trees. The sides steepen into big rock walls. We push on until our little path ends under an immense curving overhang. The yellow sandstone walls soar up over our heads in a smooth curve. We are in a kind of cave, with a flat earth floor and a roof a hundred feet high. At two points streams cascade from above, to continue down the hidden and rocky bed of the valley.

We settle in, choose our several sleeping places, cook the evening meal on Trangias, boil water from the waterfalls. Darkness falls fairly rapidly here. Bats sew their aerial patterns above us. We make a fire and gaze at the shifting colours in the embers. Five of us are white, seven Basuto, Zulu or Bantu, one 'Cape-Coloured', though this last is as dark as any of the blacks. Ages range from twenty to forty, but several have never slept out before.

The night passes, not so much in sleep, as far as I am concerned, as in something almost better, a delicious awareness of comfort and ease, and of how much more satisfactory it is to be lying in a sleeping bag than walking with a pack on.

We are up at five thirty, away before seven.

A rocky scramble takes us into the world above the cave. Up here is a large sprawling village, Lipetu, on a high broad col. We find the water supply, a covered spring, carefully protected against cattle. You dip in under the little roof with a dish and patiently fill whatever receptacle you have. It is a daily chore for women and girls, who carry large buckets and drums away on their heads. When a baby girl is born the village women notify the father by throwing water all over him. For a boy they beat him with sticks.

For a mile or two our way lies across a broad upland. Ahead we see a big valley, with tributary valleys coming down from a range of jagged mountains, the Malutis, rising to over 10,000 feet. We descend steeply into the main valley, our road having at this point deteriorated owing to erosion into a complex 'donga', like a miniature Grand Canyon. At the bottom, there is an attractive river with grassy banks and big shapely willow trees. By now it is raining hard with thunder and lightning, and we are glad to take refuge in the back of another cave or overhang. At this point it emerges that Samson, a genial but dreamy twenty year old, has omitted to bring his waterproof, and is now looking stoical and resigned in a totally wet T-shirt. He has, however, brought a large radio with twin speakers. We arrange a groundsheet over his shoulders. Since the rain has moderated from stair-rods to steady downpour, we boulder-hop across the river, walk up smooth slabs of bare rock, and pick up another red-and-yellow trail up the Menyameng valley. The hills are now shrouded in mist, the thunder has moved away, but quiet, persistent, Lake District-style rain appears to be setting in. We pass a school, tin-roofed, with a row of narrow, corrugated iron privies ranged alongside, at decent intervals from one another. The children swarm about, wrapped in pieces of blanket (the Basuto raincoat) indifferent to the rain.

About midday we come to a village, Ha Boranta, where a rondavel is under construction. The round thatched roof is complete, but it is supported only on a ring of vertical poles. The stone, mud or wattle walls have yet to be built. We ask if we can shelter under it to eat our lunch. We get out a Trangia and brew tea. As we have one or two Sesotho speakers in the group we are able to converse amiably with the villagers. They show much interest in me and concern for my well being, since a white beard is to them indicative of extreme and venerable old age. Interspersed with the mealies there is a great deal of 'daka' (marihuana) grown, and indeed towards the heads of these mountain valleys there are fields sown with nothing else. We make a joking reference to this and within seconds sprigs of the precious weed are produced for us. These local people are courteous, quite formal in some ways, but always ready for a laugh.

We plod on. The rain abates. Our intention is to bivouac under waterproof sheets somewhere in the vicinity of Ha Charlie, a highland hamlet now visible high above on the top of a truncated spur. There are some flat and sheltered places in the valley bottom, but it seems a good idea to make some of the height towards the pass we must attain tomorrow. The rain seems to be easing, and there is bound to be water at Ha Charlie.

We strike up the steep and muddy path. Unfortunately as we approach the village the rain comes on again very heavily, the stair-rods now horizontal in a rising wind. Ha Charlie, we find, has few amenities and these do not include flat or sheltered ground. In fact the village seems to have been situated with a view to catching every breeze that blows. On the very crest of the spur is a large walled kraal, which would make a tolerable campsite except that its floor is a swamp of black mud and cowdung. We huddle in the porch of a rondavel while one of our number seeks out the Chief. The Chief when he appears is wearing a khaki greatcoat buttoned askew, and has an umbrella and wellingtons. We ask his permission to bivouac somewhere near the village and seek his advice as to a possible site. He and I go and stare disconsolately at the hummocky ground in the lee of the cattle kraal. Rather than provide shelter the wall seems merely to create turbulence in the airstream that sweeps powerfully over the spur.

By this time the group have seeped gradually into the dim interior of the rondavel. In there it smells deliciously dry, with the clean fragrance of old woodsmoke. It has a neat mud floor washed with cowdung. Near the centre is a circular depression about two feet six across and three inches deep, the fireplace. There is no chimney but one can see a small chink of daylight in the apex of the thatched roof. There is a double bed with brass knobs, a cheap formica-topped table, a good-looking but rickety dining chair, and two donkey skins crudely cured and as stiff as boards. There are two eighteen-inch square windows, one blocked up, the other with four little panes of yellowing glass.

I will not dwell on the delicate moves that bring the Chief to offer us the use of the rondavel, first to cook in, and then to occupy for the night. Perhaps they are too shaming, too much like begging. But I have in mind Samson without a raincoat, and our meagre supply of cord for constructing bivouacs, and the total inexperience of most of the group. At all events the Trangias are soon in operation and hot drinks and soup and supper prepared. Our kind hosts bring in a shovelful of burning wood-coals and a quantity of firewood, a very generous gesture in a country where fuel is at a premium. We sit round the cheerful blaze, wheezing gently in the smoke, and are visited in relays by everyone in the village. We feel immensely snug and weatherproof, but as the smoke gradually thickens from the roof down we are forced lower and lower, eyes smarting, towards the ground. I recall from forty years ago a cold wet day at the Refuge de Tuqueroy in the Pyrenees when with a wood fire burning the only breathable air in that wretched hut was in a layer six inches above the floor.

Before we turn in we have to take out all the ash and embers of the fire as every inch of floor space is needed for sleeping. Our rucksacks alone fill half the rondavel. At last we are all settled in and the last to lie down is the unfortunate villager who has to share his bed with one of our party. He stands on the bed, arranges a blanket round his waist, wraps his outdoor blanket round his shoulders, and as he lies down takes off his hat and hangs it on one of the brass knobs.

I am near the open door. The smell of rain is in my nostrils. All night there is something crawling delicately about my person, never biting or stinging, just exploring. My questing hand fails to locate it. Live and let live, I finally say to myself, and concentrate on the simple pleasure of being in the dry.

In the morning the rain stops long enough for us to breakfast outside. We sweep out the hut, shake the donkey skins, leave everything spick and span. Before we depart the rain comes on again but we set off uphill into the mist on a good though precipitous path.

We reach the col. Nothing could be less inviting than the steep mountainside running with water that rises to our left. But to go down into the next valley would involve us in miles of extra walking. We turn left, uphill, into unknown terrain. A path of sorts traverses the side of the ridge, much of it across steep slabs cascading with water. Each time it debouches on to a small grassy col it is difficult to know where to look for the continuation. There are subsidiary ridges running off to the side and we are anxious not to stray on to one of them. Samson, wrapped in his ground-sheet, has more reason than most to want to get a move on, and he steps confidently out in front without the faintest idea where he is leading us. This in the end is such a distraction that I compel him to get in the middle of the group and stay there.

In a mist times and distances become distorted. We seem to spend hours and hours threading dubious paths with many an anxious consultation of the compass, but eventually that moment arrives when the valleys below begin to swim vaguely and strangely into our ken, and then show sharp and clear as one drops below cloud level. We are still on the right ridge. A world of mesas and sandstone scarps lies below us. The clouds disperse. The sun comes out, extravagantly hot. The Mountain Kingdom of Lesotho, which boasts the highest low point of any country in the world, presents once more its colour, its pastoral beauty and its rugged charm. All is forgiven. We spend a long beautiful evening, bright and sunny, and sleep under another sandstone overhang in a pretty spot full of the scent of pines and eucalyptus. Water is half a mile away but there are many willing to fetch it, We make another camp fire. We are nearly home.

Before the group disperses everyone subscribes a couple of rand for a present for Ha Charlie. Next time in town we buy candles, matches and other household goods, and Tony rides out on horseback to give them to the Chief. The Chief reciprocates with a live chicken.

OF HORSES AND HILLS

After a lifetime of rock-climbing what struck me when I first got on a horse was the sensation of being surprisingly high above the ground on footholds that moved and were as slippery as wet limestone.

I had much to learn about horses. For one thing they were not like cars or motorcycles, to be jumped on to and driven off at full throttle at a moment's notice. They required far more attention than you ever saw them get in a cowboy film. They were also sentient beings with minds of their own; they could tell right away whether you knew anything about horses or not. At one end they could bite and at the other they could kick; in some ways it was safer to be on them than round them. I saw the point of the Chinese soldier's ancient proverb: Never stand in front of a cannon, behind a horse, or anywhere near your commanding officer.

The horses of Lesotho were derived from Arab and Barb stock imported to South Africa from Java in 1653. They were rustled into Lesotho – Basutoland as it then was – in the early nineteenth century and developed into a breed of tough, enduring ponies accustomed to the harsh terrain of the mountains. They were bought up in their thousands during the Boer wars.

So here we are in a cavalcade of twenty-five horses heading for the Maluti Mountains on what we have rather grandiloquently called the Southern Cross Expedition, a high country safari for a group of American millionaires who have pledged to put money into the Lesotho Outward Bound School. By now I have overcome my fear of horses to the point of being quite fond of them and their idiosyncratic behaviour, and am here as a horse-safari instructor, no less.

Within a mile from leaving the School we are in country inaccessible to vehicles. It is mesa country, dotted with villages. The road, much scoured by erosion, and in many places just bare rock, is yellow or red, as are the cliffs and scarps of the mesas. Eucalyptus trees straggle along the watercourses, and cultivable land is mostly under maize and millet, with occasional marijuana. The red of the rock and the green of the corn, complementary colours, are lit by bright sunlight and make a beautiful landscape. After we have passed through Ha Thaba Tsalepe, to the amazement of the villagers, our way becomes steep and rocky and we dismount and lead the horses over the most difficult sections. They are unshod and will have much stony ground to cover in the next ten days.

Our first night's camp is to be at Lipetu, a big upland village, the last of any size before we get into the bare mountains. We enter it, those that can, at a fast canter to impress the locals, for whom horses and horsemanship are status symbols. We are expected, and our arrival is the occasion for a feast and a celebration. Quantities of beer and wine have been brought up separately, and more people than one could believe possible spring out of the ground, including crowds of delighted children. We unload, hobble the horses and put up our tents.

Local men dressed up in extravagant coloured finery perform traditional dances with a great deal of aggressive stamping and posturing and clashing of cymbals. The women have a quite different kind of dancing. They remain seated in rows on the ground, with rhythmic swaying and twisting of hands, arms, bosoms and shoulders. It is graceful and sedately erotic. One of the revellers thrusts a slightly soggy marijuana cigarette at me and I take a puff or two to show willing, though all I get from it is some faint anxiety about the risk of infection. When there is nothing left to eat or drink the evening comes to an end, and we turn in.

The euphoria of this start to our trip comes to an abrupt end with a change of weather. During the night our camp is battered by a storm of wind and rain with spectacular thunder and lightning, and in the morning the prospect of getting out into the rain to cook breakfast and tackle the lengthy business of catching the horses, loading them up and getting ready for departure is daunting. We wisely decide to wait and give the rain a chance to stop. Some of our party are entirely unused to camping except in huge R.V.s (recreational vehicles) and several sleeping bags are wet through. The heavy rain does at length go off but the day remains damp and dreary and it takes us three hours to get ready to move.

The five pack horses account for much of this. Loading a pack horse is not a matter of slinging a few boxes and bags over its back. The ropework required to produce a well-balanced load that will stay put all day is a work of art. In addition, getting one's own horse ready is no small task. You have to catch it, put a halter on its tossing head, take its hobbles off, brush it down, place saddlecloth and saddle, haul taut on the girth, get the bit between its big gnashing yellow teeth, and make fast saddlebags and kit bag. You are then supposed to pick up its feet and check them for stones in the soft part of the hoof.

When we do get started we find that the tracks have become slippery with mud and the horses slide and sit on their haunches in an alarming manner. One falls down altogether and the lady riding it is saved from having her leg crushed only because her kit bag takes most of the weight. After a few miles we have a steep eroded descent to make, and lead the horses down it. They are good at picking their way down difficult ground, and it is best to give them their head. They are also much influenced by their fellows, and if one bold spirit will tackle an awkward descent, the others will follow. We reach a river valley and stop under a huge overhang to dry out.

It is a lovely spot, the river overhung by big weeping willows. Two or three youths in Lesotho blankets appear from nowhere. They hold the horses' heads and make themselves generally useful collecting firewood. There is good grazing, security from further rain under the overhang, and the opportunity for the more inept campers to get their sleeping bags dry. We decide to stay for the night.

Next morning we make a good start in fine weather and after riding up a valley to its head, trying to keep the pack horses from getting into the maize crops, begin a steep and stony ascent into the upland world of the Maluti Mountains. Crossing the Menyameng Pass we camp at about nine thousand feet in a wide hollow with good grass and a small tarn with a stream running from it. It is an attractive place, austere and clean. The night is freezing cold, but we find enough dried dung to make a fire. We keep a watch through the night, one hour each, partly to keep the horses from straying too far – for even hobbled they can cover quite a distance, hopping like kangaroos – and partly in case of theft. These hills are grazed by goats tended by herd boys who lead an astonishingly spartan existence and are not above a bit of rustling.

There is a moon, and on watch there is something magical about being the only one awake in a sleeping camp in such a remote corner of the mountains. One is supposed to count the horses before reporting all well to one's relief, a chore honoured by some more in the breach than in the observance. The man who has the overall responsibility for the horses is Hlalele, and he takes his job so seriously that he is apt to prowl about at any time of the night, checking. He cannot read or write or speak English, but among horses he is the most highly educated of us all, by far.

My horse, Nandi, a good-looking light chestnut mare from the Orange Free State, has been very strong climbing the hills, but next day, now that we are in rockier and steeper places, she becomes nervous and at one point, on a slabby descent beside a waterfall, she refuses altogether. By rearranging her load we manage to get her moving again and some time later I change horses with Wendy Pieh, our leader, for an hour or two. Her little mare drifts effortlessly over the roughest ground in a smooth uninterrupted flow of movement, in total contrast to poor Nandi's jerky and stumbling progress.

Though every day we have a lengthy midday stop to let the horses graze and rest, today we are in the saddle for many hours, and finish by making a long, steep and winding descent into the upper valley of the Bokong River, a tributary of the Senqu, or Orange. There is a tiny settlement here, lost and isolated in the heart of the mountains. The one family has a few goats and a small area under maize. Two youths appear clad in blankets, loin cloths, woolly hats and wellies. They wear sporrans adorned with row after row of safety pins, and carry decorated sticks, the weapon of choice in this country.

We have been delayed so much by the storm at Lipetu it now seems unlikely that we can stick to the planned itinerary and reach the large stash of food that has been cached in a distant valley. By my modest standards we still have plenty to eat, but this is a view not shared by the American millionaires, who see starvation staring them in the face. We are camped in a charming level area of greensward beside a clean highland river rather like the upper Tweed, and all these people can think of is food. Josh Miner and I do something to allay their fears by fishing the river using spinners, and catching twenty-five innocent trout. It seems that the people living here are unaware of this source of food, and we teach the two lads the rudiments of angling. The question of the cache of extra food is still anxiously debated, however, and we finally decide to have Qamako and Peter Goth take the pack horses to pick it up, while the main party have a

rest day and then take a shorter route over the high ground to a rendezvous. The foraging party will leave a message at the summit of a pass,
reporting their progress.

The night is clear, frosty and bright with moonlight, and we are drenched
with dew. One of our night watchmen allows a couple of the horses to get
into the mealie field but we mollify the farmer next day by making
generous reparations in South African rand. To have a day of rest in this
delectable spot is worth coming a long way for. Qamako and Goth have left
early in the morning with their string of pack horses tied tail to halter in
single file, and the rest of us devote the day to reading and writing, exploring the locality, snoozing and chatting. Most of the party are elderly, though
no one, I find out, is quite as old as I. Most have been on a horse before but
only two are experienced riders. Three or four have never camped in a
lightweight tent or slept on the ground. Most of the group are quite unused
to mountain walking and could not have got so far into the heart of the hills
except on horseback, yet any fit back-packer could have kept up with us on
these travels. The couple who find the life a complete change from anything they have ever done are Bob and Bitsy Boozer, from Alabama.
Everything alarms them, the altitude, the steep terrain, the temperature
changes, the starkness of the landscape and the behaviour of the horses.
They see this as a serious expedition and not just a holiday excursion, and
considering that we are getting into country that none of us knows, I
suppose they are not entirely wrong.

The rest day does us good, and it is remarkable how much emergency
food has come to light from the personal saddlebags of the group. Crossing
the Bokong River provides a little excitement. After a lifetime of watching
cowboys splash their way through rivers in movies, I find myself at last
doing the same. Our way now takes us along a narrow path across a precipitous mountainside, where Mampoki, the tall, lanky, anorexic looking
young mare, our remaining pack horse, loses her footing and slides downhill until stopped by a stunted tree. She lies there quietly, her eyes conveying the message: You got me into this; you get me out. We dismount, climb
down, unload her pack and pass it up from hand to hand to the path. Hlalele
puts a rope around her neck to supplement the head collar. She flails the
ground with her long ungainly legs, sending scree and turf bounding down
the hillside. I think it is only through Hlalele's special relationship with the
equine world that she is finally coaxed back on to the track.

By midday we reach the high bare pass where the foraging party said
they would leave a message. Half a mile up the hillside is a rocky knoll
with a round stone hut on it. I go up to it and see that it is a partly thatched

hovel recently occupied by a herd boy, judging by the bent aluminium mug and piece of rag lying on a heap of straw. Outside under a stone is a scrap of paper with the message that all has gone well and they hope to find us on the track that crosses the watershed ridge further north.

We are now committed to finding our way along the summit crest of the Malutis. It is craggy country, but not at all narrow or precipitous, and route finding should be easy as all we need to do is follow the highest ground. Once up onto the heights it is rather like the top of the Glyders in Wales, a chaos of frost-cracked rocks. We are on top of our world, with great empty spaces all around, a high, stony desert. Various members of the group feel that their fate hangs upon our finding the foraging party, but I am not much concerned on this score, for I know that we can make it out of the hills before we are seriously short of food. It is quite inspiring to be up here on horseback at over ten thousand feet and I feel a good deal of affection for the horses, in spite of all the work they give us.

In this country one can see for miles, and before we have actually reached the track that will ultimately take us to White Man's Pass, we spot the baggage train. We meet exactly as planned and there is much rejoicing. The pack horses have behaved very well tied tail to head, and the foragers have enjoyed their adventure. We camp at the first likely spot and feast upon the fat of the land.

Next day we follow the majestic sweep of the mountains over another col and on to a beautiful spot where a river runs over great slabs of clean basalt in a series of delightful shallow falls, before turning a corner and dropping down into a deep valley. A tributary stream has good drinking places for the horses. We spend two nights here. Some of the party climb surrounding hills but I am content to sit by the plashing water enjoying the smooth waterworn rock and absorbing the atmosphere of this high, lean, empty landscape knowing that tomorrow we must go down and down and down into the world of men.

In the morning the hills are shrouded in mist but we have no difficulty in making our way up to Lekahalo La Makooa, or White Man's Pass. By the time we reach it the sun has burnt through the cloud and we look down a bare rocky defile. We now have to descend a precipitous escarpment which plunges four thousand feet to the lower valleys. In the second Boer War prisoners were employed to build a road up the escarpment in an impressive series of zigzags and hairpin bends. It now lies in ruins, but still affords a feasible way down. It is the roughest and stoniest place we have yet encountered, little better than a scree slope in places and covered throughout in sharp loose slabs of rock like a crazy staircase in the last stages of dilapidation. We lead the horses down and the going is painfully slow. Some horses keep refusing, causing traffic jams. Some stray off the road but soon find themselves on ground too steep to negotiate. The sharp stones damage the hooves and fetlocks and my poor Nandi and one or two others leave flecks of blood on the track. Back-packing, I have descended this road in well under two hours. It takes us five.

When at last we reach the foot of the pass we stop for a long rest, letting the horses graze. We are back in civilisation, or Lesotho's version of it, surrounded by local women and children and close to the big new road that is being built across the mountains to service the construction of the dam on the Orange River, which the government has been contemplating for twenty years and has now given the go-ahead to. The morale of our party, which was at rock bottom during the descent, swings suddenly up to euphoria, and Charlie Stetson, the leader of the Americans and the man who promoted the trip, takes Polaroid pictures for the local women and leads the children in comic songs.

But we still have far to go to reach our final campsite, which is in Hlalele's village, Ha Mohloane, and as our way is along the edge of the new road, we have to endure the noisy passage of heavy trucks travelling to and from the barrage. It is a dismal change from the silence of the mountains. I and several others walk in order to spare our horses which are footsore and lame. The miles go slowly by, and darkness falls.

At about this point Stetson loses his temper and declares that he is taking over the leadership of the group from Wendy Pieh and Peter Goth. It is with complete astonishment that I see this tall, handsome sixty year old millionaire throwing a tantrum like a spoilt child. We have no option but to plod on, and when at last we reach Hlalele's home, and his delightful daughters bring us water from the spring, and his friends undertake to care for the horses during the night, we make soup for the party but most of them want only to get into their tents and sleep.

We are now half a day's ride from home and thankfully leave the new road, taking byways across country. I ride Mokorotlo, a sway-backed ugly little pack horse, as tough as any mule and quite unaffected by all the hard going of the last ten days. Nandi trails along beside us on a leading rope, carrying nothing. This countryside with its yellow roads, its mealie fields, its fine sandstone crags and its hamlets of thatched rondavels, is the landscape that inspired Tolkien's *The Hobbit*. The horses know they are going home, and they find enough energy at the end to sweep into the grounds of the school at a triumphal canter.

The plan is to drive immediately to Maseru, the capital, stay the night in the Grand Hotel, and next day attend a reception at the royal palace, certificates commemorating the trip being awarded by King Moshoeshoe II. Unfortunately, a military coup has caused His Majesty to flee to Oxford, and the reception is now to be held by the Queen at the private family palace some miles out of the city.

At midday we assemble there, scarcely recognisable – especially the women – in our best clothes, and are graciously received by the Queen, large, gorgeously attired and motherly, and by the Prince, an old boy of Ampleforth School in Yorkshire. We are offered drinks and circulate in cocktail party fashion.

When we get to the formalities each of the visiting Americans receives an appreciation spoken by one or other of the staff members of the expedition, before accepting the award of an Outward Bound badge from the Prince. Hlalele, who speaks no English, is not exempt from this, and his speech is translated by Qamako. His comments are warm and touching, spoken from the heart. It has been a new experience for him, and at the hotel he entered a lift for the first time in his life. My encomium is for Bob and Bitsy Boozer, for whom it has been an ordeal but also the adventure of a lifetime. Bitsy afterwards asks me if I can give her a copy of what I have said. We then proceed to a traditional Lesotho meal with grilled steak, mealie paste, potatoes, yams, roast chickens and various sweetmeats and puddings. I am drinking a cup of the local beer made from fermented millet when the Queen comes up to me, takes the cup from my hand and drinks some herself. "No, no" she says. "It is not good. I will get you some better." And she does. It is not every day that I drink from the same cup as a Queen.

This reception is a very enjoyable occasion and we are treated with great courtesy and naturalness. We come away with a good opinion of the Mountain Kingdom of Lesotho.

Our American guests depart. Charlie Stetson has resumed his confident hail-fellow-well-met demeanour but has made no apology for his outburst under stress. Before leaving he gives me a little book he has written and had published, *Ten Ways to Christian Love*.

Looking back on the trip I have to say that it was more an exercise in horse management and people management than in mountain travel, but by using horses we entered into the spirit of the mountain life of the region. The horses became a part of the scenery, and getting to know them was an added enrichment to our experience of the hills.

IDYLLIC HILLS

To choose a favourite mountain, a favourite coastline and a favourite view, and then hold forth about them as inclination dictates, seems at first an easy and agreeable task, verging on the self-indulgent. But on getting down to it, I find I do not really have any favourites. I love them all. It is as bad as being asked who is the most beautiful woman in the world. Though Diana Rigg springs immediately to mind, to present the golden apple to her is to do a grave injustice to countless others. Especially Jenny Agutter. For with mountains, as with members of the opposite sex, though custom can never stale their infinite variety, at the same time, in a way they are all pretty much the same.

Mountains in Britain are mostly the remnants of ancient plateaux, and consequently vary comparatively little in height. Since they have all been glaciated, they exhibit much the same features, coombes, tarns, ridges, truncated spurs and so on. Here and there a crag has obstinately withstood the forces of denudation. They have rather bald heads, and their natural vegetation has been considerably impoverished by sheep or deer, or by conifer plantations. Their fastnesses are much defiled by wire fences, walls and gates. They have a poor sunshine record and higher-than-average rainfall. Yet they still fill us with a sense of the sublime and cause us to go back and back to them.

In the past they were seen merely as chaotic bits of the earth's surface which Nature had not yet seen fit to tidy up, but now they have become a stage and backdrop for our personal inner dreams, be they tragedies, comedies or romance. They are the raw material for our castles in Spain. And since it generally takes two to make an idyll, for me the term 'idyllic hills' fuels my imagination with pleasant recollections, based more upon desire than upon fulfilment I daresay, of the enjoyment of female society in the most attractive of all settings. The pastoral dream of sporting with Amaryllis in the shade is nowhere more potent than in the mountains, simple and austere though they are.

But I should strive to focus my attention on the hills themselves.

There is a mountain, however, that does stand out on its own and has made a special impact upon my imagination. It is not even a Munro, which shows how undiscriminating the Munro list is and provides me with a good reason, besides my dislike of exertion, for not embarking upon the task of ticking them all off. I refer to Suilven. The least inanimate of all Scottish mountains, it lies like some forgotten Titan, hunched up and brooding, all on its own in the middle of a great glacial peneplain. From one end it appears as an elegant spire, from the other as a huge round-shouldered hump. From the sides it is seen to be a ridge, with two dissimilar summits and a high bealach between.

I first came to it from Stac Pollaidh. We made our way across the watery moors and pitched our tent by some nameless lochan. There was a grassy level, a clean curving little strand, limpid water, a birch tree. Not a breath of wind, and no midges either. Idyllic. We ate. We lay naked in the sun, idled, slept a little. But as the afternoon turned into a long evening, perfect, with the sky like a duck-egg, we began to be troubled by that common weakness which has made the human race such a menace on the face of the earth – the urge to get up and do something. Suilven lay alongside like a lion couchant. So we set off, taking nothing with us, to climb it. There was a steep staircase up to the bealach. Our Ordnance map showed a spot height at the western end, while the eastern summit was just a mass of hachuring, denoting crags, with no spot height given We went therefore on to the western summit but seeing the other was manifestly higher, we retraced our steps and tackled it. We soon came to a *mauvais pas* and, while not altogether dismissing it, tried first to find an easier way round to the left. Our way led out on to the northern flank. We found ourselves on one of the highest of many horizontal ledges which ran across that side of the peak. They were narrow ledges, separated by rocky walls and extending down and down in a beautiful curve like an immensely steep ski-jump until they flattened out on the broad plain below. The evening was by this time advanced enough for this plain to take on a rather remote and dream-like appearance. We proceeded along the ledge until it narrowed to nothing. Three feet further on it started again. I began to feel the onset of heavy breathing as I stepped across, and a certain superstitious dread arising from being without a rope, but the ledge broadened thereafter and we got round and on to the summit, and then down the east side and back to the camp in the fading light. The yellow glow of our little fire as we brewed up showed it was darker than we thought .

On a later occasion, by contrast, we approached it from the north and once again I did not escape without a slight twinge of alarm, for this time it was violently windy and one felt one could well be blown off the ridge. Only a very short distance above us was the cloud base, and the wind seemed to be rushing furiously through the narrow gap between mountain top and cloud. By going a short way down the far side of the western summit, however, we spilled the wind and lay in comfort on the sward, looking out to sea and training binoculars on the ships in Lochinver harbour. It was like gazing out from the observation deck of the Graf Zeppelin. The isolation of Suilven from its neighbours creates the impression on its big flat western summit of a grassland floating in midair, and the landscape below looks like the Canadian Shield as seen from a plane.

It is a wonderful place.

Once as a boy I was in a railway carriage, and a woman was saying to her neighbour, "But I wouldn't like to live up there, round Ambleside. I should feel too hemmed in." I stared at her in hostile astonishment. How could anyone be so debased in her values as that. But now I would have considerably more tolerance for her point of view, and when choosing a coastline I am inclined not to select a rocky headland with pounding surf, or one of those beautiful inlets bright with lichens and sea-pinks in the Highlands and Islands, but rather a place where the thing to wonder at is the flatness. There are many such: the Solway, Morecambe Bay, the Wash, the Sands of Dee and Hilbre Island. The rising tide will send sheets of water sweeping silently over vast acres of sand, mudflats or saltings, making new shapes as it fills barely perceptible hollows. These places all have a wonderful, gleaming horizontality. One that stays particularly in my memory is the coast at Lindisfarne. I came to it once while ranging about the north of England on a new motor cycle. The road ended abruptly on the coast itself, Nowadays there is a concrete tidal causeway, but at that time there was nothing but a long perspective of posts leading across the sands to the island a mile or so off shore. A saltwater channel had first to be crossed, and a rusty taxi which had been waiting for the water level to drop now plunged into it, emerged dripping the other side, and headed for the island. Reluctant to risk my bike in the salt water I left it at a railway station, waded the channel and continued barefoot over the sands. At intervals along the line of posts there were little refuges on poles, with ladders up to them in case one got caught by the tide. On the island were fishermen's huts made of upturned boats, like Pegotty's house, and a pretty village with a little castle, an abbey and a pub. Once the tide was up there was little danger of a visit from the police and so closing time was determined more by the phases of the moon than by local bye-laws. Having missed the low water I spent the night on a sofa in the front room of the pub.

As for my choice of view it again favours breadth and openness. It is the view you get towards the end of the Ennerdale horseshoe as you descend the long, easy ridge from Haycock and Little Gowder Crag. A broad sweep of fells lies before you, but the whole landscape is dropping away seaward and gives a remarkable sense of space and light, with the

Isle of Man, often with a small cloud sitting over Snaefell, riding surprisingly high up in what one keeps assuming is sky, but which is in fact the Irish Sea. After the steep and crowded hills of central Lakeland, this is an inspiring change of scene.

These then are my 'favourites'. But they are not the only ones, and some of the places that flash upon my inward eye are so simple and unremarkable and personal that they would hardly be suitable for writing about, yet they persist in the memory as bright and significant images even after many years.

(One of a series entitled 'Idyllic Hills' featured by *Climber & Rambler*.)

A NORTHERN RIVER

One weekend, during a heat wave, my friend George Spenceley invited me to accompany him to Ambleside where he was to give a lecture. I agreed, but said since it was so hot why not spend the weekend on the water. I could bring my canoe.

We launched at Brathay and paddled down to Windermere in a beautiful sunset. We landed at a little point, brewed up on a campfire and sat watching the darkness creep over the water as we ate our supper and drank a bottle of wine. Next day we paddled down the lake, which was pleasant enough, but crowded with power boats and water skiers. One or two people, trying to be funny, said, "How!" to us as we passed.

"Why don't we go to some quieter waters?" we said, and that is what started us planning our Canadian river trip.

As a small boy, the adventure stories of R.M. Ballantyne had filled me with romantic notions of the North West Territories. Nick Nichels, in his book *Canoe Canada*, which we now consulted, wrote:

'Of all Canada's canoeing regions, none has greater appeal than the North West Territories. Much of the appeal is based on the colourful journals of the explorers, and the mystique of far off wilderness places. In reality, none but very experienced canoeists should actually tackle the waterways of this land. Such experts must possess great stamina, high courage to keep moving at all physical costs, and a spirit of determination to win. All equipment must be the best available, from special tents to prepared foods and scuba wet-suits ... There is no second guessing after a start is made and very often there are slim chances of rescue in the event of emergencies. Only the best canoeist will consider travel in the North West Territories and it would be irresponsible to suggest otherwise.'

Strong words, these, we thought, but with the natural arrogance of mountaineers the world over we assumed they were meant for ordinary tourists and not for the likes of us. We decided on the river Thelon (from the Inuit Teh-lon-deze, or Fish River) because it ended at Qamanittuaq on Baker Lake, from which it was possible to get a flight out. So that George would not start the trip as a complete novice, we arranged a half-day's paddling on the Oxford canal, and a further couple of hours on the river Cherwell.

In July we met in Yellowknife. I flew in via Winnipeg and Port Churchill and found George already there; he had come by bus from Edmonton bringing with him food for five weeks. Our plan nearly foundered because of the cost of chartering a light aircraft, but by an extraordinary stroke of luck we fell in with a Canadian who supervised the season's.flying for forest fires. He provided us with a free flight in a Beaver to Hanbury Lake. Weeks earlier we had arranged canoe hire through the Hudson Bay Company's U-paddle service. You could pick up a canoe at any Hudson Bay post and return it at any other. The charge was $70 a week.

So, with our seventeen-foot aluminium Grumman canoe lashed above one float of the aeroplane we rose into the air over Great Slave Lake and flew east. Below us we saw the country through which we were to thread our way, an illimitable maze of lakes and rivers, laced with sandy eskers twisting their way into the distance like snakes. It was a daunting sight. We touched down at Snowdrift and topped up the fuel tanks, pumping the petrol from forty-five gallon drums with a hand pump. Indian children stared at us with round eyes, ready to dart for cover. I found it hard to believe that this young pilot – he looked about eighteen – knew where he was going in such a confusion of lakes, but we eventually alighted in the middle of one of them and he said,

"Hanbury Lake. I don't want to go to the shore in case I puncture a float."

He unlashed the canoe and dropped it into the water. We put our gear into it and got in ourselves.

"See you," he said, "and good luck."

And he sped off, rose into the air and was soon a speck in the distance.

We were alone. It was three hundred miles over a watershed back to Yellowknife; five hundred downstream to Baker Lake. We were in the middle of a small lake with bare stony shores. The only sounds were the rapidly fading beat of the aeroplane, a muted roar of running water beyond the outlet of the lake, and the whine of mosquitoes.

As we landed, the flies fell upon us with shrieks of savage delight. It was as much as we could do to think straight enough to get the tent up. When we had dived inside it and zipped the fly-screens, the black-fly lined up along the apex and troubled us no further. The mosquitoes had to be pursued and slaughtered.

At the beginning, and to some extent throughout, I had misgivings about the wisdom of this trip. We were in the North West Territories, beyond the tree line, in a vast wilderness in which even downed aeroplanes occasionally disappeared and could not be found. My canoeing skills were meagre; George's nonexistent. I was a poor swimmer and a perfect candidate for hypothermia. I had been at sea and knew how treacherous moving water could be. George, a good swimmer, seemed to have no qualms on this score. I realized I was going to have to do all the worrying.

We had well over a hundredweight of food, in five big bags of heavy plastic. We had two cooking pots, two enamel mugs, two spoons, and a knife each. We had a good tent, a Saunders Base-Camp, lent to us by Peter Livesey. We were to bless him a hundred times; it was our one luxury. No change of clothing, no waterproofs.

We had a set of maps, five miles to the inch, a compass, binoculars and cameras; a fishing rod and spinners, and some fireworks – bangers – in case of bears.

This very slim outfit turned out to be a boon, for it made setting up camp easy and portaging less arduous.

Our plan was to descend the Hanbury River to its confluence with the Thelon and then continue to Qamanittuaq on Baker Lake, Chesterfield Inlet.

The Hanbury took us through remarkably varied and picturesque country. At first it was quite turbulent and rocky, and we spent a good deal of time portaging and lining. Lining involved floating the loaded canoe down rough and rock-strewn waters while we moved along the bank holding it on bow and stern painters. It meant much wading in the shallows and slipping over half-submerged rocks. We were not young. I was fifty-seven, George fifty-four but after a few days we looked about ten years older, our faces so burnt and our eyes so puffed up with mosquito bites. Some stretches were a delight to paddle through, however, and the river changed character constantly. Occasionally it meandered through great deserts of blinding bright sand, with the sun beating down upon us so fiercely that the backs of our hands, from holding the paddle, were swollen with sunburn. At other times the limpid waters flowed over huge rocks which lay in wait for the unwary, just inches below the surface. It ran through rapids we had to portage and through lakes whose exits were invisible until we came close upon them.

On our first paddling day the canoe got stuck on a submerged rock and tilted upstream. Before the gunwale dipped into the water I leapt over the side and dragged it into the axis of the current. The river was deeper than I thought, and I went right in, but I still had hold of the canoe and pulled myself aboard as we swept on down. After a few minutes I began to get cold, so we landed and I wrung the water from my clothes, put my sweater next to my skin, and got dressed again. We realized that boulder fields in moving waters were more dangerous than they looked.

We soon fell into a satisfying daily routine. For breakfast we would make a big pan of porridge, laced with soya flour, milk powder and margarine, and because of its fat content this meal would keep us going for about five hours of paddling. Whenever we heard the roar of a rapid ahead we would land and walk along the shore to investigate. Sometimes we fished, but had great difficulty in landing the fish we hooked, and it took a long time, in the absence of a landing net, to find a way of doing so. The secret was not to try and lift the fish out of the water, which caused it to go frantic and break the line, but to land, bring it into the shallows, then gaff it with the blade of a knife under the gills. At the end of the day we would make camp, light a driftwood fire, cook our evening meal and eat it together with the flies that had drowned in it. We tried drinking our tea through a head net in order to filter out the flies, but very soon these nets were found to be about as irritating as the flies themselves. The black fly were in many respects worse than the mosquitoes. Looking like tiny versions of the ordinary housefly, they would not only attack uncovered skin but also crawl in at wrist, neck and ankles. I wore Levis with metal fly-buttons, and to my disgust found these little demons even exploring as far as my crotch. I put an end to this nuisance by wearing my underpants over my jeans. This strange get-up, which resembled doublet and hose, confounded them and they turned their attentions elsewhere.

The evening was usually the very hottest part of the day, and we would be glad to get into the tent, strip off, and enjoy the Turkish bath atmosphere, free from bugs. We would write up our diaries, read our maps and take our ease. Since this was virtually treeless country the best we could do with our food was to put it under our canoe well away from the tent. We were in grizzly country, and we sometimes saw their footprints, but we had no trouble with them.

We knew from the map that a major obstacle on the Hanbury was Dickson Canyon. It was according to the map preceded by a smaller rapid, and this would alert us, we thought, to the big hazard ahead. But as we paddled down the middle of the river, towards two rocky bluffs, one either side, we became aware of a kind of mist rising above the smooth water. I stood up to investigate.

"It's the canyon," I gasped. "Quick. Let's get ashore."

There were some agonizing moments of indecision over which side to head for as we were drawn ever nearer. Then we swung right and paddled hard for the bank. We hauled the canoe ashore and went to look. I felt weak at the knees to see that smooth water, on which we had been happily floating, slide with dizzying acceleration into a cauldron of white water, which continued for over two miles through a narrow cleft. It would have been a swift and certain death.

We took a whole day portaging Dickson Canyon, for at this early stage in our trip we had a lot of food. We walked a total of fifteen miles, making three or four trips. George's feet had become soft through so much wading in previous days, and he got huge blisters.

After the canyon, the river took us through delectable esker country, braiding through expanses of clean sand and winding across rocky moorlands fragrant with moss and shrubs. The next obstacle was Helen Falls, and we made no mistake about that. We approached it down a ravine and the scene was made more dramatic by a brief darkening of the sky and some thunder and lightning. Half a mile before it was a small shelf rapid, which we might have shot had it not been for the hazard ahead. Instead we lined it, and since there was a smooth rock shelf to walk on we continued lining the canoe right to the top of the fall, where we took it out and made camp.

Helen Falls was a fine sight. The river fell in one single vertical drop of some forty feet into a rock-strewn gorge. In a cairn near our camp we found a tin containing notes from the people who had passed that way over the years. It had been put there, we learned, by Eric Morse in 1960. One note was by a man and a girl on their eighty-seventh day from British Columbia to Baker Lake. Another mentioned that the youngest member of the party was "Helen, aged ten months". We rather proudly added our names to this select little band.

The remaining few miles of the Hanbury were very beautiful and by this time we had learned how to cope with swifts, riffles and minor rapids. The dazzling pink sands along the river, and the water so clear and pure and just faintly amber, like an exclusive Speyside malt whisky, and the tiny stands of gnarled spruce, made for an unfolding scene of great beauty and variety. All too soon the Hanbury came to an end and we joined the Thelon whose scenery was on a quite different scale.

At the confluence we spotted a green tent. It belonged to a party of archaeologists who had been flown in to excavate an old Inuit site. There we found a girl from Manchester who greeted us with a broad Lancashire accent. She wore a tee shirt depicting a drunken, grinning cat, with the legend: Happiness is a tight pussy. We joined her for supper contributing a good-sized pike which she stuffed with herbs. After the meal we got underway again in the gleaming sub-arctic evening light, the river like flowing enamel, a sun dog showing in the sky. There was a chill in the air that gave the beauty a faintly ominous aspect. I was conscious of our sliding in the frail canoe over a potentially deadly element, cold water.

We were now on a much bigger river making its majestic progress across the barrens to Hudson's Bay. Much of it was smooth and placid but one was always conscious of its size and power. We made good progress at the rate of between twenty and thirty miles a day. We began to see caribou and musk oxen and wolves.

Fifty years before our trip, Jack Hornby had paddled this river with two companions, and they had built a cabin in the remarkable stand of timber, a sort of oasis in the barrens, which is now the Thelon Game Sanctuary. Their intention was to shoot caribou and overwinter there. The caribou failed them and they starved to death. Hornby was a very small man of enormous stamina, who loved the barren lands and endured years of hardship and starvation there. He was the son of an English clergyman and county cricketer, the Hornby mentioned in Francis Thompson's poem 'At Lords':

As the run-stealers flicker to and fro,
To and fro
O my Hornby and my Barlow long ago.

When I was perhaps seventeen my mother had given me a book to read entitled *Unflinching*. It was the diary of the eighteen-year-old schoolboy Edgar Christian, who, with Jack Hornby and Harold Adlard, had died of starvation in the Canadian barrens. He had been the last of the party to die and his journal stood as a poignant record of his steadfastness.

So we were now, quite by accident, on that same river. We landed where it rounded Hornby Point and cast about in the forest of black spruce until we began to find tree stumps with axe marks, and eventually the ruins of Hornby's cabin with its one foot square window. Beside it stood three mounds with wooden crosses, the initials J H, E C and H A carved upon them. We stood there for some time, ankle deep in sphagnum and fragrant moss, in a cloud of insects, oppressed by the isolation of this forlorn and forgotten neck of the woods. It had been June before Edgar Christian died. He put his diary inside the stove for safe keeping. It was found by the R.C.M.P. two years later.

Through the game sanctuary the Thelon resembled the great Canadian river of one's imagination, flowing broad and powerful through forests of black spruce, but it eventually came out into the barrens once more, spreading out and braiding through the Ursus Islands. Here we canoed in rapt silence through scenes of Saharan brilliancy, with low sand dunes, and everywhere a glassy 'mirage' of water, still or swirling, and ourselves miraculously progressing over it in our aluminium shallop. The water was clean and clear, and sliding remarkably quickly over the bottom when it was visible. The course of the river was difficult to determine. One seemed to be in a world made up entirely of water, a vast round lake with no apparent outlet. It was a bewildering, hypnotic and enchanting place.

We came out at last to Beverly Lake. It looked like the sea. From now on, wind was to be the chief danger. On big open stretches of water it could create waves large enough to swamp a canoe and convert it to a rolling, unmanageable log in the water. While we snoozed one afternoon on the shore, hoping the wind would die down, as it often did in the evening, two pale lanky wolves appeared on the bank just above us, and looked at us for some time before quietly loping off. Venturing on to Beverly Lake we crossed one of its bays in increasing wind and higher and higher waves, and were glad to get safely ashore. We were now held up for four days by a high wind. A sand island we could see out across the water had a sandstorm cloud over it for the whole time. We made a comfortable camp in the shelter of some low bushes, rested thoroughly, and could walk on the barrens untroubled by bugs. Our only worry was how long we were going to be pinned down. It was August; the northern summer was nearly over.

The wind abated and at four in the morning we embarked on an eight-mile crossing of the lake. We paddled hard, to get across before another blow could start. There was now a long smooth swell where whitecaps had been and the water looked black under the dawn sky. It was a scene of beauty and of menace and made a powerful impact upon me. Eventually we could discern a pencil line of land ahead. It was a group of low islands, which would shelter us from further wind.

From this time on we were preoccupied by concern about the wind, for Beverly Lake led into Aberdeen and Schultz Lakes, about a hundred miles in all of open water. Lake Aberdeen was fifty miles long and set in a landscape of desolation. We were frequently halted by wind and beset by other

problems. We got into shoals and had to tow the canoe like a sledge through water six inches deep. We endured a night and a day of bitterly cold rain. At the end of it we sensed that the storm was dying out and although we had just turned in for the second night we got up, struck camp, and paddled away in the dark, determined to use every bit of calm weather we could. It was a memorable and magical night. Wolves howled and loons cried. The land was just a dark smear, impossible to judge how far off. It was cold. Ice formed on the bow. At about one o'clock we were so cold we put in to the shore and crept into our sleeping-bags without properly erecting the tent. We were up with the sun at four but it was no warmer. We made porridge and ate it shivering. The scale of this watery landscape was stunning and the land was a bare and stony place, the abomination of desolation. But we got to the end of Lake Aberdeen that day, having paddled some forty miles.

On Schultz Lake I found a fillet knife, which is still in my kitchen and in daily use. I also found an old woollen sweater, full of holes. I shook the dust out of it and wore it, for the short northern summer was coming to an end. We were puzzled by what looked like buildings in the distance, but it turned out to be a bank of old snow from the previous winter. We did another night paddle and, having got through Schultz, pitched the tent and slept.

We awoke to hear a voice calling "Anybody at home?"

Astonished, we unzipped the tent and saw two smiling Inuit faces. They were just checking to see if we were all right. The young one spoke English; the older man just grinned. They were from a fishing camp and had come up from Qamanittuaq in a boat driven up the rapids by two big outboards, a practice, we were told, that often caused accidents. Next day we came across their camp and they gave us a huge steak from a lake trout for supper. We had found enough driftwood to cook on throughout but it became scarce towards the end so we picked up whatever we could and our canoe was like a floating wood pile. We had not much else, our food being almost finished.

The time came when we debouched at Chesterfield Inlet, thought in the 18th Century to be the North West Passage, and paddled the last few miles up Baker Lake. On the wide open waters now there was a long smooth swell which put us at no risk but was quite awe-inspiring. In the troughs we could see nothing but a ragged hill of water ahead; on the crests we could see the village in the distance, an unprepossessing range of prefabs at the foot of a stony hillside.

George was anxious to finish and have news of his wife. I felt relieved to be safely through, but also sad to be breaking the simple and strangely satisfying rhythm of our life in the barrens.

When our bow grated on the pebbles of the beach, thirty-one days from our start, it was an emotive moment. Little Inuit boys grasped the canoe and pulled it ashore. A young Mountie appeared and greeted us; his area of jurisdiction was about as big as Wales.

"Will our stuff be all right?" we asked.

"Yes," he said. "They won't steal anything."

"They might borrow it though," he added as an afterthought.

We returned our canoe to the Hudson Bay post and paid our dues. The manager, an Orkney man, invited us to dinner. His wife was Inuit, originally from Lake Aberdeen, a fact I found hard to credit having seen what a desolate place it was. The spot she would love to live in, she said, was Kirkwall.

The elders had voted Qamanittuaq a dry town, and the only place of entertainment was the Kapetuvik (Coffee Shop), run by Further Education. The girls in there said, "You guys got any booze?"

There was no piped water. A truck delivered lake water to the houses on request, filling the big tanks they kept in their kitchens. We visited the cemetery on the crown of a hill. The coffins were simply placed on the bare rock under cairns of stones.

In retrospect this journey seems one of the most significant and memorable adventures of my life. I can say with Pascal:

Le silence éternel de ces espaces infinis
M'effraye

These vast horizontal tracts of country and the miles and miles of clear clean water made a deep impression on me. The barrens had a haunting beauty which spoke directly to something basic in my spirit. It was all the stronger from an admixture of fear as we paddled our frail bark across this immensity. On this journey too our friendship was cemented and strengthened. For George it marked a new era of travel. He has since paddled the Danube to the Black Sea and the Mississippi to the Gulf of Mexico.

EAST BUTTRESS

Early in the fifties I went up Scafell with S.B. Beck to make an attempt on Central Buttress. At that time it had a tremendous reputation, both for difficulty and exposure, and I was strung up to a state of high resolve.

The weather was perfect and the crag was dry, but on arrival at its foot we were disappointed to see one party already on our climb and another waiting to do it. The party in action was led by the guide Jim Cameron, and he was taking a client up. I was not surprised to see him first in the queue. In climbing huts he was usually leaving as other occupants were thinking about breakfast. We knew that he would soon get up the climb, but how long the second party would take we could only guess. Waiting in the wings to start a performance such as Central Buttress can be quite demoralising. We stayed, however, and watched Jim at work. His method of doing the Great Flake was to climb the slab to the big chockstone – no longer there these days of course – put a sling on it, and climb down again protected by the top rope. His assistant then climbed up to the chockstone and suspended himself from it by a system of slings. Jim then went up again, climbed over his second, stood on his shoulder and after one more move, reached the perfect holds on the top of the flake. He then brought his client up. On this occasion, with the client standing on the second's shoulder and looking with dismay at the crack curving out above him, we heard Jim's calm voice saying, "Come on now. Make a move. You mustn't tire the second too much," whereupon the client made a struggle and overcame the crux, possibly with some assistance from the rope. The party then moved efficiently on.

With the other rope it was a different story. They reached the chockstone all right but there the difficulties began. After a while they changed the lead and the new leader made a determined effort but ran out of steam, and in retreating to the chockstone he came off and fell beneath it, to be lowered down to the stance.

I came to the conclusion that this, after all, was not my day for C.B. Instead we went over Mickledore to the East Buttress, determined to do something creditable even though we had abandoned hope of the first prize. We picked the Great Eastern Route, described by A.T. Hargreaves in the old F. & R.C.C. guide as: '240 feet. Very Severe. Rubbers. Leader needs 60 feet of rope. A fine climb with magnificent situations.'

Our equipment was simple. We had a hundred feet of rope, and two slings each, with karabiners. Nuts and other aids had not yet come into general use. On our feet we wore the rubbers referred to in the guide book, that is, plimsolls or tennis shoes. To me this climb was a venture into a new kind of territory, steeper than I was accustomed to, but it had the compensation that there were some sharp and positive holds. At first the buttress seemed to lean outwards in a disconcerting fashion, and on one stance the ledge one sat on was so sloping one could feel one's pants creeping up one's backside. After a while by climbing a steep wall we got above the impending part of the crag and were on precipitous airy expanses of rock, in the magnificent situations mentioned by A.T. Hargreaves. We finished in a state of considerable elation and self-congratulation, and when, having gone down the Broad Stand to Mickledore again, we met Betty Monkhouse, a Workington doctor, I agreed to take her up Jones's Route from Deep Ghyll, though Bert Beck said he had done enough for the day.

It is curious how much one's attitude can affect one's performance on a climb. I had brought a great deal to bear on the ascent of Great Eastern and it had fallen easily to such a determined onslaught. I came to Jones's Route quite relaxed, and found it unaccountably hard. Nevertheless, as always, to be on those superlatively fine, firm, warm rocks on a summer afternoon was about as pleasurable as anything Lake District climbing could offer. It is to me a matter of regret that nowadays the amount of climbing equipment one has come to regard as necessary makes the slog up to the crag too much for an ageing mountaineer.

Some twenty years later the East Buttress of Scafell was the place where I did what I still think of as about the hardest route of my life. It was called Hell's Groove, and I was in the company of a number of my young colleagues at the Outward Bound Mountain School. The climb was proposed by one Howie Richardson, a Loughborough-trained P.E. specialist of great strength and agility. I was really only there for the fresh air and the scenery, but somehow found myself toying with the idea of having a go. Even before we roped up I was considerably put off by the steepness of the scrambling approach. The first pitch, which had a brutal overhang on it, gave even Richardson a lot of trouble, and everyone else either came off onto the rope, or had to retreat for a rest before managing it. We were on two ropes, the first led by Howie Richardson, the second by Mike Wilkinson, a Skipton climber.

When it came to my turn, I climbed up to the overhang with little enthusiasm, and after casting about for some time became totally discouraged. For me it seemed ridiculously difficult and I said I was giving up and going down. But then, deep in a crack, I found so magnificent a handhold I was fired with a new resolve. I moved my feet up, I reached up and out and got my claws on a small but possibly adequate hold. I soon found myself out over the overhang, but needing both hands to keep in balance. Improving the situation slightly by moving one foot, I willed my left hand not to let go and reached up with my right. What was uppermost in my mind was that I could not have led it, for in my leading I never got anywhere as near as that to coming off. But I made it, and without a pull on the rope, and received the congratulations of the youngsters, twenty years my junior, who were with me.

It was not over yet, by any means. There was now a long runout of some eighty feet with almost nowhere to rest. Anyone who came off, and one or two did, swung out away from the rock and had to grab it quickly on swinging back. Perhaps I exaggerate, but if my memory serves me, I moved upwards driven by the hope of better things and the conviction that if I didn't I would become detached from the rock and pendulum away from it. Every time I defeated the crag's attempt to push me off, and every time I removed another nut and sling, I felt a fresh little surge of elation. It was in the end enjoyment of a high order, and shamelessly undeserved as I was not leading or seconding, but a mere hanger-on. Even so, I felt when we reached the top that I had something to be pleased about, and the glow lasted quite a long time.

Howie Richardson eventually settled in British Columbia where he has raised a family and continues his vigorous and adventurous outdoor life. Mike Wilkinson went out to Nigeria to be Warden of the Outward Bound School there. Though his initial contract was only for two years, he stayed on, married a black woman and made his home there. To our great sorrow, he was rock-climbing with students when they were attacked by a swarm of bees, which killed him and some of his charges.

Sharing adventures with people creates a bond, which is seldom fully acknowledged but perhaps goes deeper than we think.

CLIMBING GOSSIP, CLIMBING FRIENDS

As I look down the years, names from the past float in and out of my memory. Less evanescent are the faces that go with them, and things people said or did. There was Shepherd, for instance – I cannot recall his first name – secretary and leading light of the L.U.M.C. in 1938, medical student, keen as mustard on climbing. He had one brown eye and one blue. I came across him years later in the Mediterranean towards the end of the War, now a Surgeon Lieutenant in the Navy. Climbing, he said, oh, that, that was just a youthful aberration. Not at all interested now. He'd moved on, grown up. Unlike C.H. Oates, or Titus as he liked to be called, a clerk in the office in the Faculty of Arts but an active L.U.M.C. member. (I still have his copy of Kirkus' *Let's Go Climbing*. Did I borrow it and fail to return it, or did he give it me? I have so long regarded it as my own that I think probably the latter.) An outgoing, mustachioed character, he looked like a stage version of the British army officer, and that is what he became. He was the first person I clapped eyes on when I resumed university studies after six years of war. He hailed me with enthusiasm and suggested a weekend at Ogwen to see if we could still climb. I demurred. I was too old, I said, past it – I was twenty-six – not enough blood in my gin-stream. Nevertheless we went, and it rained the whole weekend. We slithered our way up the Milestone Buttress, Titus exclaiming joyously,

"Agility nil, old man, agility nil!"

I was hooked once more, and made haste to rejoin the L.U.M.C. The next two years was one of the happier times of my life.

A frequent companion was K.N. Davies, reading physics, a tough, powerful climber, indifferent to discomfort. We sometimes bivouacked in a gun-emplacement in the Nant Ffrancon Pass, trying to sleep on the sloping shelves by the draughty loopholes, as the floor was too wet.

Then there was Wildblood, who came less for the climbs than for the company, a boon companion, dead now, I regret to say. And June Stevenson, Jean Raffle, Mary Taylor, June Thorpe (now June Parker, author of the walker's guide to Mallorca, now dead too). And Keith Warburton, with whom I continued to climb long after leaving the university.

Nameless names, most of these, as far as the annals of climbing are concerned, but we did sometimes rub shoulders with the famous. T.A.H. Peacocke once commented favourably on the way I led Belle Vue Bastion, and once when I was feeling pleased with myself for leading Lot's Wife, I had the temerity to ask John Lawton if I could tie on to the end of his rope and try Lot's Groove. He was working in the slate quarries at that time, a fine climber and a kind, unassuming man, later to have a terrible fall on Spectre.

Once, in my early days in the Lakes, I was walking along the foot of Bowfell Buttress, when I came across a couple of climbers, one of whom, a small man, was standing with both boots in a pool of water. Seeing me looking puzzled he said, briskly, "Just tightening up my No. 1's."

It was my first meeting with A.B. Hargreaves, who climbed in No.1 Tricounis.

Going further still into the past, I regret I never knew the name of the man who first introduced me to rock-climbing, a Tynesider I met by accident just after Christmas 1937, at Grasmere Youth Hostel. He had a sixty-foot manila rope which made him an impressive figure in my eyes.

"Like to do a bit of a climb tomorrow?" he asked.

"Yes, okay," I said. But that night I hardly slept.

Next morning we went up Easedale. I had a slight sensation of floating, but the die was cast, and I was committed.

We came to Pavey Ark, the great crag that stands above Stickle Tarn, and scrambled up to where the rocks began.

It was easy! Climbing was easy. Moreover it was marvellous. These hills, that I already loved, took on a new order of beauty when seen from these lofty and exhilarating perches. It was like sharing the world with an eagle and a raven. I was hooked. I 'grasped the crag with crooked hands' and exalted in a new freedom.

We did the Crescent Traverse and Gwynne's Chimney, modest enough climbs as I later learned, but not bad for a first attempt on a January day.

I had seen as a freshman the notices in the Union inviting membership of L.U.M.C., but had been too modest to respond. I now joined, and began an association that lasted many years.

Our nearest rock-climbing was at Helsby, some twenty miles from Liverpool. The village was dominated by a crag of red sandstone, standing at the top of a steep slope. Much of the rock, which faced north, was green with lichen and looked somewhat repellent, but we grew to love it. From there we looked down on to the roofs and gardens of the village, and out to the Mersey estuary and the Wirral.

H.A. Carsten had written a guide to the crag. It was a wonderful out-door gymnasium, which gave concentrated exercise, and we would climb until we were so supple and relaxed as to be almost a danger to ourselves. Sometimes we cycled there, returning home in a very satisfying state of exhaustion.

At Easter 1938 we had a meet on Ben Nevis, which was my first real experience of snow and ice climbing. I had made an arrangement, weeks before, to be given a lift by a lecturer member of the L.U.M.C. He was to pick me up in the main street of Kendal, at about midday on the day before the meet. I stood there for nearly an hour, becoming more and more doubtful about the rendezvous, but sure enough, he finally drew up in an old open tourer Bentley. He had beside him his elderly housekeeper, so I took a back seat. I dare say I owe my survival to the fact that she was only going as far as Abington, for I was then able to get into the front and so avoid death from exposure. Even there it was a chilly, if stately ride.

We were to be accommodated in or around the C.I.C. (Charles Inglis Clark) Hut, high up the Allt a'Mhuilinn, under the great beetling crags of Ben Nevis. It was hard going, getting up there with all our food, camping equipment and climbing ropes, though our president, Graham Macphee, had hired a pony to carry some of the heavier gear. We stopped for a breather and Macphee took off his sweater.

"Are you not taking something off?" he asked me.

"No, I'm okay," I said.

"Price," remarked Macphee to the party in general, "is like an Alpine guide."

I was flattered.

"They never sweat," he continued. "They only stink."

Our first outing was a mass ascent of Tower Gully, and I felt I was having a taste of true alpinism. At the top there was a big cornice with a cave under it, in which we sat while a manhole was being excavated through the roof. When at length we had all climbed through on to the summit of Ben Nevis, Macphee, who had been filming the ascent, had us all stand in a line. He set up the camera, started its motor, and ran to join the line. The man at the other end then ran to stop it. When we saw this film later, what got the most applause was this final line-up. The row of gloved and balaclavaed climbers suddenly staggered sideways, under the impact of Macphee's nudging himself into the frame, then the screen was filled by a charging madman, followed by several split second shots of sky, climbers, snow and distant hills, as the assistant cameraman fought with the off-switch.

We did other gully climbs but our best exploit was our ascent of Tower Ridge – a party of three or four novices with only one sixty foot rope. At one point we had to bypass a huge rock buttress named, I think, the Great Tower. Our way led out along a snow-covered ledge above a fearsome drop into Tower Gully. Owing to the shortness of the rope, two or three of us had to be on this slippery traverse without any security. Hardly had we got safely round this *mauvais pas* when we heard the rush of an avalanche and far below us we saw two figures dwarfed by distance bouncing and somer-saulting down Gardyloo Gully, like dolls tied together by a length of string. They passed down and out of our sight; we were appalled, but could do nothing but continue our climb. Eventually we came to a gap before the final steep slope that led to the broad open summit. Here we had a long and demoralising wait while two experienced climbers of the meet finished Glover's Chimney. Fortunately they had plenty of rope, and we were glad of their help on the final pitch.

We returned to the hut expecting to see dead bodies there, but learned that the two climbers we saw falling had survived more or less unhurt. Had they been wearing crampons they would almost certainly have been injured but in those days crampons were not much used in British hills.

My association with Graham Macphee began in 1938 and lasted until his death in 1963. On my first winter trip in the hills he lent me an ice axe, and I lost it on my way there. I was hitch-hiking, and put my gear on the empty back of a lorry; the axe must have been bounced off. I reported the loss at a police station in the vague hope that it might be handed in.

"I want to report the loss of my ice axe," I said.

The policeman gave me a long puzzled look. Then he picked up a pencil and a pad.

"Eye-sacks," he said, "and what did they contain?"

On the meet I was able to borrow another axe for the weekend. Afterwards I bought a replacement, digging deep into my meagre finances, and took it round to Macphee's house. He was surprised, and I think it gave him a good opinion of me. Over the years our acquaintance developed into something more like a friendship. He proposed me for the Alpine Club, and when I got married he gave me a present of some antique fruit dishes. I climbed with him occasionally though he was twenty years older than I. He was an excellent second, who could put a leader on his mettle and fill him with confidence.

Though he was ambitious in the climbing world, keen to ally himself with such promising young climbers as Colin Kirkus and Bill Peascod, and contrived for many years to stay in the Groupe de Haute Montagne of the C.A.F., which required its members to keep up a high standard of alpine climbing every year, measured by a points system, each route counting for so many points, he remained an active member of the L.U.M.C. for thirty years, attending meets, and helping students by offering them lifts in the big old Humber shooting brake that had been an ambulance in the First

World War, and by obtaining for the club the use of climbing huts such as Brackenclose and R.L.H. Under his guidance L.U.M.C. dinners were conducted in a comparatively orderly fashion. I remember one for which he secured as principal guest H.W. Tilman, whom I had the pleasure of leading on a climb on White Ghyll, Langdale. Macphee's devotion to the L.U.M.C. was all the more commendable since he was so efficient and punctilious, and the student members so feckless and wayward. We were once at Brackenclose in very bad weather, and no one was disposed to go out and get wet. The Fell and Rock were very house-proud over their huts, and if a member invited guests to use them, he had to accompany them. This requirement kept Macphee with us when he would no doubt have preferred to be at home. He said that having come all the way from Liverpool he might as well get a bit of exercise by going up Scafell Pike by the most direct route. Several of us joined him, and we went up by Lingmell Col to the summit, Macphee noting with some satisfaction that he could still ascend at the rate of two thousand feet an hour. On the summit he turned to me and said, "It's not worth getting out map and compass in this weather, but I expect you know Scafell well. If you can take us to Mickledore we can go down from there."

"Okay," I said, anxious to sustain my reputation for local knowledge, "I think I can do that."

And I struck off boldly through the mist and rain.

There were unfortunately extensive snow patches and they distorted what should have been familiar ground. In five minutes I was lost. In my anxiety to find something I would recognise, I speeded up and led the party across seemingly endless hostile slopes of snow and rocks. I thought I must be somewhere on the Eskdale side of Mickledore, but since nothing made sense I began to doubt even that.

Eventually Macphee asked me in his quiet incisive voice if I had any idea where we were. I had to admit I didn't.

"Then there's only one thing to do, isn't there," he said, pronouncing every word with quiet deliberation, "and that is to go back to the summit."

We struck uphill, getting tired now, and wet. None of it was recognisable, and as we climbed I became increasingly puzzled. At last the summit cairn loomed out of the mist and rain. But it was not the big broad cairn of Scafell Pike. It was tall and slim. I could not believe my eyes.

"Scafell," I said.

We must have crossed under the East buttress without seeing it and got on to the steep broken ground round Foxes Tarn.

"Well," said Macphee icily, "at least we've Done Two Tops."

I think he forgave me, but he was not by nature very forgiving. He was once on Tower Buttress on Scafell Shamrock, when the leader fell. The only casualty was the second, for the rope somehow got round his thumb and wrenched it out. The leader was so pleased with himself for having escaped unharmed, and so indifferent, it seemed, to his second's very serious injury, that Macphee never forgave him.

Macphee was himself not universally liked. There was a long-standing feud between him and Graham Brown, and he never had a good word to say of A.B. Hargreaves. But the longer I knew him the better I liked him.

On a seaside holiday with his wife in the Canaries he could not resist climbing Mount Teide.

He did so with a guided group, but elected to go down on his own. He failed to return. The search party that found his body included Lady Hunt. Had he known she was on the island he might well have arranged to climb the mountain with her instead of the guided group, and the outcome may have been different.

I managed to reach the age of twenty-eight without having to work for a living, unless, that is, you count university life and six years in the Navy. My first job was at Workington Grammar School, and when I went for interview the headmaster suggested I speak to the head of the English Department, one S.B.Beck. It took us about two minutes to discover we shared an interest in climbing, and that is all we talked about instead of discussing the job.

As soon as I took up the post Beck and I went and did the North Climb on Pillar. Bert Beck was not a leader; he was happier seconding and did it well. His knowledge of Lake District climbing was encyclopaedic so he was good at suggesting suitable routes. When we arrived at the Nose he said, "We'll do the descent into Savage Gully, I take it," but I had an old score to settle with the Nose, and standing tiptoe on the flake below it, put to the test the old guidebook assertion that 'a man of moderate height can reach a flat hold with his right hand.' I got up it without difficulty this time, and Bert was impressed.

We climbed quite frequently together in those early days, and even went further afield, to Wales and to the Alps.

I soon made the acquaintance of another local climber, Jack Carswell, a steel worker, and in his day one of the Lake District's top climbers, though he was not interested in pioneering new routes and so has remained relatively unsung. For a time I was trying to keep up a climbing partnership with both him and Bert Beck, and it would have suited me better if we could all three have climbed together. But nothing would induce them to do so, and when I pressed them for a reason I met with a blank wall. They were starchily polite if they met, and said nothing derogatory about each other, though it was pretty clear Jack Carswell did not think much of Beck's climbing. I was mystified, but now I am older and more worldly wise I have a theory but nothing to substantiate it. Bert was a few years older than I, and had been a useful mentor and second to the young Bill Peascod. He had seconded him on the remarkable Eagle Front ascent of 1940. He was a strange character, a good and amusing companion on the hills, a second who inspired confidence, and he was always courteous and punctilious over the arrangements for days out. Yet he was extraordinarily private and reserved in other ways, living behind a protective barrier. As a newcomer to the profession I was anxious to see how he tackled the teaching of English, but whenever I went into his classroom on any pretext, he immediately stopped everything he was doing, and I never had a single scrap of advice from him in his capacity of head of department, for on the hills any discussion of our work was taboo. He would talk about books and reading, however, and he once told me his ambition was to be able to write like C.E. Montague. He had quite a flair for naming new climbs, too. Suaviter and Fortiter in Birkness Coombe were particularly apt, not only in their learned allusions, but as accurate descriptions of the climbs themselves.

He led a somewhat humdrum life and I sometimes wondered whether his reticence stemmed from some sort of disappointment with himself. He had spent his whole war as a private in an anti-aircraft battery somewhere in the Midlands, reading endlessly to pass the time, and in the common room at the grammar school he spent every lunch break in a never ending game of solo whist.

I am indebted to him for two climbing anecdotes, both concerning a friend whom he had introduced to the hills. He took this fellow up Scafell in conditions of deep snow, and touring the summit area brought him to the top of the crags. "This" he said, "is Deep Ghyll." Whereupon his friend stepped forward to have a look, broke through the slight cornice, and fell right down from top to bottom. The snow was so deep and new fallen that he escaped injury. Asked what the accident felt like he said he kept thinking he was coming to a halt, only to accelerate again and plunge over a new drop.

At another time they were on Skye, in the Cuillin, and on top of the Cioch, that extraordinary jutting rock on the Sron na Ciche. Bert Beck did not carry a watch and it was his habit, as I had noticed, to ask the time of anyone he met on the hills. On the Cioch he asked his friend the time and he dug out a gold hunter from the recesses of his clothing. He then dropped it. It slid down the sloping rock and disappeared into a crack from which it was impossible to retrieve it without blowing the Cioch apart with dynamite.

"It was my grandfather's," was all he said. That watch must still be there.

To our surprise Bert Beck suddenly stopped going climbing and fellwalking and took to touring with a caravan. We did not see much of him after that. It was only after he died, years later, that I learned he had given up climbing on grounds of ill health. He had never said a word of this to his old friends.

Frank Monkhouse was for a time vice-president of the L.U.M.C. but he spent so little time with the club that Graham Macphee ousted him. He was a lecturer in geography when I first met him, and later became professor of geography at Southampton University. He always had an eye to the main chance, and produced the textbook *Physical Geography* just in time for it to supersede Dudley Stamp's classic book of the same title. It was a textbook no Sixth Form in the country could afford to do without, and he claimed it sold more copies than *Gone With the Wind*. He was a lively and enthusiastic character and his lectures invariably went on longer than the fortyfive minutes allotted in the timetable. He was the first person to show me how to use an ice axe and when I took a post at his old school in Workington he introduced me to his widowed mother who offered me lodgings in her commodious house. Though extremely energetic and enterprising he also had the rare gift of enjoying life, as though it was an exciting game, and fun to win. At a climbing hut one evening, seeing everybody taking their post prandial ease before the fire, he had our party do the washing up for everyone that night in exchange for having our breakfast things done next morning, a shrewd bargain. On another occasion on which the party at a hut pooled its food for the weekend, a searching inquiry into who had brought what revealed that Frank had contributed a bottle of HP sauce.

He and I planned a week in Scotland, during an Easter vacation, and he sent me a suggested itinerary so ambitious I dreaded the thought. It was consequently with no little relief that I received the news that he had got mumps and had to call it off.

He often spoke of writing a book entitled *Ordinary Climber* to offset the spate of books about exceptional mountaineering achievements, and eventually, after he had retired early from academic life, and apart from updating his best selling textbooks could devote his time to the hills, he did in fact produce a book in collaboration with Joe Williams, a consistently good Whitehaven climber, called *Climber and Fellwalker in Lakeland*. It is typical of Frank Monkhouse's style, bursting with lists, sketch maps and factual information. Once a geographer always a geographer. But it does reflect his energetic enjoyment of the hills.

During this period he was living in Ennerdale in a farmhouse sold off by the Forestry Commission. He died suddenly of a heart attack while gardening. When I heard the news I immediately recalled a comment his mother had made some thirty years before, when he was outstandingly fit and active, to the effect that he had been turned down by a life insurance company, and how absurd the decision had seemed.

Jack Carswell, with whom I had a long and enjoyable climbing partnership, was a cragsman of the old school. In our early days neither of us had a car and this meant we made frequent use of climbing huts and spent whole weekends climbing. We were much dedicated to good climbing practice and aimed at being in control at all times. We climbed in nails but sought to avoid scraping the rock. All that could be heard on our ascents was the click of iron on stone and the occasional quiet instruction, "Taking in", etcetera. We had no adventures to speak of, for we climbed well within our capabilities. I did not realise it at the time, but Jack, a few years older than I, acted as if he had passed his peak, and though he had for instance led Central Buttress on Scafell, both up and down, he was now more inclined to choose Severes and Mild Very Severes. Both of us, I now think, could have climbed harder than we did. Our object, however, was the enjoyment of competent cragsmanship and our ropework remained simple. We invariably 'led through' and would often repeat climbs so that the order of our leads was reversed. It was a good partnership, cemented by mutual trust and confidence.

Crosby Fox, the mountaineering sea captain, was someone I never knew well, and this was my loss, for he was a thoroughly likeable, talented man and a keen climber. I would sometimes come across him on the Lake District crags, and one such time was when Jack Carswell and I were at Gimmer Crag in Langdale to do Hiatus, a Very Severe first climbed by George Bower in 1927. The climb starts a few feet to the left of the celebrated Gimmer Crack. We found Crosby Fox starting up the Crack with a second whose name I forget. We were just about to start ourselves when Jack suggested we should step back from the foot of the rock to trace exactly where the route was supposed to go, for we knew its upper part was not easy to follow. This brief delay proved providential, for as I was finding my way up a steep slab with poor holds, I heard a noise above me like the rushing of a mighty wind, and looking up saw a body coming my way at high speed. It was Crosby Fox, who had fallen off what was known as the Rectangular Excursion on the Gimmer Crack route. He came to a stop about two feet above my head and had I been a little further up the pitch he would undoubtedly have knocked me off. He was unhurt except for a few abrasions and had to be discouraged from getting straight back onto the rock and continuing, in the belief, popularly held, that by doing so he would avoid losing his nerve. His second was in fact more hurt than he, having been pulled off his feet and thrown against the rock, and he was quite unable to go on. When we had seen them both safely off the climb we returned to Hiatus, somewhat shaken ourselves, and had some anxious moments before it was over, wondering whether we had got off route on the airy traverse by which the little overhangs at the top are circumvented.

Crosby's life was tragically cut short when he was avalanched in the Himalaya while leading a Yorkshire Ramblers expedition.

Jack Carswell and I had something of an adventure when we first climbed The Crack. It is a fine route, one of the great classics of Lake District climbing. We were there on a hot summer day, climbing in plimsolls, and using Jack's hundred foot nylon rope. We were keyed up to what for us was a challenging climb, but at the same time confident and eager. We 'led through' as always. A long-standing climbing partnership is very satisfying in that communication is easy and often unspoken, the rope not only attaching the climbers together but also forming a sympathetic bond capable of conveying messages and indicating mood. Our climbing was always careful and deliberate and we subscribed wholeheartedly to the old doctrine that the leader must not fall. While we were happily engrossed in our progress up The Crack we only gradually became aware that the sky was darkening, the day had become still and oppressive and all the signs were gathering for a thunderstorm. We were about halfway up, and felt rather trapped, especially when thunder began to rumble and crack among the 'reverberate hills.' We needed to get a move on, but that did not mean we could be any less careful. We had just traversed back into The Crack proper when the first big drops of rain fell. I was in the Sentry Box. Jack joined me at speed and immediately made the strenuous pull-up out of it climbing straight up to the Overhang, where he belayed to a chockstone. It was now raining hard with big, fat drops, a fact I had not fully realised in the partial shelter of my stance. In no time the crag was flowing with water; it was spouting off the Overhang like a fountain. In our constricted stance, tied to the chockstone which, rumour had it, was put in years ago by Graham Macphee, we took off our rubbers and stuffed them down our shirt fronts. This revealed a big hole in the toe of one of my socks so I found myself climbing barefoot on one side. Jack gave me a shoulder to help me over the Overhang and I pressed on upstream, water pouring off my head and into my eyes. I was able to place a runner, and on the strength of it climbed the last section at high speed, wrapping my bare toes round anything that felt like a hold. Out on the top I sat in a puddle, jubilant, and brought Jack up. He'd found a sling and karabiner on the way up, he said. It was mine but it had not been attached to the rope. In my haste I had clipped it round the loose end of my bowline which was about two feet long, with the result that my flight up the last pitch had been unprotected. I suppose that gave us further cause to be pleased with ourselves, for what I remember most vividly about that climb was the wonderful satisfaction of sitting in the bouncing rain on top of it, laughing at our escape.

Jim Joyce was a consultant gynaecologist whom I met in dramatic circumstances. I had just done a back somersault off Dow Crag, and he traversed across to me from Gordon and Craig's Climb. I climbed with him occasionally thereafter and he was the doctor present at the birth of my eldest son. He lived in Eaglesfield, a village a few miles from Workington, and his wife, Heidi, was the daughter of M. Seiler who owned the Gornergrat Hotel at Zermatt and who was once President of Switzerland. Jim had met her and wooed her during his early alpine climbing. He had been an able and adventurous mountaineer in his early days and he still, in middle age, retained much of his youthful disregard for danger.

He told me that once as an undergraduate of Oxford or Cambridge – I forget which – he was drinking in a pub with climbing friends who were planning to go to Chamonix. They had already booked their journey by train and were to depart in a week's time. In his cups Jim bet them he could get there faster on a bicycle, and it was only in the cold light of next morning that he realised how rash he had been, especially as he did not even own a bicycle. As time was of the essence he rapidly bought a second hand machine, packed his climbing gear, and set off. At the end of the first day he was so saddle sore and deadbeat he nearly gave up, but as the days went by his condition improved and in the end he had the pleasure of being on the railway platform in Chamonix to meet his friends. The only trouble, he said, on the holiday that followed, was that he found his companions woefully slow uphill, while they found him maddeningly fast.

He came of a family of doctors. His father had been the surgeon who amputated Douglas Bader's legs when he crashed a plane in training. There was a touch of Bader's recklessness about Jim, I thought. He was a big man, a bit ponderous and rather pleasantly vague in manner. One or two people considered him too heedless to be safe to climb with. The climbs I did with him, however, were without untoward incident and the only time

I remember getting rather apprehensive was when we climbed the frozen waterfall at the top of Newlands Pass and found ourselves without satisfactory belays on wet rock and decaying ice. On a poor day when we had nothing much to do he proposed going up the remains of the miners' gangway on Fleetwith Pike which in its day had had a cable railway. Where the structure had collapsed into gullies there was a lot of loose and tottering masonry to surmount and some bent and twisted railway lines hanging out over space. It needed care. At one point Jim remarked, "When I bring the children up I usually put a rope on here." It was to me a revealing comment, as I feared for my own safety let alone that of small children.

A few years later he had a nervous breakdown and for a long time was a prey to severe depression. In an effort to help I drew his attention to an advertisement H.W. Tilman had put in the *Times* which ran something like: "Wanted, seacook. Small ship. Cold seas. Women need not apply." Not expecting anything to come of it, he nevertheless applied, and travelled to Devon to see Tilman. They got on extremely well and he was hired. Unfortunately, while waiting to start the voyage he lost confidence and pictured a situation in which, through seasickness or other failing, he could not do the job and would consequently let Tilman down. He confided these misgivings to Tilman, who said he had someone who could join as cook at Belfast but not before. Jim thought the safest course was for him to go as far as Belfast and then make room for this other volunteer.

On the voyage round Land's End and through the Irish Sea they met heavy weather but Jim had no trouble with seasickness, enjoyed Tilman's company immensely and bitterly regretted having to leave at Belfast. The episode did however do something to assist his long climb out of the pit of depression.

Later, he suffered a ruptured aorta, but fortunately an expert heart surgeon was to hand, whose intervention brought about a dramatic change in his life expectancy, from ten minutes to what turned out to be ten years.

Another doctor I climbed with was Tony Drummond, a consultant psychiatrist. He came to Eskdale Outward Bound School to do a Mountain Leadership Certificate course, and became instantly hooked on climbing, the more so since on the course he met a keen woman mountaineer, whom he later married. He was a man who once he had taken up an interest would pursue it with passionate thoroughness until he knew everything there was to know on the subject. He had devoted the same intensity and energy to fly fishing and the tying of flies. I had some enjoyable days out with him; he had a lively intelligence and an original and inquiring mind.

There was one climb we did which I will not easily forget. It was supposed to be Great Gully on the Wastwater Screes, and I thought I knew it. But, where the gully divides into two, somehow we took the wrong turning, and, coming to an impasse, instead of retreating started up the scrappy crag face between the two branches. I led for a whole rope's length without finding a decent belay. It was disconcertingly steep, and desperately loose. The belay I finally took was suspect in the extreme, and as Tony came up he threw down rock after rock. Seeing them bounding and crashing down, and sometimes bouncing out into space, had a damaging effect upon my morale. We were now committed to this route, for there was nothing fit to abseil from, and to climb down would have been as difficult as to continue upwards. It was curious how steep and exposed it all seemed; if the rock had been sound we would not have noticed it. I led off again, pressing each hold into place rather than pulling on it and so wholly absorbed in disturbing nothing that I almost forgot to be frightened. It was only when at a stance, hooked to some doubtful belay, and looking straight down into Wastwater, while the rocks Tony dislodged bounded towards the lake and I imagined our two bodies doing the same thing, that I felt scared; action is a great antidote to fear. We got up of course.

Whenever I drive down Wasdale I look up and pick out the big inverted triangle between the branches of Great Gully that we went up that day. Even from the road it looks steep and open, and that climb remains in my memory as one of the small private adventures of my life.

Though I only did one or two rock climbs with him I knew John Cunningham quite well from the South Georgia Survey Expedition 1955-56. This was the trip that got him interested in the Antarctic, where he subsequently spent many years.

He was an extraordinarily gifted man, good looking, well built, competent and intelligent. I first met him when he arrived in South Shields to board *S.S. Southern Opal*, the supply ship of Christian Salvesen's whaling enterprise. In South Georgia we used two-man tents and our policy was to switch tentmates frequently, but on our first eight week journey we did not do so, as we were conducting a bit of research into the rival merits of pemmican and Army meat bar. Consequently I spent the whole journey sharing with Cunningham, a supremely efficient camper, and I learned a lot about his life and adventures. He had many tales to tell of the Glasgow shipyards and his exploits with the Creagh Dhu Mountaineering Club.

He had been a wrestler in Glasgow and recounted with relish the tricks of that rough sport, such as wearing a sweaty singlet to put an opponent off, and rasping him with a two day growth of beard. In pursuit of greater suppleness in climbing he and a fellow member of the Creagh Dhu joined a ballet school, but they were so much in demand for hoisting ballerinas into the air and catching them as they leapt, that they soon lost interest and returned to simpler forms of work-out.

He and Hamish MacInnes emigrated to New Zealand, taking up the offer of a ten pound passage, lured by the expectation of bigger mountains, but they found it hard to get to them at weekends and missed the proximity to the hills that Glasgow had provided. He claimed that they used to tell the Kiwi girls they had worked in the oatmeal quarries of Aberdeenshire, and were believed. When they decided to return home the authorities said they were under an obligation to remain, having been given an assisted passage, but they had saved enough money to repay the full cost of the fare and so took their leave.

This was in 1953. They knew the English were planning an assault on Everest, and they assumed that being English they would fail and retreat leaving various camps and equipment behind them. John and Hamish therefore went home via Nepal and made a beeline for Everest, telling the headmen of the villages they passed through that the main party with the paperwork and permits were behind. When they learned with surprise that Everest had been climbed they started up Lhotse but had to retreat as their food, which had largely consisted of a sheep on the hoof, had run out.

I tell this as I heard it from John Cunningham. He had of course a talent for embroidering a tale, and this caused him, several years after the South Georgia trip, to give serious offence to some members of the expedition. *Mountain* magazine did a profile of him in the form of a question-and-answer article – always an unsatisfactory and lazy way of reporting an interview – in which he claimed, or at least was reported as claiming, that, having fallen into a crevasse he was left to get out of it without any help from his companions. This was absurdly inaccurate and I imagine he was just flippantly making light of the incident, but it provoked some of the members to demand a retraction.

He and his Creagh Dhu pals came and climbed in the Lake District. They insisted on calling Wastwater Loch Wast, and Scafell Ben Sca. John did Botterill's Slab on Scafell and declared it a V. Diff. I suppose that is how it seemed to him after his ascents on the Etive Slabs. I joined them one Sunday in Langdale. It was a summer day of drizzling rain. I found them camped in the valley, making a late and leisurely breakfast. They always referred to the cooking tins as the drums. They seemed in no hurry to attempt any climbing but eventually proposed having a look at Kneewrecker Chimney on Raven Crag, on the grounds that since it was overhanging it might be dry. We did it in two ropes, one led very smoothly by a climber called, if I remember, Bill Smith, and the other, with more apparent difficulty, by John. I followed at about the limit of my powers. We then did Bilberry Buttress, the climb with what we used to call the piano-playing pitch, where your fingers range anxiously along a horizontal ledge on to which you hope to mantelshelf.

That was before Cunningham went south again and it was the last time I saw him. He later qualified as a teacher and worked in outdoor education. Like many climbers he was not much of a swimmer, and he drowned trying to save a student who had fallen from a rock into the sea on the coast of Anglesey.

So many of the people with whom I shared some of the best times of my life are now dead.

An old mountaineer I was glad to be acquainted with was Howard Somervell, who was on Everest in 1924. Retired near Rydal, he was good enough to come and talk to the Outward Bound students about the expedition and his life as a doctor in India. He was an inveterate smoker, and since at that time I usually had some strong, cheap and nasty Swiss cigars called Stumpen, he was keen to help me smoke them.

An accident had brought the Everest expedition to an untimely end, and Somervell had as a result been able to travel for some time in India. What he saw caused him to spend most of the rest of his life as a medical missionary there. He claimed to have done more cataract operations than anyone living. He was warm-hearted and hard-bitten. He was also a very good landscape painter, portraying mountains as powerful three-dimensional forms.

Once, during the few years that I was a member of the Alpine Club – until I resigned as meetings and lectures etcetera took place in far-off London – I attended a lecture at South Audley Street. Most of those present looked very elderly, the kind of men you would expect to see ensconced in leather arm chairs behind copies of The Times in some well-appointed club. Howard Somervell was in the chair. Before the lecture there were one or two deaths to report and clearly he had arranged for friends of the deceased to say a few words of condolence and appreciation.

It was interesting to see with what gruff absence of sentimentality this elderly body of men acknowledged the departure of their fellow members, especially as most of them could not have been very far from the end themselves. When the last brief obituary had been spoken, one of the audience stood up and said he would like to add to what had been said of one of the deceased. In addition to his alpine climbing, he said, this member had been active in recent years in other fields, and he gave in great detail a long list of the many societies, parish councils, good causes, artistic interests, pastimes and hobbies the man had played a part in. This catalogue of activities and good works went on for so long, and was so full of trivia, that one or two of the audience became inclined to chuckle.

At last the speaker sat down. There was a pregnant pause. Then Howard Somervell said, "Well, gentlemen, we seem to have lost a Very Versatile Membah," which brought a hearty burst of laughter.

There is something to be said for such a cheerful sendoff.

Louis Wuilloud was a friend of André Roch, and I got to know him and his family very well over the years. He was a Swiss guide, and also an electrical engineer. He lived in the Valais, at Champlan, a village overlooking Sion. He and André were very different in almost everything except their devotion to the mountains. André was a cosmopolite, Louis a Valaisan speaking no English. André was of no religion, Louis a devout Catholic with an even more devout wife and eight children. He was employed by the Forces Motrices de Mauvoisin, the huge hydroelectric scheme in the Pennine Alps. Two of his sons were also guides, and his whole family keen skiers, particularly Marianne, the eldest girl, who skied with fluid grace at very high speed. All the girls became nuns, at the behest, no doubt, of their mother, and one of the boys a priest.

Louis was a great exponent of Valaisan life and culture, and himself an expert at the arts of tossing the flag and playing the accordion and the alpenhorn. He would sometimes point the great horn over the garden wall where the ground dropped precipitously away into the Rhone valley, and send the melancholy booming notes across into the far mountains. He was also a vine-grower and wine maker, and his uncles owned a vineyard called Diolay in the valley, where, in a very beautiful old house, there was one of the most famous libraries of viticulture in Europe. The house had a great cellar with a gravel floor and a range of wine barrels and spirit casks. The Wuilloud wines were never advertised but bought up by regular customers. Their labels all carried the statement 'Ni filtré ni sucré '. To Louis, no picnic was complete without a bottle of wine and a flask of spirits. A favourite pleasantry of his was to point to the sky saying, "Regard l'aigle!" before taking a swig of *marc* or *lie*.

He was strong and tireless, working in his garden before and after going to work at the hydro plant.

On two occasions he included me on inspection trips to the tunnels which delivered water to the dam at Mauvoisin, flying to the heads of glaciers then skiing down to the tunnel entrances. Our pilot was the famous Geiger, who first pioneered a glacier flying service. One of these flights was to the Glacier de Corbassière, under the Grand Combin. Cloud was very low that day and the pilot landed in the poor light with a bump that gave my neck quite a whiplash. He laughed an apology.

We then made what was to me an adventurous descent of the glacier, and its snout. Louis and his assistant cast about in the snowy wilderness for some time until they came upon a marker. Digging down through the snow they revealed a manhole with a padlocked lid. This gave access to a vertical shaft. A ladder led down to a metal grid, and a further ladder down to a lower grid. We descended several of these ladders to reach a horizontal tunnel. Louis here switched on the lights and we continued underground, checking various water courses, and looking into one or two quite comfortable small rooms fitted out with bunks, seating and cooking facilities. It seemed quite unreal that all this should exist beneath the wild desolation of snow, ice and rock that we had just left.

Eventually we retraced our steps and climbed back up the ladders to the real world. The descent of the glacier had been mostly on powder snow. Now we skied through variable snow conditions, and in my anxiety to keep up I found it strenuous. The final descent into Fionnay was down a steep slope of lumpy avalanche debris, and I arrived in the village with my shirt so wet through with sweat that the manager of the *Centrale* there lent me a dry one. We drank quantities of tea.

The other flight was to the head of the Glacier de Brenay, under the Pigne d'Arolla. This time the cost of the plane was shared with a customs officer called Fournier, who wished to check the telephone at the Chanrion Hut. It was being used, he said, by smugglers. Fournier had with him a big dog, a bouvier, and when I went to pat it he urgently warned me off. In the plane no one wanted to sit next to this dog, and when we got out, and the plane turned round and sped off we kept an anxious eye on it as we put on our skis and rucksacks. The plan was to split up into two parties, one to do the hydro work, the other to go by the Chanrion. We were to meet for lunch at an agreed point. I went on the Chanrion route; it involved easier skiing, but on the other hand it meant I had to stay with the dog, who added to my problems by repeatedly treading on the backs of my skis and showing an unwelcome interest in my sticks. On a long traverse across a steep slope I was relieved to see it lose its footing and go tumbling down some hundreds of feet. Fortunately it came to no harm.

As we made the pleasant easy run back down the valley to the rendezvous, the dog went ahead, and finding the other party already there, gave them a basilisk stare and carried off their sandwiches. Fournier arrived too late to do anything about it.

Touring the Forces Motrices was of particular interest to me as I had seen both the barrages, at Fionnay and in the Val des Dix, while they were being built. The dam walls were riddled with tunnels and vertical shafts, like a Gruyère cheese, and it was a thrill to be taken inside them. On one occasion Louis took me and my wife and young family out on to a narrow iron balcony three quarters of the way up the eight hundred foot curving wall of the Mauvoisin barrage. This was a barrage voûté, like a gigantic saucer standing on edge with its back to the water, and in it was a shaft with a plumb line. The concrete of the dam was plastic enough to move outwards as much as four inches from the pressure of water behind it, and the plumb line monitored this movement.

Louis Wuilloud was a good man, generous, meticulous and hard working. Life to him held few uncertainties. He was happy, successful and proud to be Swiss. He saw no reason to travel beyond the Valais for he thought it the most beautiful place on earth and he did not wish to go anywhere where a different language was spoken. His one trip to England was to Folkestone, as a member of a group of Valaisan folklore enthusiasts, to toss the flag and play the alpenhorn at a festival.

At the age of seventy his health declined suddenly, and when I last saw him he was a bent and shrunken version of the powerful, stalwart figure I had known for so long. He died soon after. I shall always remember his power-packed personality, and in a way he still exists in his sons, now family men themselves.

OLD SOLDIERS

'Old soldiers never die, they only fade away', said the old song, and the same can be said for old climbers. However little actual climbing we do, we still regard ourselves as climbers, and in theory if not in practice the feel of warm dry rock is still one of life's pleasures. We live largely on tall stories of days gone by. Beerbohm Tree's quip might well apply to the old climber: 'What an old bore; even the grave yawns for him.'

A few years ago my fading away was afforded a period of remission, so to speak. Colin Greenhow, a B.M.C. guide, would come into the Lake District to climb with clients, and his wife who came with him would call me and suggest a climb. It was a good arrangement. She usually picked the routes, and for the most part we 'led through', that is took alternate leads. This caused me to do climbs which, left to myself, I would have thought beyond me. Sheila was tall and slim and a good and careful climber, patient and systematic in placing protection, and in this way she was a good influence upon me, for I have never fully grown out of an inclination to concentrate all my energy on getting up the pitch rather than seeking nut placements. On one of our climbs, Troutdale Pinnacle Direct, leading the steep rib that takes you to the bottom of the big slab, I conscientiously placed three runners, but as I moved up, the spiral spring on my stich-plate neatly lifted each one off so that I did the whole pitch without any protection. Sheila forbore to mention it, thinking it might put me off. After that I discarded the spring of the stich-plate and have never missed it.

We contented ourselves with Severes and Mild Very Severes and though she could have climbed harder than that, for me, over seventy, it was like an exhilarating return to former glories. On a climb on Sergeant Crag – it was either the Great Wall or Broadway – I was in the lead, and finding progress up a steep little wall difficult, I moved off to the right into an open chimney. As I came up level with the top of the wall a bird shot off it like a bullet, leaving a nest with four eggs in it. We climbed past the ledge as quickly as we could, the bird, a peregrine, circling about uttering shrill cries. From the top of the climb we cautiously went down again on a top rope until we could see the nest and were glad to note that the peregrine was sitting on the eggs again.

One of our best excursions was to Scafell, where we did once more an old favourite of mine, Moss Ghyll Grooves, on which I led the crux, so vividly described by Blanche Eden-Smith on the first ascent with H.M. Kelly. This pitch had become a little harder since the grass ledge from which the traverse was made crumbled away beneath the feet of my friend Roger Putnam some years before. It is a climb of great character with wonderful situations, and to do it again after so many years was very gratifying, and demonstrated the interesting fact that owing to the great advances made in climbing safety I could now, as an old arthritic man, do routes of much the same standard as I did in my early days.

During this brief partnership with Sheila Greenhow I did two climbs I had never got round to in my more active years. One was Savage Gully on Pillar, a Very Severe which I had always fought shy of but which proved not particularly difficult except at one place where a bulge had to be passed by means of some awkward side-stepping. The other was Engineer's Slab on the Ennerdale face of Gable, which, owing largely to Jack Carswell's awe-struck description of it, had always loomed large in my imagination as a trap for the unwary. It was first climbed in 1934 by F.G. Balcombe after hours of gardening, and was not repeated for twenty years.

Sheila phoned me to say she would be going to Wasdale with Colin, where he was to do some guiding, and how would I like to do Engineer's Slab on Gable. I was torn, as so many times before, between a disinclination to be terrified and the lure of brave deeds on a big crag. "You'll have to lead it," I said, and she agreed.

We arranged to meet at the foot of the crag itself so I approached from Honister Pass and she from Wasdale Head, a plan that worked very well, with no waiting about by either party.

Engineer's Slab, as Jack Carswell had pointed out, was more a wall than a slab, and it was situated high up on the mountain. We approached it by way of an enjoyable route put up by A.H. Greenbank, and rated Severe. A short traverse then brought us to its foot. I must confess I was not happy about it. It was an imposing enough rock face with no ledges that I could see, but what impressed me more than that was its reputation, or rather the aura that it had acquired over the years in my imagination. If Sheila had cried off I would have been entirely in agreement.

There was no chance of that however, and we started. As it turned out the rock was sound, the holds small but good, and the opportunities for inserting nuts quite adequate. Belays tended to be in niches, so there was something pretty unrelenting about the steepness and exposure, and at one point a layback was required, though it was not really strenuous. It was in fact a quite delightful climb. I began to wish, without saying as much, that I had not insisted on Sheila's leading it. Even seconding I found it an inspiring climb, high up on the mountain with a fine sense of exposure, and one of the best I had done. The final pitch was up a chimney. Here the angle was slightly less steep but it proved the hardest part of the climb by far. It was holdless and greasy and Sheila had a severe struggle. Even following with the solace of a top rope I found it hard work. It reminded me rather of Smuggler's Chimney on the same crag, which we always used to call Struggler's, but this was in a much more dramatic situation.

One of the great attractions of Engineer's Slab is that it lands you just about on the very summit of Great Gable. We sat there well pleased with ourselves, Sheila full of the glow of having done a good lead, and I well content to have at last set foot on the route that had haunted the back of my mind for so many years.

FAIN WOULD I CLIMB; YET FEAR I TO FALL

Written on a window pane by Sir Walter Raleigh. Queen Elizabeth wrote under it 'If thy heart fails thee, climb not at all.'

Climbing, like sex, is fun to do, but boring to discuss, and the question of why people climb is of more interest to those that don't than to those that do. After all, to ask a climber why he climbs is rather like asking a fish why it swims. Many climbers, however, get cornered into attempting to rationalise or justify their enthusiasm. I like the story of the mountaineer's little son, who, at the seaside, while other children built sand castles, spent the day digging an enormous hole. When asked why, he replied, "Because it wasn't there."

When Tom Patey wrote on the subject he agreed with Darwin that 'Man with all his noble qualities still bears in his bodily frame the indelible stamp of his lowly origins.' Climbers, Patey averred, were 'the only genuine primordial humanoids.'

But what makes some people and not others revert to this animal behaviour? It is partly, I think, that climbers have managed not to grow up. They are like young animals at play, practising, for fun, the skills which will give them a better chance of survival. So climbing, at its purest and simplest, is play, and climbers are big kids.

This is no bad thing. There is much to be said for remaining childlike, for there is no joy to equal the joy of a child. 'Heaven lies about us in our infancy,' said old Wordsworth, and 'Shades of the prison-house begin to close about the growing boy.' So climbers escape every weekend from the prison-house, to disport themselves on the rocks with the pleasure and spontaneity of youth.

You might not think so, of course, as you anxiously palpate the rock for anything that might serve as a hold, or grope the chalk bag and nervously wipe the sole of your boot down your calf, but fundamentally climbing is still play. You have only to watch children playing to see with what seriousness they enjoy themselves, and the total absorption a climber experiences while working out a series of moves on which his life may depend comes from the same fount of joy. Come to that, the more serious the enterprise, and the higher the stakes, the purer the enjoyment. So whereas in the past we got our reward from climbing Severes, with the sketchy protection of a manila rope tied round the waist, we now, with modern gear, have to go to Extremes to get the same payoff.

This atavistic explanation provides the central truth about climbing, I believe, but motivation in human beings is seldom that simple. No doubt there are as many and as varied reasons for climbing as there are for getting married. Love and procreation may be the fundamental reasons for marrying, but people do it also for money, sex, social advancement, career, safety, companionship, and so on. Similarly, with climbing, though doing what comes naturally is at the heart of it, there are other considerations.

Some do it for social reasons; they join clubs to share adventures with friends. Some are keen to identify themselves with what they see as an elite. Others are thrill seekers; they do it for kicks. Then there are those who need to test themselves, and improve their self-image.

A large body of climbers do it for aesthetic and sensual reasons, because they love the beauty of the hills, the open air, and the feel of rock under their fingers. Most, I imagine, do it simply out of a sense of adventure, on the basis that 'he that loseth his life' – or at least risks doing so – 'shall find it'.

For a small number of climbers the goal is to be the best, and to that end they embark upon rigorous weight-training and working-out. Such climbers are gymnasts and athletes as well as courageous cragsmen. They are greatly admired by the ruck of climbers, though not much emulated.

One of the attractions of climbing is that almost anyone can manage it, and often climbers with what Menlove Edwards called 'an ineptitude for high places' remain keen and devoted all their lives. I remember one who was so slow, and who got so alarmed on the crags, that no one in his club wanted to climb with him, and he became known as Thank God Chalmers, from his habit of praying fervently as he struggled from hold to hold. Yet he persisted all his life, repeatedly making the long journey from London, where he lived, to the Lake District, for weekend meets. In the days of petrol rationing he travelled by train, bringing with him a motor scooter on which to get up Langdale. He even bought bottles of cigarette lighter fuel to eke out his petrol ration. He climbed in the Alps, too, employing guides, who no doubt earned their fees.

A surprising number of climbers and mountaineers have started life as weedy youths and have found in the hills the means to health, vigour and self-esteem. I am one such myself. As a small child I had fits – now known as febrile convulsions – which caused my mother to regard me as 'delicate,' and I was discouraged from rough sports. Though not averse to taking risks, I shrank from getting hurt, and was anxious to avoid the kind of knocks you were prone to in games like soccer, rugby and even cricket. At cricket I fielded at long-stop. At soccer I would run purposefully away from the ball, as if cleverly anticipating a pass, though in reality trying to avoid the action. Camping, hill-walking and scrambling, however, were activities in which you did not get hurt at all, and yet could still feel a sense of adventure. When one December day in 1937 I met a man carrying sixty feet of thick and hairy manila rope, and joined him for a climb on Pavey Ark – Crescent Traverse and Gwynne's Chimney, as it turned out – I was astonished to discover that from climbing you could get the maximum of exhilaration for the minimum of skill and effort, and as long as you were careful you did not get hurt in the least. What is more, I found the drama and beauty of the mountain landscape immensely enhanced by foregrounds of soaring crags and plunging rock-faces. I was wholly taken by the romantic notion of the sublime and terrifying aspects of nature.

What I find hard to explain to myself is the obsessive nature of climbing. Once bitten I thought of little else. If I saw a mantelpiece, I wanted to mantelshelf on to it. I eyed the façade of every building in town, not from architectural interest, but for feasible routes. Bouldering on rocks, bridges and walls became almost a sport in its own right.

Perhaps it was obsessive because it was so serious. In the early days, when protection was so poor, you stood to get hurt, even killed. This made it something either to devote your whole attention to, or to give up altogether.

Speaking for myself I have to a large extent seen climbing as an escapade. Much of the fun has been in getting away with it, unscathed. "Yah! You missed me that time!" is what I feel on escaping in triumph at the top of a climb, having cheated once more that old adversary, the force of gravity. A touch of hubris, one might call it, an assertion that I am still alive and indestructible in spite of all my fears and weaknesses. For most climbers, I imagine, much of the pleasure is in tinkering with the safety margins. If climbs are too easy, you may find them enjoyable enough, but you finish the day vaguely dissatisfied. If, however, you have been sorely tried, and not found wanting, you sit at the top with such a feeling of quiet exaltation it is hard to exaggerate it.

I always claimed not to be interested in competing, and I never had any dream of being a star like Colin Kirkus or Maurice Linnell. I wanted simply to think well of myself, and take a modest pride in my strength and nerve. That did not, however, rule out the desire to be seen to be competent, and to gain acceptance among my peers. One of the pleasures of leading a decent climb was, I am bound to admit, letting everybody know about it.

Climbing, in fact, is a sport full of covert competition. That is why the introduction of blatant competition climbing – coming out of the closet – caused such a fluttering in the dovecotes of the B.M.C. On scrutinising my own motives on this issue I have come to the unflattering conclusion that it was not competition that I objected to; it was losing! The surest way not to be beaten by the 'flannelled fools and muddied oafs' of the sporting world was to decline to play. That being so I needed some other way of creating an acceptable self-image, and climbing was the answer.

This line of thought runs counter to the widely accepted notion – widely accepted at least by climbers – that there is some intrinsic merit in being a climber, that he is braver, nobler and more capable of higher aspirations than the ordinary person, that he belongs, in short, to an elite. It was an idea fostered – unintentionally no doubt – by those early gatherings of Olympian young men around Geoffrey Winthrop Young at Pen-y-Pas, and by the exclusiveness of the major climbing clubs. I suppose frequently choosing to 'screw one's courage to the sticking place' on rock-climbs cannot but improve one's character a bit, but what if your climber is driven to this extraordinary behaviour of putting his life at risk, in order to compensate for some inadequacy buried deep in his psyche? Perhaps there is a grain of truth in the observation I once heard from a farmer's wife watching climbers on Troutdale Pinnacle: "They want their heads looked."

Despite the recent emphasis on gymnastic ability that climbing walls and competitions have brought about, climbing is still a largely cerebral activity, requiring forethought and calculation, and a certain emotional, and even spiritual input. Fine classic routes can be climbed by people of very moderate agility, and though it is putting it too strongly to say "It's all in the mind," there is some truth in that assertion. For this reason climbing can be enjoyed for most of a person's lifetime.

Climbing is many things, a sport, an aestheticism, a bit of lifemanship, a home-wrecking addiction, a wantonness, but it does transport us to a kind of Xanadu. What differentiates it from other sporting interests, what makes it more than a sport, is its romanticism, the compulsion to transcend the ordinary and aspire to greater heights and enlargement of spirit. Climbers who stick at it all their lives, even when their powers are waning, their bones getting more brittle, and their climbing very small beer compared with what is being done all around them, these are true romantics, seeking they know not what, and undeterred by the manifest uselessness of what they are doing.

Acknowledgements

In writing this book I could not have had a more able, meticulous and supportive amanuensis than Jean Altshuler, nor a more encouraging and supportive adviser and publisher than Peter Hodgkiss. I am much in their debt. I owe a great deal too to the many friends who shared my outdoor life, and helped shape my opinions, not least my old colleagues from Outward Bound and the B.M.C.

A few of these articles were first published elsewhere:

'Short of the Folding Stuff' in the *Alpine Journal 1986:*
'Way Out West', 'Youth at the Door', 'Training for the Haute Route' and 'Ha Charlie' in the *Fell & Rock Journal* :
'Bridging the Gap' in *Mountain* :
'Look ! No Boots', 'Idyllic Hills' and 'Adventure by Numbers' in *Climber & Rambler:*
'Bridging the Gap' and 'Adventure by Numbers' also appeared in *The Games Climbers Play,* Diadem Books.

Lines quoted from poems are as follows:
In 'Getting Out' p.7 Richard Lovelace's 'To Lucasta'
In 'Batura Mustagh' p.45 Laurence Binyon's 'For the Fallen Sept 1914'
and p.46 the epitaph in Wasdale churchyard to Broadrick, Garrett, Ridsdale and Jupp, killed on Scafell in 1903.
Some of the details of the Batura Mustagh expedition I owe to John Edwards who wrote an account in the Alpine Journal.